Distracted by Alabama

Distracted by Alabama

Tangled Threads of Natural History,
Local History, and Folklore

James Seay Brown Jr.

THE UNIVERSITY OF ALABAMA PRESS
Tuscaloosa

The University of Alabama Press
Tuscaloosa, Alabama 35487-0380
uapress.ua.edu

Typeface: Garamond Premier Pro

Cover design: Lori Lynch

Cataloging-in-Publication data is available from the Library of Congress.
ISBN: 978-0-8173-2117-8
E-ISBN: 978-0-8173-9393-9

For Andrea, Josh, and Katy

Contents

Epilogue   275

Figures

Acknowledgments

Most of the folks I'm indebted to for my knowledge of the book's subject matter are talked about (and thanked, explicitly or implicitly) in the text proper. But there are some I still need to thank who have helped out with the creation of the book during these past few years.

Old friend George Elliott, pursuing a photography hobby in retirement, was ever ready to run me off an eight-by-ten glossy photo, color or black and white. Dozens and dozens of them. Only late in the process, when I learned he spent four hundred dollars for print cartridges every time he ran out, did I learn just how generous he was. Samford faculty colleagues from years past, Mike Howell in biology and Jonathan Bass in history, sent me not just single photos of fish collecting and folklore excursions but whole files of photographs from which to choose. Joey Brackner, the state folklorist, also spent time digging around for needed photos from decades past. As someone who has trouble finding last month's bank statement, I bow to their superior organizational skills and appreciate the time they spent on my behalf. Bill Mathews and Jo Kittinger gave me photos of people holding salamanders better than any I'd ever made. My granddaughter Alison Brown made me freehand copies of needed hieroglyphic cartouches. Birgit Kibelka, local landscape architect, helped me get better-quality Google Earth–based screen captures of the maps showing Ross Creek culvert.

Ivy Alexander, administrative assistant for Samford's history and classics departments, was ever ready to print off drafts when I needed a hard copy. Once, when I was visiting my older daughter in New Hampshire, I suddenly needed to write a letter that was to be printed on Samford University letterhead, and my closest supply was about twelve hundred miles away. It was a weekend, and I texted Ivy about my dilemma. No problem, said Ivy; it will be my pleasure first thing Monday morning to print out your letter on letterhead and send you an electronic copy. An amazing combination of administrative efficiency and good humor, she's still my warmest contact with Samford some six years after retirement.

It's been almost forty years since I had a book published by the University of Alabama Press, and as you can well imagine some protocols have changed. Wayne Flynt, for years on its editorial board, was kind enough to read and comment on early chapter drafts. I appreciated senior acquisitions editor Claire Lewis Evans's unhurried and thoughtful phone calls on what to tackle and when, especially knowing the extra pressures of both time and finances that she was under as of at least March 2020, with the arrival of COVID-19. And "Reviewer B" of the manuscript, who was later revealed to me to be Marty Olliff of Troy University's history department, seemed to sympathize from the first with what I was trying to do. There were a couple of times in the process when I was close to abandoning the whole venture, but his positive endorsement kept me in the game.

And to my wife, Linda Faye, who throughout the project kept the home fires burning, including doing all of the bookkeeping—while I disappeared most mornings to Samford University Library or chased around the state doing interviews or making photographs—I didn't say it enough, but I really, really appreciated it all.

Distracted by Alabama

Introduction

My first full-time job was professing history at Samford University. It also turned out to be my last because I did it for forty-five years, from 1971 to 2016. I was hired to teach Russian and general modern European history, to cover a secondary field in modern East Asia, and to teach lots and lots of survey history of Western civilization (later world history) courses. I hope I did those things creditably, but I know I didn't do the specialty courses exceptionally well. I didn't even turn my Russian history dissertation into a published book with an academic press, which—looking back—seems inexcusable for even a moderately ambitious scholar.

Partly I didn't focus more on Russian history because we had such a small department, and it was mostly made up of American historians. There were usually only two of us to cover the entire rest of the world over recorded time, and I only had the chance to teach Russian history every fourth semester or so. Like the cowboy who rode off in all directions, I eventually spread myself thin by working up courses in Middle Eastern, Latin American, and African history and even in folklore. I wound up taking history students to twenty-two countries on five continents in travel/study courses, doing things as interesting but ill-advised as getting stranded for a time in central China in the aftermath of the Tiananmen Square massacre of 1989. Not much of a specialist but one heck of a generalist, I could tell myself.

But partly it was that from the very first I was fascinated with Alabama, and a lot of my energy and time went into exploring different parts and aspects of it. To some extent I was interested in its political and social history, but mostly I was drawn to its natural history and its folk culture, those last two often closely intertwined. So it is that today, instead of being recently retired from some Ivy League college and still much in demand by congressional committees and think tanks to explain Russia's past and future, as I'd planned, I'm here in Homewood south of Birmingham proper as a naturalized resident, same address since 1975. My Russian history interests remain, deep down, but I haven't traveled there since 1993—ancient history now, it seems, with Boris Yeltsin filed away in past centuries with Ivan the Terrible—and my language skills are rusting away. There are some consolations for those disappointments. First among them is a clutch of my former students out there doing all kinds of neat (if mostly non-Russian-related) stuff that I myself could never have done, who tell me that I inspired their work, at least in part. Second is that there are institutions and things folkloric and natural history–oriented in and around Alabama that I have had a hand in creating or studying or just had a ringside seat for observing their development. The back story of these last is the main subject matter of the book in hand.

This is basically a memoir, which means that it's not exclusively on Alabama, but about how Alabama experiences shaped me and informed my mostly non-Alabama intellectual interests, or sometimes the reverse, how my broader interests shaped my appreciation of things in Alabama. It is organized by topic, and the topics are researched some more some less, including some oral histories I did just in the last few years. The chapters are strung together roughly chronologically, based on when I first had a close encounter with the main subject of that chapter. This chronological treatment begins with chapter 1 about the Cahaba River, which I discovered three days after moving to Birmingham. To look ahead selectively, chapter 2 begins with the spotted salamander migration in Homewood that I discovered that first fall and winter here, 1971–72; chapter 5, which deals with Sacred Harp singing, starts with my first attendance at such an all-day singing and dinner on the grounds in 1974; chapter 10, on snaring river redhorse sucker, dates from 1978–79, when I first interviewed those who did it and then was taken snaring myself; and chapter 12, about old-time railroad work gang calling, was set in motion in 1981 by some oral histories I was doing just then. There are a few cross-references from chapter to chapter in the book, but each chapter can still be read as a stand-alone article (over half of the twelve indeed started out as articles in journals or magazines).

Writing the book these past few years was a mostly pleasant ramble down memory lane, but there was a deeper inspiration for it too, I think, or at least an aspiration—to create a book worthy of inclusion in a category of the arts that I've long loved.

Certain locales, even those we've never visited, are vividly alive for us solely because they were sharply focused on by a single painter, photographer, poet, nonfiction author, or even novelist or short story writer. Just in terms of the American landscape, I think of how Georgia O'Keeffe deepened our view of New Mexico, Ansel

Adams of western mountain ranges, Rachel Carson of the edge of the Atlantic, Sidney Lanier of coastal Georgia's live oaks and sawgrass swamps, Henry David Thoreau of a hundred-acre lake south of Concord known locally as Walden Pond, Aldo Leopold of an economically marginal sand-blown farm a couple of counties north of Madison, Wisconsin. Apparently all it takes is one careful observer (and thoughtful expresser of those observations) to bring any patch of the earth to rich, vibrant life in the minds of readers or viewers.

Just a couple of summers ago (July 2019), my son Josh and I—who for twenty years now have been meeting in Biloxi annually for a three-day fishing trip to the Chandeleur Islands south of there—finally took the time to visit the museum in nearby Ocean Springs featuring the art of Walter Inglis Anderson (1903–65). He was something of a Gulf Coast Vincent Van Gogh whose art took over his life, or perhaps more accurately one whose considerable mental problems were expressed in his art. At times in his life he'd abandon the family and take an old rowboat some fourteen miles out to Horn Island, a briar- and scrub-grown barrier island most of us wouldn't look at twice, or would just value for its beaches. He'd live there on canned goods for a week or two at a time, and feverishly paint the individual animals and plants and the general landscapes and seascapes that he saw all around him.

Whatever personal demons drove him, his idée fixe as an artist was that a good artist, by concentrating on one slice of nature closely enough, could present its rhythms and patterns of life clearly enough to awaken an understanding of it in the rest of us. For my son and me, at least, it worked like a charm. We were enchanted by his naturalistic alligator gar swimming vertically down three offset sheets of typing paper; by his two blue crabs facing off (blocky, stylized, but absolutely aware and alive); by his shorthand version of all local nature on the walls and ceiling of his secret little room; by his public school auditorium wall mural still preserved there. Anderson's brilliantly simple repetition of reed forms and bird wings will inform my view of marsh reeds and flocking seabirds the rest of my life. His art makes you think about running out to Horn Island with canned goods, a ream of typing paper, brushes, and paints, and—even if you know you'll never actually go—makes you feel as if he'd already transported you there for a little while.

It's the same with human communities in their natural settings. Just in terms of writers, I think of James Herriot's books on Yorkshire as seen through the eyes of a transplanted Scottish vet; Peter Mayle's *A Year in Provence*, about local life in the southeastern corner of France as viewed by a British couple who were new landowners there; Pearl S. Buck's *The Good Earth*; John Steinbeck's *Cannery Row*; William Faulkner's word pictures of "Yoknapatawpha County"; and even closer to home, Carl Carmer's *Stars Fell on Alabama*. Readers will probably each have their own long list of similar favorite books, because this exploration and memorializing of communities is one of the things literature does best.

The book in hand may not be of the caliber of those listed above, but it's hopefully of the same genre. The dozen chapters are some testament to how intrigued and involved I've been with aspects of a most interesting place. It's a bit strange to me, looking back, that I didn't have this same interest and involvement in the area around Cookeville, Tennessee, where I grew up and came of age. Only after coming to Alabama and only after getting interested in fiddle music hereabouts did I discover that a national championship–caliber fiddler had lived in Cookeville when I did, and was even kin to some of the folks I knew who worked at the local college. Maybe it was just that things were so different here in Alabama that they caught my attention—more different than I'd expected because I was only about two hundred straight-line miles from my old hometown. Maybe it was that my view of things around me was newly informed by historical patterns that I had learned in grad school and in my efforts to hone my craft as a young teacher.

I hope readers of this book find the writing engaging enough to rise to the standard of "creative nonfiction," and the various subjects and people written about to be worth their reading time. My fondest wish is that the book would pique the interest of those who have never visited Alabama or are relative newcomers, as well as add a thing or two, even a topic or two, to the knowledge of natives who know the state like, well, natives. But if it shouldn't happen to interest many readers, I'll still be comforted by the knowledge that at least it will be a recorded chapter of family history for my three children, who grew up in the midst of all this through no fault of their own. It probably permanently warped their lives. I remember that when Andrea, the oldest, was in the pre-K program at Vestavia Hills Baptist Church, she took an IQ test administered there by a Samford education student. That was about the time when I was first picking up white oak basketry as a hobby, learned at the hands of an old-timer, as talked about in one of the early chapters of the book to come. Later, the student, laughing, showed my wife the test. One of the questions went with two pictures, one of a man chopping wood and one of a man reading a book; it read, "Which man is working?" And of course Andrea, to the detriment of her calculated IQ, had answered that it was the man reading the book . . .

chapter one

Immersed in the Cahaba River

First Encounter

I moved from Nashville to Birmingham in mid-June 1971 with my wife, Linda Faye, and our two-year-old daughter, Andrea. We came, out of graduate school poverty, in a Chevy II with some unrepaired body damage, and in one of the smaller U-Haul trucks with all our worldly goods. My wife's fifteen-year-old brother, Mike, came along, to help with the move into a rental house back of Samford campus, about a ten-minute walk from my new office. Mike and I rode down in the U-Haul, towing the Chevy II; my parents brought my wife and daughter down in their car, stayed the night, and went back home.

After two days of unloading and roughly setting up the house, Mike and I had outlived our usefulness and were given time off to go fishing. We went with fishing rods, a few hooks and sinkers, and a fine-meshed seine, this last in hopes that the local countryside would support the kind of river wade fishing with hellgrammites (the aquatic larvae of the big delta-winged dobsonfly, looking for all the world like black, flattened, rubbery caterpillars with impressive pinchers) that we did back in the Tennessee hill country. Not having a map and not knowing much about the area, we headed the Chevy II as directly away from downtown Birmingham as we could judge. At every major fork or intersection in the road we took the low road on the time-tested theory that rivers seek the low ground. Sure enough, on a country road named Grants Mill we crossed a nice-sized little river with visible pools and shoals, signposted "Cahaba River." We parked, walked down into the rocky shoals right under the bridge, and indeed seined up hellgrammites. We put them in empty Coke bottles so we could carry them in our pockets, hid the seine on the bank, and started wade fishing up the river. Unfortunately, the recent hard rains had the river "as muddy as a clayhole," as the country expression has it, and we only had one bite. But that was a big fish that bent Mike's pole into a sharp arc as it went zipping by him, before it came off. "We'll come back here when the river clears up," was our thought—and come to think of it, I've probably been wading in or canoeing on that stretch of river an average of once a quarter for half a century now.

Vignettes from Early Years on the River

In my mind there are still some surprisingly vivid memories of the Cahaba from those first five or six years we lived in Alabama.

Early that first year in Birmingham I found my first huge elephant-ear mussels in the shoals just above Grants Mill falls, looking like something that could have come from a tropical sea. Having read that mussels were a staple of the riverine Native American diet, I collected some, brought them home, cubed the meat, and made a Cahaba River version of clam chowder. When finishing every bite, I remember, there were these almost unchewable rubbery cubes left in the mouth, and my appreciation for Native Americans increased.

I mused about the ruins of Grants Mill itself, the mill that gave the road its name. The thick iron bars that anchored the mill dam to bedrock at the top of the falls (before the dam washed out in a 1947 flood, I was told) were, and are today, still there; the stonework where the waterwheel stood is still mostly intact on the left bank.

When my older (and then still only) daughter, Andrea, was about five years old, in 1973 or 1974, she went through a *Wizard of Oz* phase so thorough that for a time she wanted to be called Dorothy. When we went to the pound to get our first dog, there were some handsome choices, but there in the next-to-last cage was a Toto look-alike, albeit longer legged, which we of course got and of course named Toto. I used to take Toto with me wade fishing the Cahaba, and I still have a memory of wading up to the deep hole underneath Grants Mill waterfall, and Toto swimming right across the hole in front of me like some aquatic creature. It spoiled the fishing that day but obviously created a lasting tableau in my mind.

An older colleague in the history department and a native of Alabama, Wayne Flynt, did a lot in those years to introduce me and my family to Alabama—driving us up to Cheaha the first time, showing us Hatchet Creek and other favorite locales of his. He taught me to play handball and introduced me to the faculty crowd that played. I taught him to wade fish with hellgrammites and introduced him to the Cahaba and some its larger tributaries that I was just exploring.

Once in those first few years I was in Birmingham, we two were fishing a good hole in the (upper) Little Cahaba River off Sicard Hollow Road when a big fish— the first really big fish Wayne had hooked—snatched his bait and immediately broke his line. I asked him how he had his drag set, and he said he had screwed it down as tight as he could; wasn't that right? I explained what the drag was for, and he caught more big fish later! But the very next time we fished that same stretch, you could tell he was itching to get to that particular hole. Then as we got close, we saw a couple skinny-dipping in the pool. They hadn't seen us yet, and I was all for quietly circling around them in the woods, leaving them undisturbed; but no, that was Wayne's big fish hole. He waded all the more noisily; they were alerted and took to the bank and threw on some clothes and were the picture of demure innocence when we got there. As it turned out, poetic justice was served; no fish bit in that hole after all the commotion. I laughed and laughed about Wayne and the skinny-dippers in his big fish hole, and I got a lot of mileage out of the story in later years. Not long after, on a similar wade-fishing trip, in an errant cast I hung my lure in a streamside bush. When no amount of yanking got it free, I waded down to it—and was immediately stung by a couple of red wasps from a cloud of them coming off their nest in that much-shaken bush. I dropped my rod in the water in the panic of my retreat. To get it back, after self-control returned, I lowered myself in the shallow water until only part of my brimmed hat and under it my nose and eyes were above water, with a little opening in front of my eyes under the brim to see through. I slithered downstream, retrieved the rod, and then with much more difficulty slithered back upstream in reverse, to Wayne's uproarious laughter—laughter repeated again and again in later years.

In the summer of 1977 I took a couple of my favorite former students out wade fishing in that original Grants Mill stretch. I had caught what fishermen usually call "spring lizards" for us to use for fish bait (mostly dusky salamanders, and excellent fish bait they are, though it's a practice I've foregone in later years, as you'll understand by the next chapter). About the time we parked at Grants Mill Bridge a summer thunderstorm broke loose, and we retreated back up to the little country store that used to be at the corner of Overton and Grants Mill Roads. The storm blew over fairly quickly, the sun came back out, and we went back down to the bridge and started wading upstream. We caught and strung a few small bass, and worked up to the lip of the hole just above the falls that was too deep to wade. We were all three on the left side of the river, looking upstream, in the shade of some overhanging branches—I think I could take you to within ten feet of the spot today—with our salamander bait cast out into the deeper water and resting on the bottom. A flotilla of three large-mouth bass as fat as footballs came cruising by in front of us, hunting in a pack to see what food the rain had washed in from the banks, I'd guess. One slowly, casually, nosed down and inhaled the salamander being fished by one of the students.

The student was using an old and cranky closed-face Zebco reel, and when he tried to set the hook, the line just came freely out of the reel. It rocked the big bass a little, but it just sat there, broadside to us, only ten to fifteen feet away. "What do I do now?" he said. I told him to grab the line ahead of the reel and try to set the hook again. He did, and the big fish (six and a quarter pounds, it turned out) was so close to us it threw water on us with its tail, and the line cut into the student's index finger. It was probably worth it to him, because for the rest of the afternoon he delighted in comparing his monster on the stringer with our little ones. A few years earlier I'd learned from some Japanese guys about my age (students in a volunteer ESL class I was teaching) how to make a *gyotaku*, a fishprint, by inking one side of a fish and then pressing paper over the fish to get the mirror-image print. Back at my house we tore up a brown paper grocery sack, got my daughter's blue tempera paint to use in place of ink, and made such a fishprint. All these years and years later, the former student still has it framed and on the wall.

Discoveries in Graduate-Level Biology Classes

Bob Stiles, ichthyologist, joined the Samford faculty in 1972, one year after I did. Back then the biology department (as did history, religion, and English) had a full-fledged master's degree program. By 1973 I was taking some of his graduate courses, and for credit. One of them was Vertebrate Field Zoology, which naturally enough as taught by an ichthyologist spent a good bit of time on fish. I enthusiastically seined rivers and ponds as a member of the class group, and often singly on my own time (all these years later, my by now very good and old friend Bob Stiles still occasionally wears a T-shirt that shows a kneeling fisherman at confession, labeled "Forgive me, father, for I have seined"). Lots of the seining went on in tributaries of the Cahaba or the main river itself.

But it was Bob's History of Biology class that did more than anything else to connect lots of academic fields for me. Here things that were commonplace and old hat to biologists and physical scientists hit me with the force of revelation. The crust of the earth is spreading out from the mid-ocean ridges. How do we know that? Because every few million years, the earth, which is an iron-cored magnet, switches polarity north to south or vice versa, and when the lava freezes into a solid just after it oozes out of that crack, it locks in the polarity of the time of its birth. Dragging a magnetometer across it reveals mirror-image sides, with alternating bands of north, south, north, south polarity and matching widths facing each other on either side of the mid-ocean ridges. One spreading tectonic plate then dives under another with all sorts of interesting geological results, and over time—lots and lots of time, because they generally move at about the same speed as fingernails grow—the tectonic plates underlying continents drift around, with the continents sometimes combining and at other times separating. And evolution, which works on the same unimaginably long time scale, reflects it: acacia trees and marsupials (except the Virginia opossum, which apparently wandered up the isthmus connecting South and North America), for example, are limited to the southern continents because they evolved after the southern Gondwana separated from the northern Laurasia when the original super-continent of Pangaea broke apart. All the undescribed varieties of the little *Ulocentra* snubnosed darters in the Cahaba and other Alabama rivers had come about by a similar process over geological time. It was all presented through the lives and adventures of the discoverers of these things, and it linked history and biology firmly together forevermore in my mind.

In 1974 Mike Howell—the original Samford ichthyologist, who'd gone off to teach at Cornell University in 1972—came back and rejoined Samford's biology department. So all of a sudden this medium-sized department in a smallish university had not one but two full-time ichthyologists. Mike was a fisherman as well, and at least as I remember it, I got him interested in the stretch of the Cahaba River above the old Grants Mill site, telling him and his fisherman son about some large bass I'd caught there and larger ones that had gotten away.

HIRED PADDLER ON A US FISH AND WILDLIFE SURVEY OF THE RIVER

In 1981, when I'd been in state a decade and had spent about as much time with the university biologists as with the historians, Drs. Howell and Stiles contracted with the US Fish and Wildlife Service to survey populations of two rare and possibly endangered small fish in the Cahaba—the Cahaba shiner and the goldline darter. As per the contract the ichthyologists were to sample the river from Trussville down to Booth Ford, a curvilinear seventy-five miles as the river ran. Sampling was to be not once but twice over, spring and fall, with sample sites being on average a mile and a half apart.

Their plan for doing this was to take two canoes with two people in each one, with two vehicles to do the necessary car ferrying before and after, and bite off the river in six- to eight-mile chunks. The four paddlers would get out at likely spots to seine for the two little fishes, and rod-and-reel fish for bass in between (this last not mentioned in the grant but not technically forbidden either). Since I had a canoe, was a keen fisherman, and was an enthusiastic if not particularly skilled puller of an end of a seine, I was hired on as the almost-invariable third member of the party; the fourth varied trip to trip. As I remember it, the pay for me and my canoe was twenty dollars per day, which for me was pure gravy; I'd have paid twenty dollars per day to be allowed to do it, and life has been downhill ever since that high point. Peering into a seine with these pros, I got fairly adept at recognizing particular minnows and

Figure 1.1.
Goldline
darter

The goldline darter (*Percina aurolineata*) is a small but beautiful member of the perch family, never getting quite three inches long. It has been federally listed as "threatened (vulnerable)" since 1992. (Photo courtesy of Mike Howell.)

darters at a glance; all these years later I still think *venusta* instead of blacktail shiner, or *nigrofasciata* instead of blackbanded darter, when I happen to see one (usually a bycatch when I'm seining for hellgrammites).

The scenery was phenomenal, and we had some adventures. On the one trip when Mike Howell himself couldn't go with us, the rest of us rashly decided to bite off something like sixteen miles of river instead of our usual six to eight. It was late in the fall when the days were shorter, and early on the fishing was so good that we went too slowly. By late afternoon it already looked as if dark might catch us, and—improvident, matchless, and flashlightless—we swapped some fish to a bank fisherman for some matches just in case worst should come to worst. Sure enough, we were benighted, and we knew nothing else to do but wade and paddle in the dark until we should run out of energy, following the stars appearing downriver between the tops of the trees on the banks, paddling until we suddenly hit rocks, wading and barking our shins on rocks, falling in unseen deep holes between the rocks, wondering just how nocturnal cottonmouth moccasins were—all with having little idea how

Figure 1.2. Cahaba River research trip

Bob Stiles at left, author in center, Mike Howell at right. Digital copy, made in 2000, of a ca. 1981 slide, somewhat compromised by fungus on slide emulsion. Included here anyway on the theory that every memoir needs at least one hazy picture of happy people, brightly colored and suffused with light. (Photo courtesy of Mike Howell.)

far we still had to go. We were rescued when we came across a streamside bonfire of some campers, students from Montevallo. One of them kindly drove the four of us to our car, and the next day we came back to retrieve the canoes. Another time we got locked in by the coal company gates down near New Slab, and I had to walk and jog five miles in the dark to collect the upstream car. Again, we had to come back to retrieve the downstream car the next day.

When in 1982 Professors Howell and Stiles submitted the 148-page report on where we'd found the shiner and darter, to be published by US Fish and Wildlife, I was listed third as a junior author—a battlefield promotion from hired paddler, I thought.[1]

THE HISTORY OF THE RIVER

Speaking of history, over the years I've tried to read some history dealing with the Cahaba and sites along it, but I have found only limited sources. It is generally celebrated as one of the few free-flowing rivers of the state, though with some qualifications on the "free-flowing" as it passes close to Birmingham. The substantial dam on the river just downstream from Highway 280's twin road bridges is less than a quarter mile downstream from where the (upper) Little Cahaba joins the main Cahaba; if you look upstream over the lake (while driving slowly across the bridge or while stopped in traffic on it!) you can see the mouth of the Little Cahaba. The dam was built in 1890 as part of supplying water to a fast-growing Birmingham. In times of low water it shunts the flow of the Little Cahaba *upstream* in the main Cahaba to the pumping station on Sicard Hollow Road, a little over two miles away. In 1911 the dam that creates Lake Purdy was built about five miles up the Little Cahaba from its junction with the main Cahaba, so as to store water—to be released in the dry season to go down the Little Cahaba and up the bed of the main Cahaba and wind up at that same pumping station. Greater Birmingham still gets about half its drinking water from this century-and-more-old system. Though I'm sure a major price in aquatic life was paid for all this, robbing the downstream of its two major upstream sources in the dry season, I'm certainly one of the drinkers of that water.

Downstream from the sizable dam at 280, over the course of the next three miles there are four low dams, mostly the remains of old water mills. After that, though, the main Cahaba is indeed free flowing—all the way down through Shelby, Bibb, and Perry Counties and even on into Dallas County, where it finally joins the Alabama

River. More than that, its main downstream tributaries also have substantial un-dammed stretches. The first major tributary is Buck Creek, coming in from the east. It is free flowing for almost two miles, up to the dam in the city of Helena. Shades Creek is the next; it comes in from the northwest and has no dams for a remarkable thirty miles upstream. The last major tributary, and biggest of all, is the (lower) Little Cahaba, coming in from the east. This river traverses nineteen free-flowing miles from its junction with the Cahaba up to the first concrete low-water bridge to cross it (a barrier to fish only in low-water times), and another seven miles up to its first little dam, in the town of Montevallo. I gradually learned about the migration of aquatic life in that considerable free-flowing network of rivers and creeks; it preserves at least a partial picture of what the natural environment was like all over Alabama just a century and a half ago, as you'll see in some later chapters.

Since "Cahaba" was in the title, I was initially excited about historian Harvey H. Jackson III's *Rivers of History: Life on the Coosa, Tallapoosa, Cahaba, and Alabama,* which came out in 1995. It's an interesting and well-written book, but except for a few sentences here and there (not counting his treatment of historic Cahawba, a town fronting on the Alabama River just downstream from where the Cahaba runs into the Alabama, and from 1820 to 1823 the state's first capital) there's almost nothing on the nearly two-hundred-mile-long Cahaba River and its whole watershed. The subjects at the heart of the book—steamboat traffic, river towns, and the huge hydropower dams that came later—needed little or no treatment of the Cahaba. I wondered why the Cahaba was even listed in the subtitle. The single important exception came late in the book, a two-page essay on the movement for environmental quality of the rivers, which was led by people interested in the Cahaba River more so than by people interested in the three other, much-larger rivers. Jackson himself seemed surprised by that: "Ironically, one of the places where a passion seemed to exist was in a city seldom associated with a river—Birmingham."[2] And then he had some interesting things to say about the Cahaba River Society, about which I already knew a little something.

LEARNING ABOUT THE CAHABA RIVER SOCIETY

Looking back over the decades, I'm amazed that the Cahaba is still swimmable in many places and fishable in most. In that first decade I was experiencing the river, it was going visibly—and olfactorily—downhill in terms of water quality mainly because of its proximity to the state's largest urban area, with its antiquated sewage disposal system. I remember in 1981, on that US Fish and Wildlife grant to survey the river for those two little fish, that it stunk horribly when we canoed by the mouth of Patton Chapel Creek, with its sewage treatment plant overload pouring into the main Cahaba. As per the grant we had to seine soon thereafter on our way downstream. One of the four of us, probably not coincidentally, got really sick soon thereafter; we all suspected *E. coli*. That the Cahaba is still there today as a recreational destination seems to be mostly owing to the Cahaba River Society.

My main contact with the society over the years has been with Dr. Randy Haddock, its field director (who just retired in 2020). For some twenty-five years he led the youth and college group river trips I requested from the society. For many of those years he guided my spring folklore classes down the lower Little Cahaba, river flow permitting. Occasionally, when the upper part of the river was too high and dangerous because of its rapids, we'd go on the lower Cahaba itself in the coastal plain below the fall line near Centreville. Once I was on a trip he led through the mile-long canyon that Shades Creek, a Cahaba tributary, cuts through Shades Mountain, as good as any place to say "the Appalachian mountains end here." Apart from these river trips we've had a lot of other contact, and I count him as a friend. Although I'm usually a paid-up member, my association with the society has been episodic; so recently I sat down with him to try to get his overview of the society and its work.

One of the first questions I asked Randy was why he thought the environmental quality concerns about rivers in Alabama had been led by Birmingham, a question raised in my mind by Jackson's *Rivers of History*. Randy's take was that environmental movements happened here first simply because Birmingham had more people than any other urban area in the state. I reflected that even if those with serious environmental concerns were a small subset of the whole population, in a big city they were thrown into contact enough so as to feed off one another's energy and eventually to organize. Randy made it sound like the assembling of fissionable material: at some point you'd cross a line of critical mass, and a self-sustaining chain reaction would occur.

Randy himself came to Birmingham from Missouri as a freshly credentialed biology PhD hired to do some specialized biomedical research at the University of Alabama at Birmingham (UAB). His heart was more in field biology, he says, and early on he was snared—even more than I was—by the Cahaba River. The Cahaba River

Society was founded in 1989, and Randy worked for it full-time from 1991 until 2020, with volunteer work there even before that.

I think I first heard of Randy when I was told about his identification of the pollinator of the Cahaba lily. A beautiful species of white spider lily, the flower grows in rocky shoals in a narrow band of rivers across the South, not just in the Cahaba (though maybe a quarter of all the Cahaba lily sites are indeed in the Cahaba and its tributaries). For a long time it was a mystery who or what pollinated the flower. In early June 1991 (the lily's blooming season is roughly the last half of May and the first half of June), Randy told me, he got himself to one such lily-growing rocky shoal on the main Cahaba down in Bibb County about ten at night, and settled down among the tall flowers with a butterfly net. "Settled" is probably too tame a word for it; if you've been on any of those lily shoals you know the lily bulbs are underwater, down in the cracks and crevices of rugged bedrock ledges. I can only image the discomfort of an extended stay there at night, and I didn't think to ask him about how much blood he lost to mosquitoes or whether he too wondered about how nocturnal cottonmouths were. About midnight he caught the perpetrator in the act: a night-flying sphinx moth (the plebeian sphinx moth, to be precise, *Paratrea plebeja*, though another lily-pollinating sphinx moth has since been found, and today Randy thinks most any sphinx moth of the right size might occasionally do the job!). Randy still has that original specimen, though it has suffered from much showing. From wing tip to wing tip it is about an eighth of an inch shy of three inches across. The last time I went down to Hargrave Shoal to see the lilies bloom in late May, one of our group found a huge dragonfly emerging from its impressively large nymph case. Coincidentally, Randy was down there too, with a small group including some travel writers. We called him over to identify the insect. It was a "dragonhunter," Randy said, the largest of Alabama dragonflies and so named because it eats other dragonflies.

The actual formation of the Cahaba River Society is a most interesting and implausible story. Back in the 1980s Don Elder was first chair trumpet in the Alabama Symphony Orchestra and also played in the symphony's brass quartet. Though the symphony was based in Birmingham, it played all over the state, and the brass quartet, being more mobile, presumably did even more so. All four of the brass quartet members were fishermen—what were the odds?—so they often extended their musical stays near fishable waters. But apparently their first love, certainly Don Elder's, was the Cahaba River. Don could see it going downhill, environmentally speaking, and began gathering folks interested in the same problem for discussion sessions in

Figure 1.3.
*Cahaba
lilies*

This photograph was made on Hargrave Shoals one year on the twentieth of May; local lore has it that the Cahaba lilies bloom from Mother's Day to Father's Day.

his living room. Funding in the form of grants from a couple of local businesses let them incorporate, rent office space on Seventh Avenue South in Birmingham, and get a phone line. Randy remembers in the early years that the phone never stopped ringing; it was a focus for an unexpected amount of love and interest that local folks had in the river.

In 1997 the Cahaba River Society put out a beautifully done pamphlet called *Cahaba: A Gift for Generations; A Series of Historical Essays Revealing the Cahaba River Past, Present and Future.*[3] It's only twenty-six pages long, but it is a full seventeen by ten inches in size and is in color. The two-page spread on mussels, for which the Cahaba is a world leader in sheer numbers of species, has photos of twenty species, including those with such wonderful names as pistolgrip, Southern fat-mucket, monkeyface, and three-horned wartyback. It explains how well mussels show the health of the river: in 1938, scientists were able to collect an astounding forty-two species; in 1973, only thirty-one; in 1994, down to twenty-seven . . . My favorite part of the pamphlet is a three-page historical essay called "The Struggle for Cahaba River Preservation." It deals with the major personalities who began in the mid-1960s to try to get federal legislation to protect the river, though never successfully.

THE CAHABA RIVER SOCIETY'S STILL-REVERBERATING "BIG BANG"

In the first few years of the society's existence, Don Elder and friends tried to systematically explore the state of Jefferson County's sewage disposal system, obvious source of many of the river's problems. It turned out that although the stormwater system and the sewage disposal system had been built as separate entities, the sewage system was so old, leaky, and poorly maintained that to some extent the two had merged. As a result, billions of gallons—*billions*—of untreated sewage were going into the local watershed every year. There were regular "collection system overflows" and "bypasses" that the county claimed it had the right to release as emergency overload in a major rain event. It seemed to Don Elder and Cahaba River Society friends that this was happening in every rain; how could the county call it an emergency? Such releases and overflows weren't just into the Cahaba, but into rivers all over Jefferson County. It turned out that Village Creek got the worst of it; a billion gallons flushed into it alone just in one bad year. In this era, when Village Creek flooded it carried raw sewage into people's homes. Learning about this really helped society members explain to residents and business leaders the necessity of cleaning up the sewer system: it wasn't only for the Cahaba River's benefit.

Locally, the Cahaba River Society is known to most folks—so long as they're old enough to remember—for its subsequent lawsuit against Jefferson County. Ironically, though, Don Elder and the society's other early decision makers were apparently for long undecided about launching such a suit. Things changed in 1993, when some citizens who lived out on the river approached a private lawyer and brought suit. This action forced the hand of the Cahaba River Society: if its members wanted to be able to provide critical information on the state of the river and keep some control over the whole process, they had to join the suit. Bob Tate, a society board member and veteran local lawyer near retirement, took the case pro bono for the society. The plaintiffs documented over four thousand violations of the Clean Water Act, and this prompted the federal Justice Department to launch its own lawsuit against Jefferson County.

Jefferson County settled both lawsuits in December 1996 by signing a consent decree. The county agreed, first, to repair the sewer system according to a set timetable. Second, in place of a fine the county agreed to a suggestion of the justice department lawyer for a Supplemental Environmental Project (SEP). The SEP would let the money the county paid for damages be used to buy land in parts of Jefferson County that would help preserve or increase clean water sources—particularly greenways and buffer zones alongside waterways.

The amount to be paid by the county for this SEP was apparently arrived at in the following interesting fashion. When the director of the Environmental Services Department of Jefferson County was testifying under oath, he was asked for his estimate of what it would have cost to modify the sewer system so as to have avoided all the "overflows" and "bypasses" that violated the Clean Water Act. He said it would have been at least $30 million. So the judge, and eventually the county attorneys, accepted that as the amount for which the county owed restitution. In accordance with the terms of the SEP, each of the five Jefferson County commissioners was assigned $6 million for the acquisition of such greenways and stream buffer zones in their districts. A land trust—the Black Warrior Cahaba Rivers Land Trust (in Jefferson County the creeks south of Red Mountain are in the Cahaba drainage, creeks north of it are in the Black Warrior drainage)—was set up to administer these lands, and Jefferson County was to support its operation for its first ten years. Today the land trust raises other monies and acquires lands even outside Jefferson County, and to reflect its broader scope it has been renamed the Freshwater Land Trust. The total bill for all this for Jefferson County was in the neighborhood of $1.2 billion. It was to be paid off gradually from increased sewer fees, though the rate increase would have been moderate compared to what happened next, which sent the fees sky high.

The Jefferson County Sewer Construction Scandal

At this point the top administrators of Jefferson County's Environmental Services Department—encouraged privately, it seems, by some big real estate development firms—proposed a huge new expansion of the sewer system. They justified it as required by the 1996 consent decree, plus a need to add new customers to soften the blow of the rate increases now necessary. Soon it seemed to Cahaba River Society folks that more than half the money being spent by the county's Environmental Services was for things other than correcting the specific shortcomings itemized in the consent decree.

The biggest single new project was probably the "Cahaba Trunk Sewer" that was to be bored, crossing underneath the bed of the river over a dozen times. Its estimated cost swelled from some $80 million to $140 million, including $3 million for a huge boring machine. But when the county began purchasing rights of way for the trunk sewer in the vicinity of where Highway 280 crosses the Cahaba, the Birmingham Water Works Board (owner of easements along the river thereabouts) asked for a formal assessment of the project. It turned out that the substrate from the bottom of the riverbed down just a few feet to the top of some of the proposed tunnels was mostly shale, less solid rock than had been assumed. This made the trunk sewer, on which work was already underway, now look really dangerous: there was the distinct possibility of the trunk sewer flushing directly into the Cahaba.

As all of this gradually came out, especially in muckraking (a particularly apt adjective here, no?) reporting in the local newspapers, opposition to the project grew. Not all the opposition was environmental; for one, it began to be clear that Jefferson County ratepayers, most of whom lived in Birmingham, were being asked to pay for a whole new sewer complex for the high-rent properties east and south of town. In early 2020 I was talking about this with Beth Stewart, who was in her twenty-fifth year as executive director of the Cahaba River Society. As she remembers it, the real turning point was when Greater Birmingham Ministries joined the opposition coalition. Immediately thereafter a key Jefferson County commissioner pulled his support for the sewer expansion project.

So the whole Cahaba Trunk Sewer project was abandoned. The $3 million boring machine was simply left down in its tunnel because it couldn't be backed out. At the time, I thought the Cahaba River Society might be blamed by public opinion for having seemingly started this whole expensive process, but as the mismanagement and outright corruption of the sewer expansion project gradually came to light, it removed doubt in any impartial observer's mind about where the blame lay. In summer 2005, the FBI indicted twenty-one defendants involved in this whole mess for bribery, conspiracy, or obstruction of justice. Within three years there were fifteen convictions for bribery alone: they included three county commissioners; the director, assistant director, and chief engineer of Jefferson County's Environmental Services Department; and nine individuals from real estate development corporations. Meanwhile, the ballooning financial burden for Jefferson County ratepayers was compounded by some risky bond refinancing swaps, as well as the 2007–8 financial crisis, which led to the failure of the new bonds' insurers. The former head of the Jefferson County Commission and later mayor of Birmingham was arrested by the FBI in 2008 for bribes taken during all that refinancing flimflam. The financial downhill slide continued until 2011, when Jefferson County filed for Chapter 9 protection from creditors, making headlines nationwide as the largest US municipality ever to declare bankruptcy.[4]

As late as January 2020, Cahaba River Society folks were still monitoring meetings in which Jefferson County representatives reported to a judge on progress made since the 1996 consent decree.

Dealing with the Sediment Problem

After the first decade or so of its existence, the Cahaba River Society felt that point source pollution had been dealt with to some extent. It began focusing on the larger problem of nonpoint source pollution, particularly sediment loading. In a way this problem is much more complicated because it deals with the whole watershed, not just a few fairly easily defined sites. With more and more impermeable surfaces—newly paved roads, new parking lots, new roofs—the runoffs after rains are becoming "flashy." The runoff may be short term, but it's high volume, often ripping parts of the banks off the creeks and rivers, and those dissolved banks add *their* silt load to the already overloaded flooded river. Muddy runoff from construction sites whose builders aren't concerned with such runoff—from anywhere in the whole Cahaba River watershed area—is also a real issue.

I could personally testify to the river's problem with sediment. Once, back in the heyday of the development of the big Liberty Park housing subdivision, I was in a canoe on a deep hole on the Cahaba where a little tributary comes in from the direction of a section of Liberty Park. There had been a big rain, and the tributary water was yellow-brown with rainwater runoff from who knows how many careless construction sites. The main river was still clear, and the two kinds of water weren't mixing. The tributary water, heavily loaded with yellow-brown silt, sank, and had moved upstream as well as downstream along the bottom of the main Cahaba as far away as I could see. It looked as if a clear river about two feet deep was flowing over a perfectly flat yellow bottom. The mushy silt left on the bottom after such events chokes out the mussels, which, if left alone, would filter an amazing volume of water every day.

Since that remarkable 1996 lawsuit settlement there have been ups and downs for the Cahaba River Society. In 2004 a regional planning commission led a focus on a new river protection and stormwater management plan, complete with buffer zones along the major waterways, that was much in the news and attracting a lot of support. But a quick backlash rose up against it, seemingly organized by one of Birmingham's biggest law firms, which recruited some major developers and contractors to oppose the plan. And the backlash was indeed successful in weakening the plan, setting back stormwater management plans for the local area by a decade.

When Beth Stewart followed Don Elder as executive director of the Cahaba River Society in 1995, the lawsuit against Jefferson County was as yet unresolved. It seems to me, looking at things as an outsider, that her long-term plan of building one-on-one relationships—with mayors and city council members as well as with major players in the development community—is really paying off. Fifteen years after the antienvironmental backlash to the stormwater management plan, city leaders and developers in the greater Birmingham area now frequently initiate contact with the society for advice on ecologically responsible development. Beth tells me that every single city and county in the upper Cahaba watershed has either adopted improved stormwater design requirements for development or is in the process of doing so—which means that the basic recommendations from the regional planning commission for 2004 are finally in place.

So much for a sketch of the Cahaba River Society (and the Freshwater Land Trust), from what I've known for a while and what I learned more recently. Of late, though, I've become aware of other environmental organizations concerned in whole or in part with the Cahaba River. Naturally enough I've been curious about their relationships with the Cahaba River Society, too.

The Glades and the Nature Conservancy

The Cahaba lily has been adopted as one visual symbol of the Cahaba River Society, most visibly on personalized "Save the Cahaba" car license plates. Back in the late 1980s Larry Davenport, who'd joined the Samford biology department to teach botany, was just getting into his work with the Cahaba lily, for which he is now widely known. Bob Stiles and I took him out and showed him some of the stands of it we knew about—a stand on Buck Creek not far downstream from the dam in Helena, for one, that you could just about drive to. I took Larry on an all-day canoe trip on the (lower) Little Cahaba from Bulldog Bend down to the Highway 26 bridge on the main Cahaba just to show him all the lily shoals down that lowest stretch of the Little Cahaba. There was a scattering of lily stands all down that particular run of the lower Little Cahaba, but the main attraction was one spectacular stretch of Cahaba lilies at least a quarter of a mile long, a great sloping, watery field of lilies growing from bank to bank, that Larry really got excited about. But on that very trip we missed the bigger botanical scoop.

In 1992, not all that long after the trip Larry and I made, Georgia botanist Jim Allison and three friends were canoeing that same stretch of river. Less than two miles downriver from the canoe put-in at Bulldog Bend, on the right-hand side, a rocky outcrop virtually devoid of vegetation slants down to the river. I'd almost swear that when Larry and I canoed that stretch earlier we actually stopped there to rest, to eat or drink something; I know for sure that I have stopped there on some of the couple dozen or so times I've floated that run. But Jim Allison must have done more than just stop. In wandering up on top of the rocky slope he found what at first sight looked like an unimpressive, thinly vegetated rocky flat, but on closer inspection the vegetation included plants he didn't know at all. It turned out to be the corner of some one thousand acres of land that is by far the most botanically diverse small area in the whole state of Alabama, with sixty-one rare plants and eight entirely new to science. Apparently it's all owing to the geology, the rock being an unusually pure Ketona dolomite that has much less silica than dolomite limestone almost always has. The soil from the weathering of the rocky flat is both shallow and very high in magnesium, and the rocky flat itself is perhaps of great geological antiquity—hence the assemblage of rare and even unique plant species there.[5]

Today it's protected as the Kathy Stiles Freeland Bibb County Glades Preserve, thanks initially to Jim Allison but latterly to the Alabama chapter of the Nature Conservancy.[6] The Conservancy as a national movement had gotten started back in the 1950s as a spin-off of the academically oriented Ecological Society of America. Alabama was one of the last two states to get a chapter. That happened in 1989, the same year the Cahaba River Society was formed, coincidentally.

There's not exactly a network but certainly a mosaic of other organizations interested in whole or in part in the health of the Cahaba: the Cahaba Riverkeepers, who publish data from regular water monitoring sites every week; the Alabama Rivers Alliance, which includes over sixty watershed groups in the state (including Friends of Shades Creek, often mentioned in chapters to come); the Cahaba River Wildlife Management Area; and the Cahaba River National Wildlife Refuge. And for all I know there may be other organizations out there working to preserve the river. I hope so; it's a treasure that needs all the help it can get. Recently I saw a quotation attributed to John Muir (though perhaps falsely) that I hadn't seen before: "The human spirit needs places where nature has not been rearranged by the hand of man." I immediately thought of the free-flowing parts of the Cahaba system. *Recreation* is a word that over time has been cheapened with use: it's literally a *re-creation* of the person. Being out on the surface of the Cahaba or just walking along its banks does that for lots of us.

Last Reflections, Last Request

Over the years the Cahaba River has figured into my family's life in what seem today to be unusual ways. A family in the church we've belonged to since 1975 owned a home fronting the Cahaba somewhat downstream from the Highway 280 dam. On one Sunday in 1981 my two older children were both baptized there—Josh about nine years old and Andrea twelve—by our most flexible pastor, Otis Brooks. It was a half-humorous, half-serious family belief that if God ever spoke to us in audio frequencies, he would probably sound a lot like Otis.

In the decades since we moved to Alabama, I've collected the kind of wildlife memories in and along the river that anyone does who regularly visits the same natural locale year after year and in all seasons. I saw a hawk repeatedly dive on a family of black ducks in a pool there, without success, and it permanently expanded my understanding of the verb *duck*. I've seen a sizable cottonmouth there, its back half anchored in roots a foot or so above the water, trying to lift a one-and-a-half-pound bass it had by the back up out of the water—a bass bigger than anything I'd caught that day, I thought wryly. More than once, rattlesnakes, puffed up with air so as to float high, have swum across the river close to me. Lots of times I've seen deer swimming across (once a deer pursued by hounds, though they stopped at the water's edge); beaver more times than I can count; and several times otters. I've been cursed hundreds of times by kingfishers whose domains I've floated into, and hundreds of times more have earned that Jurassic croak from a disturbed great blue heron, flying off. Flocks of turkeys have flown noisily across the river over me, usually by ones and twos at a time until the whole flock was over, and—since their talents are more in running than in flying—usually crash-landed in the woods and brush on the other side.

A few years ago my son, Josh, visiting from his home in Houston, went canoe fishing with me. We went, just for old times' sake, to that familiar stretch of the Cahaba above Grants Mill Road bridge where I'd taken him so many times when he was young. I tied on a gaudy, angular floating crankbait that he made fun of at first sight, but it proved to be the lure of the day. Twitching it as it floated near the bank got me several good fish, and then—generously, I thought—I swapped rods with Josh so he could try it out. A really big bass exploded on it, broke the line, and made off with our one and only lure of the day.

We were about a quarter of a mile above the falls, just before where the river—if you're looking upstream—takes a sharp left bend. We were fishing the left bank, and were just about to ease the canoe around the inside of the bend when a mature, white-headed, and white-tailed bald eagle came flying down the river under the tree canopy, maybe hunting for ducks. It saw us and immediately flared, just a few yards from us—rowing the air with what I remember as an impressive square footage of underwing and tail surface—immediately heading back upriver whence it came. I know eagles are slowly moving back into this country, and that they love to be close to water, but neither of us had ever seen one on this stretch of the river in all the years we'd been on it. Then, as we continued around the bend, there was a swirl and a splash out in the middle of the river. It didn't look like the roughly oval rise of a gar coming up for a mouthful of air that we often saw there. Sure enough, as we paddled up even with that patch of disturbed water, floating there was the gaudy crankbait Josh had lost to a big fish back down around the bend.

So now I think of it as "miracle corner." There used to be a huge beech tree on the steep bank on the outside of the bend, especially handsome in the light green leaves of early spring and the coppery ones of fall, and how they were reflected in the water. For a while there was only its splintered stump, and even that is gone now, but I've still left instructions with the kids to scatter my ashes thereabouts. Maybe they'll help another beech grow.

Figure 1.4. Cahaba River at Grants Mill

In the foreground is the eroded old sill log and a massive anchoring iron rod, about all that's left from the original Grants Mill dam. The bend the author thinks of as "miracle corner" appears upstream in the far distance.

chapter two

Homewood's Salamander Migration and Festival

Friday morning, April 11, 2003, was cool and shady in the parking lot of Samford University's soccer fields off South Lakeshore Drive, but the gathering crowd was not there for soccer. This was a strange occurrence indeed, a formal City of Homewood dedication of a quarter-mile-long stretch of South Lakeshore—a two-lane blacktop road leading in to Homewood High School from the northeast—as an official salamander crossing zone.[1]

Some of Homewood's finest were directing traffic into the lot, where a portable lectern had been set up. The mayor and several city council members were mixing with members of the Homewood-based Friends of Shades Creek and with local college and high school biology students brought for the occasion by their teachers. Altogether there were probably between two and three hundred people, including a half dozen reporters and a couple of TV camera crews. Everybody seemed to be in a good mood, either from the harmless absurdity of all this in the middle of a Second Gulf War in which people were getting killed, or from pure wonder at the environmental progressiveness demonstrated by a city dedicating a salamander crossing.

How it came about, and what it helped lead to, is an interesting tale. I don't know all the ins and outs of it, but I am positioned so as to know as much of the whole tale as anybody, probably. For me it all started the very first fall and winter I was in town, 1971–72, when I got involved in Birmingham's herpetology society and learned about the annual spotted salamander migration off the wooded slopes of Shades Mountain. "Herpetology," you may already know, means the study of reptiles and amphibians. The first part of the word translates literally from the Greek as "creepers" (presumably referring to the creatures, though at times on the hunt it might seem to apply to their collectors as well!). The way I'd tell the story would be to begin with the creatures themselves.

The Cycle of Life

Salamanders of the genus *Ambystoma* tend to be stout bodied and strikingly patterned, as shows in the common names of some species such as tiger, spotted, marbled, and ringed. Often called the mole family of salamanders, they all generally live underground in loose forest soil made from decaying leaf litter and old logs and limbs. They burrow deep in summer heat and drought and also in winter cold, and come up nearer the surface in the more temperate times of the year. But their eggs must hatch and the larvae develop in fairly still water, so their other main habitat requirement is standing water somewhere within salamander walking distance of home base in the woods. Best is a vernal ("springtime") pool: a wet-weather pond that fills up in winter and dries out in summer so there is no permanent population of salamander-larvae-eating fish. What this requires of almost every adult *Ambystoma*, once a year, is a trek from woods to pond, driven by the urge to breed, and back again. Time of year depends on the species, and for those species with wide distribution, also on latitude and elevation. Whenever they migrate, all kinds choose the hardest of night rains in which to move, probably the better to avoid predators in this most exposed hour or two of their year.

With this underground lifestyle and rainy-night breeding runs for all the *Ambystoma* species, then, the general public almost never encounters them. The occasional one may show up in a basement or a springhouse, or be dug up in an excavation, or be found under the bottom layer of logs in somebody's stack of firewood. Most of the year they are hard to find even for field biologists who go looking for them. But even amateurs can find them in migration time. All it takes is driving the roads in likely areas at ten miles an hour with your lights on bright, on nights of heavy rains. You'll likely need an explanation ready for police officers who come up behind you, having seen such slow and erratic driving only from the most drunken of the drunk. Think up false but plausible answers in advance to queries from concerned neighbors who catch you at it; their knowing the outright truth may damage your social status. But

Figure 2.1.
*Marbled
and spotted
salamanders*

A large marbled salamander and small spotted salamander.

the find, we amateur herpetologists would all agree, is worth it. It's like an Easter egg hunt but with more beautiful eggs, and they're aware, and they're mobile.

The two most common *Ambystoma* species in Alabama are the marbled (*A. opacum*) and spotted (*A. maculatum*) salamanders. Marbled salamanders are jet black with a white or silver mottling or mantling on the top of the head, back, and tail. They are short, chunky salamanders: a really big one might reach a little over five inches long. The marbling on the backs of males tends to be more pure white, and that of females silvery gray and contrasting less dramatically with the black background. This species typically breeds, in our latitude in central Alabama, in late September or October, migrating in the first cold rains of fall (though exceptional drought in late summer and fall, as happened for example in 2016, can delay things by months). They rendezvous in the damp depressions that will shortly fill up as wet-weather ponds. There in the depression, underneath a layer of dead leaves or under logs, they mate. The female lays dozens of surprisingly big (for her size), round grayish eggs there. She guards them until the depression begins to fill with water, usually in the rains that come in late November. Adults then migrate back up into the woods on the next heavy night rain.

The best way to find the salamanders, then, is nighttime driving on slick old country blacktop roads in the first cool rains of fall. The leaves haven't yet fallen thickly, and even a single pine needle shows up on the wet and shining road in your headlights. There will also be a scattering of different kinds of frogs and "lesser" (non-*Ambystoma*, that is) salamanders. You'll see the occasional snake, which will appear as big as a python to eyes trying to find small things. Then, all at once and usually in a low place in the road, you may come across two or three marbled salamanders in a row, sometimes more than one visible in your headlights at the same time. They will be walking so directly toward the depression where they'll breed (which will soon become a pond for their larvae to hatch and grow up in) that you can actually triangulate its location from their angles in crossing the road. If you know where the breeding site is, of course, you can tell whether they are going to or leaving from it by the direction in which they cross the road.

Then there are the larger spotted salamanders: average adults are upward of six inches in length, with nine inches not uncommon. They are dark chocolate brown on the back and grayish below, with two rows of irregular but usually fairly round yellow spots, one starting behind each eye, running down the side of the back, and picking up again on the tail, where both spots and rows merge and become even more irregular. The spots are a bright chrome yellow, though sometimes the ones on the head tend toward orange.

Spotted salamanders migrate in the first heavy, relatively warm (upward of 40 degrees Fahrenheit) rains of winter. In the vicinity of Birmingham, this most often means late January or early February; in Tennessee, where I grew up, it can be early March; in New Hampshire, where my older daughter lives, it can be late April or even May. Wherever they are, they tend to head for the same breeding sites that the marbled salamanders visited in the first cold fall rains, though now in late winter these are full ponds, and the mating is underwater. Male and female spotted salamanders—the females visibly pregnant with eggs, and the males sporting pouches on either side of their cloaca swollen with spermatophores—hike down to and then into these ponds. Then, walking in slow motion on the leafy bottom of the pond, they go through their ritual mating. It is sometimes described as a dance, and its culmination is near when an interested female follows closely behind a male. On the leafy floor the male deposits what looks like a tiny white mushroom, and the following female picks up this spermatophore with the lips of her cloaca for internal fertilization. Then his job is done, and hers is as well after she lays her eggs. On the next heavy night rains, they crawl back up into the woods for another year of solitude. "Let there be spaces in your togetherness," the philosopher Kahlil Gibran advised loving couples, though he probably would have judged this to be extreme.[2]

If you want to catch one to look at it or help it across the road to protect it from other traffic, you can usually just pick up individuals of all *Ambystoma* species. They can run a little, but the run is slow and doesn't last long, and they are neither slimy nor slick like some other salamanders—just damp. Almost never in my half century of tracking such migrations has one offered to bite me when I picked it up by the middle, and even if you should choose the very rare belligerent, it's got no jaw teeth other than microscopic. But an easier way is to take a square plastic refrigerator carton, put it on the road with the open side in front of the salamander's nose, and then tickle the end of the salamander's tail: it will almost always run straight in. Then you can examine it at your leisure—meaning back inside your vehicle, out of the heavy rain—without ever touching it (except for the tickle).

The Rest of the Life Cycle

To round out the life cycle of the spotted salamander: as the female lays her egg mass, she attaches it to dead limbs or plant stems that hold it up off the leafy bottom of the pond. The egg mass then absorbs water and swells to the size of a child's fist or even a softball, clear jelly with little black dots scattered evenly throughout. Over the next few weeks, the jelly, especially on top, turns light green or brown with algae. Just in the past few years biologists have discovered that some algae are actually incorporated into the cells of the spotted salamander egg to provide oxygen directly—apparently the only known instance of this in vertebrate animals. Fairly quickly the little dots become miniature tailed creatures circumscribed each in a small sphere, occasionally wriggling to change position in the sphere or exercise growing muscles or, who knows, just because wriggling is fun.

When a salamander larva hatches from the jelly, it can easily be distinguished from a frog tadpole because of its external gills, little feathery structures on each side of the head just back of the jaw. The larval spotted salamander is a fully mobile little hunter from the very first and soon begins to stab away at beasties in the water too small for the human eye to see. These leafy-bottomed, wet-weather ponds abound with life, are a veritable soup of life.

Late in spring the *Ambystoma* larvae, both marbled and spotted, transform into miniature adults by absorbing their external gills and coming out of the water. They make their first land journey then to the woods of their ancestors. It takes a really keen and lucky eye to see these thin, two- or three-inch-long salamanders crossing a rainy night road. And if you do find one, it's hard to tell what species you've found because it won't yet have developed its adult color scheme. Handle these juveniles with care, because this may be their first walk of many. There are records of spotted salamanders that lived upward of thirty years.

Thoreau has a luminous passage in *Walden* on his delight at hoeing a field. His hoe tinkles on worked stones from unchronicled bygone cultures, accompanied by the sounds of a brown thrasher singing, nighthawks spiraling up and booming down, and two "hen-hawks" circling, sometimes approaching and then flying away from each other, like his thoughts. Then comes this sentence: "Or I was attracted by the passage of wild pigeons from this wood to that, with a slight quivering winnowing sound and carrier haste; or from under a rotten stump my hoe turned up a sluggish portentous and outlandish spotted salamander, a trace of Egypt and the Nile, yet our contemporary."[3] He was writing in 1854, five years before Darwin's *The Origin of Species* came out with the implications that the spotted salamander's origins were so far in the past that they made ancient civilization in Egypt look like yesterday. The perceived scale of time has changed from Thoreau's day to today in the question of origins, both for *Ambystoma maculatum* and for *Homo sapiens*. Still, Thoreau captured the essence of the encounter between old and young with his "yet our contemporary."

The State of the *Ambystoma* Salamanders Generally

Spotted and marbled salamanders generally range across the whole of Alabama— and for that matter, almost the whole eastern United States except for the Florida peninsula—though their need for old woods in proximity to wet-weather breeding ponds tends to limit them to scattered, isolated patches. There is concern these days about declining amphibian populations of all species, worldwide, for reasons not yet clear (acid rain? air pollution? stronger UV light? fungal infections? other? all of the above?). Over time, habitat destruction has probably done most to reduce *Ambystoma* populations in Alabama: wetland drainage, woodland conversion into pasture or field, or clear-cutting in a way that allows sheet erosion to remove the topsoil. Even the stocking of bass, bluegill, or catfish in natural, permanent, formerly fishless ponds is a slow death sentence for local *Ambystoma* stock as all the breeding adults and larvae get eaten up year after year. But where suitable habitat remains, life seems to find a way to survive. Even in the city.

Birmingham and suburbs grew so fast over the past century that they left isolated patches of countryside as islands in the urban flood. That archipelago of green spaces was taken for granted by us for the last couple of generations; you don't really appreciate the water till the well runs dry. Recently, however, especially in Homewood (just south of Red Mountain from downtown Birmingham), these green islands are quickly being discovered and developed, given the current demand for housing here. This demand is probably mostly a combination of convenient location and reputable public school system—plus, we are a remarkably nice bunch to live among, don't you know—but homes in Homewood can cost tens of thousands of dollars more than comparable real estate in some neighboring cities. Whatever the reasons, neither steepness of slope nor difficulty of access now deters development, and many Homewood residents feel a new concern about the last syllable of the city's name.

Discovering the Local Herpetology Society

Salamander chasers have known about a population of both spotted and marbled salamanders on the northern slope of Shades Mountain (generally across Shades Creek from what is today Samford University) for decades, from even before Samford (originally Howard College) moved to Homewood from Eastlake. Here's how I found out about it, and why I was interested in the first place.

Ever since my first elementary school encounters with salamanders, I had a hobby of finding and sometimes collecting them—that is, of going herping. One of the only times I'd ever been in Alabama before we moved here in 1971 was a Saturday road trip with a fellow graduate student at Vanderbilt who was putting himself through the PhD program in German history by collecting and selling herps. He'd gather frogs and turtles around Reelfoot Lake one weekend of the month, then salamanders from near the Smokies another weekend, stashing them in stacked-up refrigerator cartons in his fridge (he was divorced, perhaps not coincidentally) until he had a shipment. Then he'd sell them to what was then, it seemed to me at least, a surprisingly large and worldwide market of amphibian and reptile fanciers, shipping his herps by air freight to places as far off as Japan in big Styrofoam containers. So in or about 1969 I came down with him to the vicinity of Three Forks of the Flint River east of Huntsville to collect hellbenders, the heaviest of North American salamanders and one of the largest kinds in the world, reaching several pounds in weight and upward of thirty inches in length. Such commercial collecting of most herptiles is illegal now, and rightly so; it pains me to think back on that day, as rare as hellbenders are in the state nowadays.

So it was that I arrived on Samford's campus as a professional historian and an amateur herpetologist. Almost immediately I discovered there was indeed a local herpetology society and that, conveniently enough for me, it held its monthly meetings on the Samford campus. The next year Ken Marion came to town from Missouri to join the University of Alabama at Birmingham (UAB) biology department. A PhD herpetologist, he gradually took over the group and gave it more structure as well as a new meeting place at UAB. As of this writing he's still going strong as its leader nearly fifty years later. But in that first year I was involved, the herpetological society was less a scholarly organization and more a colorful group of hobbyists, meeting monthly, swapping stories, and bringing the occasional herp to show.

The members were mostly interested in snakes. There was an older gent named Tommy from out toward Anniston who was famous for displaying snakes from his private zoo in school settings. He'd slipped one night cleaning out his rattlesnake cages and gotten nailed on the back of the hand, and spent three days in the hospital in serious trouble from reaction to the venom and then six more days in even more serious trouble in reaction to the horse-serum antivenin he'd been given. There was a younger guy named Danny who lived down around the narrows of Old 280 who had a collection of some 150 snakes, including several subspecies of copperheads and a reticulated python so big that when you fed it you hoped to avoid being on the menu yourself. He ran a flower shop for his day job, and he traded snakes internationally as a hobby—having them delivered to the flower shop.

Danny told a memorable story about getting such a package. As I recall the story all these years later, he'd been expecting a colorful water snake of the genus *Natrix* when a package arrived. There were just a few customers, and they were in the back of the store, so he figured he could take a quick look at his new snake and they be none the wiser. He reached his bare hand down into the bag and came up with a most venomous four-foot-long Siamese cobra, genus *Naja*, at which point he realized with unusual clarity that he'd misread the label on the package. We asked him what in the world he did then. He said he couldn't throw it, since there were customers in the store, so he lowered it into a big flowerpot and put the base over the top. After all the customers left, he got his long snake tongs and oh-so-carefully put the cobra into a proper container.

Danny told us he'd gotten a request one November from a snake-handling church over on the Georgia line. The congregation wanted to have a service, taking literally that passage in Mark (verse 16:18, here from the King James Version): "They shall take up serpents; and if they drink any deadly thing, it shall not hurt them; they shall lay hands on the sick, and they shall recover." Unfortunately for the church leaders' plans, the snakes had all gone underground for winter. So Danny agreed to give them some venomous snakes, and if memory serves he said he decided to give them copperheads instead of rattlesnakes because the latter have much more potent venom. In turn they invited him to the church service. They did things in order, he recalled, not just throwing the snakes around, but letting people who felt the spirit on them come up front to the box to pick one up, or receive it from another person. Nobody got bitten, at least that time. And it was a good thing, because part of the logic of the whole happening was that if you did get bitten, it was God's will, and in that case there wasn't any use getting professional medical care from some human.

My reaction to that was to favor other scripture, particularly Matthew 4:7, "Thou shalt not tempt the Lord thy God." But Danny had an interesting take on it from the point of view of a longtime snake wrangler. He talked about how when you first go driving the roads for snakes at night, and you come across particularly pugnacious ones, you tend to pin them down firmly and grab them tightly, and they try their best to bite you. After you've done that for a few years, he said, you're not all that concerned whether they do bite you, and when you lightly scoop them up, they usually don't try to bite. He figured if literal believers in that verse in Mark truly thought they were right with God and had been called to handle serpents—even if they were country folk who generally thought the only good snake was a dead snake—they wouldn't be pinning and grabbing, and the snakes probably wouldn't bite. He thought maybe it was a 70–80 percent effective lie detector test. And he reasoned that was why the Siamese cobra hadn't bitten him earlier—he had thought he was picking up a harmless water snake and was not all that concerned whether it bit him, and that somehow communicated in body language.

The venomous snakes in the northern half of Alabama—various kinds of rattlesnakes, and then the copperheads and cottonmouths that are fairly closely related to each other—are all hemotoxic snakes; that is, their complicated stew of injectable poisons generally indiscriminately attacks the fluids and tissues it contacts. But there is also a large set of snakes, worldwide, whose venoms tend toward the neurotoxic, and they are generally more dangerous because many of their chemicals selectively paralyze the nervous system. Danny's Siamese cobra was one such, of course, but in south Alabama we have the beautiful but deadly little coral snake, and it has been seen as far north as Sylacauga.

On Venomous Snakes and Egyptian Pharaohs

Coincidentally with learning about all this, I was just beginning to teach Western Civilization 101, which got off to a running start with ancient Egypt and Mesopotamia before hitting its center of gravity in classical Greece and Rome. I had never taught 101, even as a graduate teaching assistant at Vanderbilt, and in fact had not had a course in it since my sophomore year in college. So in those first few teaching years I was scrambling to sort out whole ancient civilizations and then craft lectures with a "hook" to get my students interested.

In this quest I found an argument somewhere (which I could not refind in later years, so this is not going to be footnoted!) that talked about the totem animals of Egyptian nomes, or city-states—a bull for Memphis, a crocodile for Crocodilopolis, a cat for Bubastis, and so on—a living animal cared for by a special priesthood because it was believed to contain the life force of the city-state. While the animal was young and healthy, it led a charmed and pampered life. But when it got old or sick, it had to be ceremonially killed, without bloodshed, while its chosen successor stood next to it so the life force of the city could jump over into the new body for another generation. Usually they'd strangle or drown the old one; shedding much of its blood would have let the spirit leak out too, you can understand. Then the priests would eat special parts of the body at a ritual feast, and the rest of it would be embalmed. So at Memphis there were rows of huge sarcophagi holding bull mummies, at Crocodilopolis lots of long caskets, at Bubastis lots of little caskets, and on like that for the other nomes.

The real punch line of the argument was that the pharaoh (from *per-ao*, "great house") was for all of Egypt what the bull was for Memphis. When young and healthy, no pharaoh would have been in danger of assassination from any other Egyptian, because of their belief that his sudden death would have killed the life force of the land, too: no babies, calves, or foals, no sunrise ever again, just death moving through the streets like the green mist in the old *Ten Commandments* movie. But by the same token, when the pharaoh was old or sick not a hand could be raised to save him, because the life force of the land couldn't be allowed to sicken and die. The chief priest would presumably dress up as Anubis, the jackal-headed god of death, and bring the chosen successor—usually the son of one of the pharaoh's sisters—into his presence. There, without the shedding of blood, the old pharaoh would be killed. How? By hemotoxic viper. *Fu* or *f* was the onomatopoeic name Egyptians used for vipers, from their hissing or spitting, and Egypt has several spectacular and deadly kinds. And there, sure enough, in the early Old Kingdom king list this royal method of death is woven into the names of the great pyramid builders: Khu-fu, Kha-f-re, Se-ne-f-ru. In each case the hieroglyph for *f* or *fu* is a pictograph of a snake with a little "v" of horns on its head—obviously from the horned viper of the Sahara and much of the Middle East that has such little scale-like projections sticking up behind its eyes.

"Hemotoxic" means attacking the red blood cells, but it's a bit of a misnomer because it attacks tissues generally as well. Death by hemotoxic snake venom is, by all accounts, exceedingly painful. About this same time, beginning to take groups of Boy Scouts and church youth groups day hiking out at Oak Mountain or weekend backpacking up in the Bankhead National Forest or around Cheaha, I was becoming acutely aware of the presence of venomous snakes. There were on average some five hundred venomous snakebites yearly in the United States, mainly in the South and West, and they seemed to fall predominantly into two categories of people: macho young adult males usually illuminated by alcohol, of the "Here, hold my beer and watch this" variety (by whom I was entertained but for whom I was not responsible); and adventurous boys between the ages of five and fifteen who were bitten on the hand, foot, or fanny because they didn't look where they reached, stepped, or sat (by whom I was also entertained and for some of whom I was indeed responsible).

One of my doctor friends convinced me to get an antivenin kit, store it in the refrigerator, and then tuck it in my backpack on hikes. I did that for several years. Later another doctor friend convinced me to throw it away, because I'd have no idea whether the bitten person was allergic to horse-serum-based antivenin, which as I

Figure 2.2.
Royal cartouches
from the Old
Kingdom

Pharaoh names in hieroglyphs of (*top to bottom*) Snefru, Khufu,
and Khafre; in all three cases the horned viper symbol reads as
the /f/ sound. (Renderings courtesy of Alison Brown.)

should have learned from Tommy's case could be worse than the reaction to the snake
venom itself. But for years afterward I kept the little "levels of envenomation" foldout paper that came with the kit. Level 1: puncture wounds; could be from barbed
wire, thorn, or snakebite. Level 2: swelling and reddening around the site, fairly obviously venomous snakebite. Level 3: swelling spreading up limb (if limb was bitten), darkening around wound. And then on up to levels 4 and 5, with just a trickle
of bleeding from bodily orifices, to a state of drifting in and out of consciousness, to
death. All in all, it was a reading that made you want to stay on the concrete sidewalk
and off the grass even in suburbia, much less hike up in the Sipsey Wilderness.

But to round out the pharaohs and venomous snakes story, the argument continued that sometime late in the Old Kingdom some pharaoh gave it some thought
and substituted an asp, the neurotoxic Egyptian cobra, for a hemotoxic viper. One
bite from the cobra, pressed to your chest, and you just went to sleep in a few minutes

without all those agonizing hours of pain and unsightly trickles of blood from bodily orifices. So about the time the "f" and "fu" horned viper hieroglyphs drop out of the names on the king list, what should pop up on the front of the double crown of Upper and Lower Egypt but a rearing cobra? And then, much later, a yearly antelope sacrifice was substituted for the generational human one, and the pharaohs slid out from under their original responsibility altogether. What a great story, no? I hope it's true, because I told it to a generation of freshmen history students.

But I have wandered widely with this snaky detour out of a salamander migration and festival story. The relevant point for this story is that by the time I got to Homewood in 1971, members of the local herpetological society—even though snakes held primary place in their hearts—had already been following the marbled and spotted salamander breeding migrations across the valley from Samford for years, and that's where I learned about it.

THE SAMFORD BIOLOGY DEPARTMENT'S NATURE TRAIL

South Lakeshore Drive is on the other side of Shades Creek from the stately, divided, four-lane Lakeshore Drive proper. It lies right at the base of the steep northwestern face of Shades Mountain. Fifty years ago it was an uninterrupted two-lane blacktop that ran fairly straight and right at two miles between Old Montgomery Highway and Columbiana Road. Except for a few houses near the Columbiana end and a National Guard armory on the other, it was for long a totally undeveloped paved road running through the woods. As I heard the story from older faculty members at Samford, the biology department had created a nature trail on that northeast-facing hillside of Shades Mountain, above South Lakeshore. A piece of the trail still ran along the hillside east of where the new Homewood High School was built in 1972.[4]

For the next decade the trail was apparently beautifully maintained, both the actual pathway itself and the range of labeled species of plants along it. There was a sizable gated-off parking lot on the south side of South Lakeshore, perhaps a couple of hundred yards east of today's high school. Other zones of the hillside were set aside for study and experimentation. The nature trail and nature study areas were the creation of Professor Herb McCullough, chair of the Samford biology department. The trail was heavily visited by garden clubs, biology classes, and even religion classes that made use of the little outdoor theater or chapel of which you can still see the ruins today, just up a little creek from the old parking lot. But these groups had to have

Dr. McCullough's permission, and then he or a student assistant would have to go unlock the parking lot gates. Retired biology faculty members still remember a thick, venerable logbook that stayed in the office for years, one that recorded every single such group reservation since the dawn of the trail.

Then around 1971—and the biology department and its chair apparently learned this from the newspapers at the same time as the general public—the university swapped some lands with the city, giving the latter a diamond-shaped piece of land on which to build Homewood High School. Dr. McCullough was apparently so displeased that half his natural land had been given away with not so much as a word to him that he washed his hands of the whole, and the remnants of the nature trail gradually deteriorated.

In terms of *Ambystoma* salamander habitat on that northern slope of Shades Mountain facing Samford University, the high school development took the middle chunk of both woods and wetlands. But on either side of the high school the wetlands and old woods remained, and the salamander migration continued across these two stretches of South Lakeshore—with the longer stretch and greater population west of the high school, as I can personally attest. Occasionally an evening event at the high school would coincide with the appropriate hard seasonal rains, and a great slaughter of spotted or marbled salamanders, not to mention other amphibians, especially leopard frogs, would occur. It was accidental murder, not premeditated, and indeed the drivers probably never even knew. And it never seemed to cut into the basic *Ambystoma* populations enough to lessen the next year's migration.

Twenty or so years ago, around 2000, Samford decided the economic climate was right to develop the remaining hillside and floodplain lands west of the high school for office buildings, retirement homes, and apartment complexes. Some of it was done, most regrettably, by bulldozing the land off the forested slope there and filling in the floodplain, and then declaring the raised land no longer floodplain and therefore open to development. Since then Shades Creek, in revenge for having lost its floodplain thereabouts, rises up and floods Lakeshore Drive itself every three or four years. More to the point of this story, southwest of the high school most of the hillside woods and all the vernal pools that held standing water in the winter were destroyed in the process, and the salamanders seem to be totally gone there.

The shorter stretch east of the high school, a little over a quarter mile long, still has all its wooded hillside south of South Lakeshore (except for where the buildings and parking lots of Covenant Presbyterian sit). Just as important, it still has roughly half its wetlands north of the road (mostly in the old channel of Shades Creek from before the Lakeshore development of the late 1920s). As a result it sustains a remnant population of spotted salamanders. But the destruction of this remnant was a near thing.

THE HOMEWOOD FOREST PRESERVE

Those thirty-three acres of wooded hillside east of the high school, the site of the remaining piece of Samford's nature trail, by then forty years old, were also in the process of being opened for development by the university. Some of us on the Samford faculty argued against the destruction of the last of the nature trail. The City of Homewood, its decision makers probably not wanting to see more apartment buildings go up so near the high school, bought the thirty-three acres, though with no consideration at the time that this would be permanent green space. Since "Samford nature trail" was no longer an accurate description, we all began calling it Homewood Forest. This was kind of a grandiose expression—Sherwood Forest it ain't—but it had a ring to it, especially when the city later bought another thirty-two acres just uphill, taking it almost to the crest of Shades Mountain.

At this point in the story, lots and lots of people got involved. So there are a slew of names coming up, sometimes one or more a sentence, and if you aren't from Homewood (or maybe even if you are!) you won't know many of them. But I'm doing this partly for the historical record (though some of this is hearsay), and partly just to show how many folks it takes to make a real community happening work.

Hans Paul was on the Homewood Environmental Commission, originally the Homewood Tree Commission. He recently told me that he first found out about the thirty-three acres when he, Henry Hughes, and Michelle Blackwood, also on the Environmental Commission, were trying to do something about tree canopy preservation and restoration in Homewood. So Hans, Henry, Michelle, and Wendy Jackson of the fairly new Black Warrior Cahaba Rivers Land Trust made a presentation to the city council on somehow preserving it as green space. As Hans remembers it, the presentation fell flat. At that point all the city was willing to do was allow a nine-year lease on the forest, essentially a pledge not to develop it for that long. Walking out after the meeting with the council head, Hans asked him what he, Hans, had to do to make a longer conservation easement happen. "The citizens will let us know when we need to do this," was the reply. And a light went on for Hans and coconspirators.

So regularly scheduled nature walks on the property were the beginning strategy, aimed at recruiting a critical mass of Homewood citizenry, who would let the city council know they needed to do this. Henry Hughes was one of the regular guides; an urban forester by training, he pointed out to interested walkers two-hundred-year-old white oaks, a near-state-record hop hornbeam right beside the remaining nature trail, and a large white ash that is fairly rare this far south. In general he talked about the botanic superiority of this rather natural old-growth woods to those city parks where leaf litter is never allowed to accumulate, much less decay, and where tree saplings and wildflowers are mowed down as soon as they come up.

Coming down the steep zigzag path to the flatter land by the road at the end of one of these walks, Henry and his hiking group found a painter with his easel set up in the woods, painting en plein air. Everybody introduced themselves, and it turned out to be Craig Galloway, then a professor in Samford's Divinity School (and today a professional artist). This encounter with an artist painting from nature in the woods inspired Henry to create an art and music venue, with all the art to celebrate the local environment. Henry knew Phillip Morris, the editor of *Southern Living* magazine, who was then still going strong at the ecologically designed buildings of Southern Progress (the magazine's publisher) just across Shades Creek and Lakeshore Drive from the thirty-three acres, and Morris agreed to host the event there. The first year, 1999, was a remarkable success, with lots of participating artists and what I'm told was a good crowd. There was even a music performance by Galloway and his wife, Deb, with him on guitar and her on cello. But for the second year attendance dwindled sharply, as if the year before was one and done. In 2001 and 2002 a new version of "the yearly event" was held in Samford's science building, courtesy of Betsy Dobbins, biology professor there and a member of the board of Friends of Shades Creek—the key institution in all this to be described shortly.

Meanwhile, the nature hikes went on. Greg Harber, who was very active in Birmingham Audubon, led bird walks there. Among other things he praised the dead trees left standing, quoting a popular birders' saying that "the tree may be dead, but it's full of life," and pointing to prime woodpecker feeding sites including for the spectacular and increasingly rare, crow-sized pileated woodpecker, whose call sounds like something out of a tropical jungle. Other natural history specialists took their turns too—Samford biology professors Mike Howell and Ron Jenkins on spiders, for example. I did one a few times featuring some traditional herb lore and, after a short detour off the main trail, described the functioning of a classic Alabama whiskey still from the ruins of three in the little creek valley just east of the high school (the Homewood police told me they knew all about them, dating back to the late 1960s, though they wouldn't tell me whose they were). It didn't hurt that a few local Boy Scout troops came to testify to the city council that they did their tune-up hikes on the remnant nature trail there.

And sure enough, gradually public interest in this green space built up.

FRIENDS OF SHADES CREEK

A most essential ingredient in all this was that during this same time Michelle Blackwood, Henry Hughes, and others were creating Friends of Shades Creek, an environmental organization that has grown since that day in numbers and scope of activity. It was the Friends of Shades Creek that took the spotted salamander as the poster child for efforts to preserve both the wooded slopes and the lowland wet-weather ponds. In fact, Friends of Shades Creek was started more than for any other reason to save what could be saved of that wooded northwest face of Shades Mountain above Lakeshore Drive.

Although lots of folks played "necessary but not sufficient" roles in this whole thing, I think everybody concerned would say the key individual in it all, the real leader, was Michelle Blackwood. She's a near neighbor of mine in the Edgewood area of Homewood, and she recently shared a part of her story with me, a part I didn't know much about. In the spring quarter of 1998, she was finishing up an art major and an environmental studies minor at UAB. For that last quarter she signed on for an internship in the relatively new Alabama Rivers Alliance. The alliance, of course, encouraged the creation of local watershed groups—usually triggered by some threat, as when the folks interested in Turkey Creek, with its extremely rare fish species, were disturbed by plans for construction of a huge jail right on its banks. And at the same time, Michelle was active in the Homewood school system, in which she had two kids. With her environmental interests and contacts and her detailed knowledge of what was going on in the schools in general and the city council in particular, she was the real creator of the Friends of Shades Creek.

Around the year 2000, Samford's newest vice president for business affairs, Bill Mathews, became an active member of the Friends of Shades Creek and a member of the Homewood Environmental Commission, and seemingly tried to serve as "honest broker" between university and city on developmental issues. An enthusiastic amateur naturalist himself, he heard about the spotted salamander migration of midwinter to early spring and tried, though without success, to find it. Michelle reacted by getting up a list of those who wanted to be called when the spotted salamanders were migrating, and details about how late at night they were willing to be called.

This has been a seasonal marker of mine for decades, ever since I learned about the migration that first year I was in Birmingham. I still watch for likely warm rains from the first of January, and then automatically wake in heavy rains at night. I'll typically say to my wife, quietly and apologetically, "I think they might be running," and she'll say, less quietly and not apologetically, "You're crazy," put a pillow over her head, and go back to sleep, while I dress, get rain gear and flashlight, and slip out of the house to the car. More often than not they will not, indeed, be running, but when they are it's a magical sort of thing. The great seasonal migrations of pioneer Alabama, when elk, woodland buffalo, and passenger pigeons circled through, are no more and never will be. Many smaller migrations, though, are still there if you look for them: in the springtime shoaling of the river redhorse sucker, when the tulip poplars are in full bloom; in May, when the spawning freshwater drum all come back downriver in the same four- to twenty-four-hour period after a big rain and a muddy river rise (chapters featuring these two to follow); in winter, when the cedar waxwings come in greedy flocks and strip berry-bearing trees clean.

Earlier I'd taken Michelle out to see the annual spotted salamander run, and she became as enchanted with it as I'd always been. Michelle and I struck a deal, then, that if and when I found the spotted salamanders migrating I would call her and she would play Paul Revere. In early 2002 I found them running at three o'clock in the morning. I called Michelle, she called around, and before half an hour had passed, a dozen people had each seen at least one spotted salamander crossing the road. She remembers having to work up her courage to call Bill Mathews, somebody she hardly knew. Sure enough, to her consternation, Bill's wife, Melinda, answered the phone, and Michelle—an unknown woman calling Melinda's husband in the dead of night—awkwardly talked to her about the salamanders running. Melinda handed the phone to her husband, and indeed he came to the migration, says Michelle—but Melinda came with him.

At any rate, word of this strange yearly phenomenon spread—semisecretly, as with a cult—and in late January 2003 I found them running at the more reasonable hour of nine in the evening, and several dozen folks turned out in response to Michelle's call this time. This night's migration was more concentrated. Not only were lots seen crossing the road, but in the lone wet-weather pond on the hillside side of South Lakeshore many of them were seen crawling and swimming around the leafy bottom, beginning the mating ritual. And here were highly placed administrators of UAB and Samford, plus otherwise upstanding businesspeople, professionals, and good family folks, all willing to risk their reputations by such behavior—though I might note some brought children as an excuse. My wife later remarked drily that the ranks of insanity were growing. This may also have been the reaction of Homewood's mayor at that time, Barry McCulley, when he first heard about it from some police report about flashlights in the woods near the high school at eleven o'clock at night and suspicious answers to straightforward police questions.

Ah, it's a tangled chain with many links. Enter Don Stewart, who had just moved to Homewood in 2002 to open his own art gallery. Don was coming out of careers in medicine and marketing to pursue his first love, art, but even earlier in life he had majored in biology, and he still had a soft spot for the environment. He started sitting in on meetings of the Homewood Environmental Commission, and he joined its discussion on how to get the Homewood public in general to recognize the value of what was left green on that north-facing slope of Shades Mountain. It was here one evening that he heard Bill Mathews say he had great pictures of spotted salamanders from the yearly migration. Agreeing that this unusual salamander life cycle might be a visible thread to tie wetlands and woodlands together for schoolkids and their voting parents, Don broached the idea of a salamander crossing and maybe even a festival to folks at the Homewood Chamber of Commerce. They saw this as a city uniqueness, perhaps even a source of future tourism, and took it to Mayor McCulley. Meanwhile the mayor had heard from Bill Mathews that indeed there was such a salamander migration and that he, Bill, had actually been out there waving one of those mysterious flashlights in the woods.

So the mayor responded to the chamber of commerce proposal with some enthusiasm, and the folks at the chamber asked Don, on the spur of the moment, to make a presentation to the city council. That was scheduled for March 17, 2003, and "salamanders" was the last item on a full agenda. It was a particularly contentious meeting, especially heated on the subject of where to locate soccer fields. Don figured they probably wouldn't even get to the salamander issue, much less react to it positively. But he finally was given time to present, and much to his surprise the city council members were virtually unanimous in support. Even more surprising was that the subject generated great good humor among council members, with lots of laughter and slapping of one another on the back, those same backs they might have been afraid to turn a few minutes earlier. Spotted salamanders were a lot like pandas, Don reasoned with me later: they're not of any obvious use, but they put everybody in a good mood. And so a city celebration of the spotted salamander crossing site on South Lakeshore was set for three and a half weeks later, and came off on April 11 as described at the first of this chapter.

A nice article about it in the next day's *Birmingham News* called the gathering, accurately enough, "a cross-pollination of traditional city promotion and ecological concerns."[5] Ken Marion, the aforementioned herpetologist at UAB (and by this time chair of the biology department there) had loaned us his six-year-old, seven-inch-long, raised-from-the-egg spotted salamander for the occasion, and it was viewed by most and photographed by many. Don Stewart spoke, as painter of the larger-than-life spotted salamanders on the road as well as designer of the black-and-yellow diamond-shaped "salamander crossing" road signs. He reminisced about his early training in amphibians under the legendary Dan Holliman of Birmingham-Southern College's biology department. Michelle Blackwood for the Friends of Shades Creek, Hans Paul for the Environmental Commission, and someone from the chamber made some remarks. I rambled on about the life cycle of the amphibious guest of honor. But the best line of the day was the mayor's: "Nature and a community can coexist when we care enough to do something about it." Then we all went back to work or class, still smiling.

There was some casual conversation at the Friday dedication of the spotted salamander crossing zone back in 2003 on how attractive to collectors of road signs these one-of-a-kind signs—well, two-of-a-kind, since there was one at each end of the quarter-mile stretch of South Lakeshore—would be. Think of it: such signs going up on a main road to the high school a month before graduation was surely a challenge for any self-respecting, red-blooded senior class. Sure enough, within three days they were both stolen. One was returned later—under heavy parental duress, it was said. Replacements apparently cost the city seventy-five dollars apiece. The new ones were welded to their posts, but adolescent sign collectors are generally a creative and persistent lot, so to date the city has given up on replacing them.

The April 2003 Homewood city dedication of a salamander crossing was kind of a sudden and spontaneous sideshow to the longer effort to get preservation status for the thirty-three acres. Henry Hughes, central to the movement to get the forested slope protected and a salamander festival going, told me that he didn't even

*Figure 2.3.
Spotted
salamander
crossing sign*

One of the original salamander crossing signs on South Lakeshore just east of Homewood High School.

hear about the Saturday salamander crossing dedication until after it happened. But it probably helped with city politics. The city council, having seen preliminary plans for covering the slope of Shades Mountain just east of the high school with condos and apartments, seemed to be united against having apartments right next to the school grounds. The city bought the thirty-three acres from Samford and—not having any particularly pressing plans for it—was amenable to giving that nine-year lease on the property to Friends of Shades Creek.

Later, for the same reason, the city bought an adjoining thirty-two acres, bringing the total area of green space to sixty-five acres. In 2008, when Hans and friends were about to ask timidly for perhaps a twenty- or at most fifty-year dedication of the land as green space, Hans says that someone on the city council encouraged them to ask for it "in perpetuity." And so they asked for, and they won, a permanent conservation easement for the sixty-five acres now known as the Homewood Forest Preserve. It's administered by what was then the Black Warrior Cahaba Rivers Land Trust, today the Freshwater Land Trust.

The Salamander Festival, 2004–Present

As a result of all the foregoing—the work of dozens and dozens of folks involved over the years and particularly the leadership of Michelle, Hans, Henry, and Betsy—there's a most interesting yearly salamander festival in Homewood. Its first modern iteration was in 2004, hard on the heels of that 2003 salamander crossing event. It's settled down date-wise to the afternoon of the last Saturday in January—just around the time of the expected spotted salamander migration to the vernal pools and back again—and place-wise to the Senior Center in Homewood on Oakmont Avenue or the building and grounds of the Shades Valley Community Church just up the street. Upcoming years will probably look a lot like 2020's, the last one before this writing. Betsy will have organized the animal display tables and have gotten there early with Michelle for setup. As usual, Craig and Deb will staff the sign-in and information desk up near the entrance of the hall. Carl will have his Alabama fossils at a side table down the entrance hall. At the end of the hall, Ken, Megan, and Kristen, herpetologists respectively with UAB, Birmingham-Southern, and Samford, will be there showing off herps. They'll have herpetology nature guidebooks including Joe Mitchell and Whit Gibbons's *Salamanders of the Southeast* scattered around.[6] They'll let the kids handle the more placid ones, including spotted and marbled salamanders. All three will have half smiles on their faces the whole afternoon, the effect of a growing crowd of hundreds (around 650 in January 2019, over 800 in January 2020) turning out to share their lifelong passionate interest in amphibians and reptiles.

In the main room there'll be a table for food and drink, courtesy of Michelle, Jane, and friends. Booths around the walls will represent local environmental groups such as the Cahaba River Society, Alabama Audubon, and the Alabama Rivers Alliance. Folks from the raptor rehab center from Oak Mountain, as they have the past couple of years, will probably parade hawks and owls around the hall. Herb may come with his great string band. If he doesn't, Rob will come with his bluegrass group, most recently named the "Over-the-hillbillies." James will be there with "Mr. Shady," a manikin fully dressed in clothing articles recovered from the creek in yearly trash pickup days. Crafting tables will set up around the far side of the room for kids— Carol and Carolyn will be presiding over the making of spotted salamander replicas of black and yellow clay, or helping kids try their hand at Japanese-style fishprints using rubber fish models, or assisting with some other craft. Henry will preside at a Botanical Gardens table with lots of local plant demos. Some storyteller will be given the mic at center stage to tell the children present the story of the salamander migration, and Olivia, dressed in her spotted salamander costume, will crawl across the floor in delightful imitation—maybe again this coming year as a couple of years ago accompanied by a little girl in her own matching costume. Ellen and Todd will bring their microscopes, with Todd providing the mulch to be examined. Melanie will bring in some high school kids to help out with what needs helping out. Henry or Michelle or somebody they've picked will emcee, recognizing dignitaries and naming the Volunteer of the Year.

I will only get glimpses of what's happening in the main auditorium because I'll be out in the hall or a side room as an honorary herpetologist, spelling the real professionals out there, delighting to help children touch or even hold spotted and marbled salamanders. It's my "catcher in the rye" moment of the year, showing kids something way more interesting than electronic games or videos. Anticipation of it and buoyant memory of it, even as I write, give me the same half smile as on the faces of herpetologists Ken, Megan, and Kristen. And at the end the cleanup crew will include many spouses of the folks named above. It's a good-hearted bunch, all these nature-minded and public-spirited adults who help put it on. The band may be paid a little something, but otherwise not a soul is there for the money; if anything, it costs almost everybody there a certain amount of cash and a lot of hours of preparation time.

The salamander crossing signs on South Lakeshore may be gone, but I hope the spotted salamanders themselves can stay. All it requires is to keep the woodland as is and the remaining wetlands as are, to refrain from mounting a string of street lights along that stretch of South Lakeshore, and maybe to protect an occasional badly timed migration from the cars letting out of an evening high school function by temporarily diverting traffic southwest.

It's not just about salamanders and a few hobbyists' strange fascination with them. It's green space for psychological health and even a degree of physical health with all those trees filtering the air of urban pollution and softening the roar of urban noise. It's to keep the barred owls that nest there, the pileated woodpeckers that live there, the mink whose footprints you see there. It's for the liverleaf and anemone that bloom in early February, the carpet of dogtooth violet that blooms in low places there on the Ides of March, the clouds of understory red buckeye that bloom later, the perfoliate bellwort and Indian pink beside the nature trail—in many ways a richer natural mix than even the Birmingham Botanical Gardens' wildflower section. The wonderful hiking trail is open to all and worth an hour of your time if you enjoy nature. So is the end-of-January salamander festival, especially if you've got children or grandchildren to bring along.

Figure 2.4. Ellie and a new acquaintance

Making friends with a marbled salamander at the salamander festival. (Photo courtesy of Ellie's grandmother Jo Kittinger.)

And so a formerly invisible, intangible connection between the hillside woods just east of the high school and the wetland ponds below and even across the road has been made visible and tangible by the publicity given the spotted salamander migration. The revealed magic of this remnant seasonal migration—that children instinctively recognize and that gets reawakened in some adults in the yearly celebration—has hopefully secured the preservation of this green space and its associated creatures for our grandchildren and their grandchildren to come.

A week or so before Homewood's 2020 end-of-January salamander festival, I went driving down South Lakeshore about midnight on the promise of some coming showers that might bring the spotted salamanders out. It was my forty-ninth straight year of doing so, I now calculate. The rains turned out to be just light and intermittent, so there were only frogs on the road, mostly leopard frogs jumping across in continuous two- to three-foot-long bounds, rarely stopping. The third one of those I braked for, right in front of the headlights, was swooped down on by a barred owl. The owl sat there for ten or fifteen seconds, swiveling its head several times from looking straight toward the headlights to looking straight away, and then flew off with its catch back into the woods. The road was steamrolled asphalt; the car and headlights were, if not of the latest model at least one of the later ones; and it was happening in an incorporated city. And yet it was a dramatic and elemental natural drama, fit for being narrated by David Attenborough in some high-budget, prize-winning nature film. Nature and a community can coexist when we care enough to do something about it.

chapter three

The Archy Culvert, a.k.a. Ross Bridge

Discovery and Rediscovery

Sometime in 1971 or 1972, early in my stay in Birmingham, I was out hiking where the main north–south railroad through Birmingham (then still the Louisville and Nashville, L&N; today the CSX line) crosses Shannon Oxmoor Road, some eight or nine miles southwest of downtown Birmingham. At that time in the flat area south of the railroad crossing there was a fenced-in horse-riding business where you couldn't hike. All along the main tracks southwest of that, though—as well as in what seemed to be an older railroad bed alongside it and a nearby, parallel, high-voltage power line right-of-way—there was good blackberry picking, among other things. I don't recall exactly what I was doing there on this particular day, but I ran into an old-timer who was also out knocking around the woods and fields. We struck up a conversation, and on learning that I was fairly new to the area, he asked me whether I knew about the old Civil War–era, slave-built stone culvert a ways off in the woods. I said I did not. He offered to hike me out to see it, and, being of the age of innocence and immortality, I went with him. And it was a remarkable sight—not just a functional culvert or viaduct to let Ross Creek, a sizable stream, under an old railroad causeway, but a hand-cut stone work of art.

I didn't think of it again for decades, until around the year 2000 when the City of Homewood began exploring purchase of the long-defunct horse farm land for ball fields and such. I told my neighbor Michelle Blackwood and others in the newly organized Friends of Shades Creek that there was a truly interesting structure out

Figure 3.1. West face of the Ross Creek viaduct

The Ross Creek viaduct as we found it, before the vegetation was removed for photographing and measuring.

there, possibly on the land that interested Homewood. Intrigued, especially since Ross Creek is a tributary of Shades Creek, she got together a group for me to guide there one Saturday.

I remembered the old stone viaduct as being maybe a quarter mile down the tracks from the Shannon crossing. We hiked down the old rail bed about that far and found a creek but no sign of any viaduct, much less one with a railroad causeway over it. The other hikers looked at me skeptically and then wound up going off exploring on their own. Much puzzled and a little bit embarrassed, I set off farther down the modern tracks. Another full mile down the tracks, there was a level, long-radius curved path leading off to the left, obviously an old railroad grade where steel had long been pulled. Another quarter mile and more down this path through the woods, I found my causeway and scrambled down its steep slopes to see one face of the old stone viaduct that went through it. I guess a mile-and-a-half hike in my late twenties felt like a quarter-mile hike did in my late fifties! I went back, rounded up the members of the group, and guided them there, partly just to prove I wasn't crazy. They were as wowed by their first sight of the structure as I had been.

Alerting Hoover to What the City Now Had

Then Hoover, instead of Homewood, annexed the property and slated it for development. I think it was my Samford history department colleague Marlene Rikard, longtime resident of Hoover, who told us how to get in contact with city council members about it, just to make sure they knew what they now had. Michelle Blackwood for Friends of Shades Creek and Randy Haddock for the Cahaba River Society asked to be allowed to present concerns (about such a major development in the Shades Creek and thus Cahaba River drainages) to the Hoover City Council.

Michelle in particular spent most of her time talking about the viaduct or culvert, explaining that it would make a wonderful nucleus for a fifty-acre park in the new upscale housing development being planned, and a natural central point for rails-to-trails walking paths. By this time I'd done a rough perspective drawing of it, showing the perfect fifteen-course Roman arch running the length of the sixty-two-foot-long culvert, dropped keystone and all. Michelle brought color photos with her that also showed the unusual, perhaps unique, semicircular walls of each outside face of the viaduct, and passed the pictures out—one to each council member—so they could see what it looked like. Since the planners had their easels and maps set up with US Steel Real Estate and Daniel Corporation's development plans, she told me, she was able to show exactly where the structure was located on them. It was Michelle's impression that neither the developers nor anyone on the Hoover City Council knew that the structure was even there, much less that this new property annexation made it one of the oldest substantial man-made structures in the city.[1]

The current head of the council showed considerable interest. When asked, Michelle assured him that it was still there and said she'd be happy to take him to it. Henry Hughes went, too, and the three of them hiked in from Shannon crossing— that mile-and-a-quarter distance down the main modern tracks and the remaining quarter mile or so along the old causeway. As Michelle remembers it, when they finally got there the council member was much impressed.[2]

So the Hoover city government responded positively to the idea of preserving it. Daniel Corporation, the residential developer, agreed to dedicate a two-acre

Figure 3.2.
Perspective
drawing of
the culvert
before
cleaning

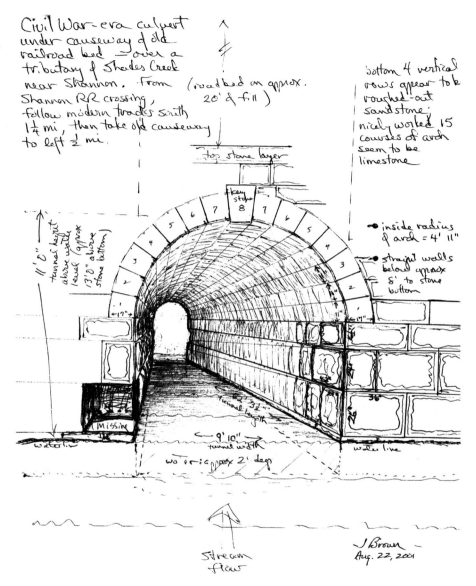

Civil War-era culvert
under causeway of old
railroad bed → over a
tributary of Shades Creek
near Shannon. From   (roadbed on approx.
Shannon RR crossing,   20' d fill)
follow modern tracks south
1¼ mi, then take old causeway
to left ½ mi.

bottom 4 vertical
rows appear to be
roughed-out
sandstone;
nicely worked 15
courses of arch
seem to be
limestone

top stone layer

key stone

8

• inside radius
  of arch = 4' 11"

• straight walls
  below approx
  8' to stone
  bottom

11' 0"
tunnel height
above water
level (approx
13' 0" above
stone bottom)

←17"→

Missing

water line

← 9' 10" →
tunnel width

water is approx 2' deep

water line

Stream
flow

J Brower
Aug. 22, 2001

A drawing the author did for Friends of Shades Creek in an attempt to show the dimensions of the vaulted structure. The drawing is dated August 22, 2001; it had been a long time since the author's college freshman engineering course in mechanical drawing.

preserve/park with the viaduct at its center. A bit sadly, from our point of view, this was just a fraction of the fifty-acre park Michelle and Friends of Shades Creek had suggested, and with almost none of its rails-to-trails plan. Neither, as Michelle remembers it, was there a word of thanks then or later to Friends of Shades Creek for alerting the developer to this architectural gem. After all, for the real estate development corporation, it went some way toward turning proximity to a very busy (and noisy!) railroad track from a negative in terms of residential development to a positive. The main sales office in the development for the first dozen years or so actually had a railroad theme inside, and it still looks like an old-fashioned railroad terminal from the outside. At that first meeting of the city council, the developers were calling it the Shannon Valley development. One of the developers asked Michelle whether any Native Americans had lived there, with perhaps an Indian name still attached to the site? She said there were undoubtedly Native Americans, and names for local geographic features, but if so no one we knew remembered them. But she told him what little we then knew of the Ross family, whose name was given to the creek. She gave him my phone number, and when we talked and emailed later, I reiterated basically the same information.

At the next city council meeting the developers made revised presentations, and all of a sudden the development's name was Ross Bridge. As of this writing the Ross Bridge development website, anchored by a beautiful color picture of the east face of the viaduct and the deep pool there, still opens with a couple of pages of text about the old viaduct, including this paragraph: "Beyond its uncontested role as one of Birmingham's beloved historic landmarks, the impact of the bridge at Ross Creek is quite clear—as it was the inspiration behind our distinct community here at Ross Bridge! We think you'll agree—there's no question that Ross Bridge offers home buyers an opportunity to live in a remarkable . . ."[3]

Well, for starters, "the inspiration behind our distinct community" seems to reverse historical causality. And of course it's not a bridge at all: it's a culvert or a viaduct. I'm guessing "culvert" was a less upscale word than "bridge" in the eyes of the real estate developers. But at least between the city of Hoover and the US Steel and Daniel Corporation developers the beautiful stone culvert and the causeway over it are preserved and celebrated.

Around this time, some industrial historians specializing in Alabama were invited to take a look at the arched culvert. They were of the general opinion that such a sophisticated and obviously expensive stone structure could not have been built with money from the South, especially during the Civil War; it had to have been the product of new northern money that flooded in years later. After all, the railroad tracks coming up from Selma hadn't made it north over Brock's Gap in Shades Mountain until 1871, six full years after the Civil War ended; why would they have needed a causeway and culvert before then? I was disappointed to think my old-timer should have been so mistaken, but I had neither the inclination nor knowledge to dig into local history enough to prove this new claim right or wrong. It was not until 2017—some forty-five years after I first saw the culvert and over fifteen years after I first hiked with Friends of Shades Creek folks out to see it—that things began to happen in a rush to bring it all into focus.

Figure 3.3.
Location of the old causeway (overview)

The background is aerial photography from 2003 as used in Google Earth. The black line is the modern CSX railroad (formerly L&N, and on a route unchanged since it was built in 1907). The thicker aqua line is Shades Creek, and the thinner one is Ross Creek. The short red line is the old railroad causeway over Ross Creek, and the white lines are the remains of the pre-1907 railroad bed. The yellow circle, centered on the culvert or viaduct, is exactly one mile in diameter.

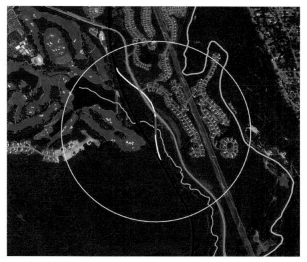

Figure 3.4.
Location
of the old
causeway
(zoomed in)

On the close-up map the aerial photography background is more recent, circa 2019, clearly showing golf course and housing developments. This figure features the same one-mile-diameter yellow circle centered on the viaduct, and the same red causeway with white lines tracing the pre-1907 railroad bed. The added green line is the Ross Bridge Parkway, dating from 2006.

MARJORIE WHITE TAKES AN INTEREST

In or about late 2015, Marjorie White of the Birmingham Historical Society began assembling a team to work on a history of Shades Creek and the communities that had grown up along it and its tributaries, which of course included Ross Creek.

I only knew of Marjorie and her work at the Birmingham Historical Society in a vague sort of way. I'd first met her way back in the mid-1970s (1975?) when she and some friends had taken our Samford history department's experimental New Horizons in History course. The course was the brainchild of department chair David Vess, and was primarily intended as professional development for middle and high school history teachers. The general idea was to let teachers explore some new teaching approaches. In addition to David, three of us team-taught the course: Wayne Flynt, just getting his teeth into his study of "poor whites"; Leah Atkins, becoming known for her work on Birmingham history; and me. It ran four weekends spread over the fall semester, three hours on Friday evening and an eight-hour, all-day session on Saturday. We taught it in 1974, 1975, and 1976, and then in 1977 Wayne went off to chair the department at Auburn, I went off on sabbatical, and we never did it again. But while it lasted it was a strenuous but exciting (at least to us) course, one that will figure into several chapters to come.

The main point here is that although I'd met Marjorie in that New Horizons course, and later knew hazily about her heading up the Birmingham Historical Society and spearheading its work, that was about it. I was not much interested in local history per se, being much more attracted to local natural history and folklore.

As I remember it, sometime in fall or winter 2016 mutual friends directed Marjorie to me for information about the historic structure at the heart of the fairly new Ross Bridge community—maybe pointing her to me because in introducing the structure to them I had been somewhat proprietorial about its discovery. Marjorie and I arranged to meet out there and explore, a much easier exploration than it used to be because the new Ross Creek Parkway runs within sight of the culvert. On the day of our explorations, Marjorie brought with her Birgit Kibelka, a landscape architect, though I didn't know where Birgit fit into the picture at the time. Remarkably, almost unaccountably, Marjorie had never seen this fascinating structure, despite the fact that she had led history efforts locally for over forty years and had been all over Jefferson and surrounding counties like a herd of sheep! She and Birgit were as enchanted by their first sight of it as I had been, and very much intrigued by the local lore that said it dated to the Civil War and had been built by enslaved laborers.

Documentation Day

What happened next was that I was invited by Marjorie to participate in a February 20, 2017, cleaning and documentation day for Ross Creek culvert. The basic idea was to start by getting rid of the vegetation sprouting from the cracks in the structure so that it could be properly photographed and measured. Since the water in the pool at the downstream end was deeper than head high, some sort of stable flotation was needed for cleaners and measurers. I threw my two canoes on the ladder rack of my old pickup truck, parked on the road within sight of the culvert, and slid them down to the water. There I lashed a hickory walking stick across the middle thwarts of the two canoes and then tied the bows and sterns together to make one fairly stable platform of the two. I brought waders for sloshing around in the shallows of the upstream end and down through the sixty-two-foot tunnel made by the culvert.

Figure 3.5.
Ross Creek
culvert,
elevation
from the east

One of the official Historic American Engineering Record photographs made on that cleaning and documentation day, February 20, 2017, by photographer Jet Lowe. Note hiking stick lashed across middle thwarts of canoes, bows and sterns tied together for stability! (HAER AL-214-1, courtesy of the Library of Congress, where all HAER photographs are deposited.)

We were a crew of eight, some of whom deserve more description in a minute, tearing vines and oakleaf hydrangea sprouts off the surface of the feature, measuring, and such. The day was sunny and got quite warm for February, and after a while it all started to feel like real work. I asked Marjorie what the going hourly rate was for manual labor in such historical enterprises. She shot back that according to her records to date, it was something less than a penny a day per person for the contracted, enslaved labor that built it in the first place. I told her I hoped the paymaster would at least round off...

On the documentation team that day was photographer Jet Lowe. He used what looked to me like a Mathew Brady rig from the Civil War, setting up a big box camera on a tripod and throwing its attached cloth over his head when looking through the viewfinder. Also there as chief of measuring was Richard Anderson. Marjorie had told me that Richard was somewhat frail, suffering from some illness, though I didn't know on the day just how seriously ill he was. There was Birgit Kibelka, the landscape architect I'd met earlier, who also turned out to have some canoeing skills. Katie Tipton, later identified to me as a great editor, was there on this day as a champion puller of weeds and measuring tapes. Carol Slaughter, a geologist, was there to try to identify the stone used. Betty Anderson helped out too, rounding out the eight-person team. And then I went home and generally forgot about it again.

"ARCHY CULVERT"

Less than two months later, at a quarter to five in the afternoon of April 10, 2017 (according to notes taken on my iPhone), I was once again knocking around the thickets and fields along the old railroad bed south of Shannon crossing. This particular afternoon I was cutting saplings with forks in them for a "thumbstick" class I was going to teach at the Birmingham Audubon Society's Mountain Workshop the next month. Up the gravel trail came a four-wheeler, and the rider turned the motor off to talk. He turned out to be William Preston, born, he said, in 1961, and raised in Shannon, though he'd been working out of state for years and had only recently returned to Alabama. He had actually worked at the local horse-riding business as a teenager, and thought it had closed about 1980. And did he know about the old stone culvert that let Ross Creek under the old railroad causeway? Of course, he said; the deep hole at the downstream end was once the local summertime swimming hole for the whole Shannon community. There was even a rough road down through the piney woods to it, and he could remember a picture in his grandmother's house of a 1965 pickup truck parked next to the swimming hole. The adults called it the arched culvert; the kids all just called it archy culvert, William told me. So much for my self-image as the last surviving human who knew about the old stone culvert and brought it to everybody's attention. Apparently everybody, but everybody, who grew up in Shannon still knew about it too.

Two months after that, Marjorie gave me a copy of the newest Birmingham Historical Society *Newsletter*, for June 2017, twelve dense pages entirely devoted to explaining the history of Ross Creek culvert.[4] I'm but a so-so local historian, more interested in impressionistic scenes and patterns of memory than in essential facts and dates (readers of the book to this point will probably agree), and in general more interested in the area's natural history and folklore. I was blown away by the report's specificity on how this structure had come to be, and how Marjorie's team in their collective research had essentially rewritten the foundational history of Birmingham.

In early 2019 Marjorie presented her and her team's new book on Shades Creek (*Shades Creek: Flowing through Time*) in a series of talks to various organizations in and around Birmingham.[5] The very first day the book was on sale—at Homewood's yearly salamander festival the last Saturday in January—I bought the book and got her to sign it. It's a beautiful work, replete with full-color photos and wonderful maps. But I was surprised that only a couple of pages were devoted to the Ross Creek culvert. It seemed to me that *that* whole story needed to be popularized as well—particularly how Marjorie knew what team to assemble to document the structure so quickly and so well. Marjorie agreed to let me sit for an oral interview with her mainly about that. The Samford Traditions & Oral History Recording Initiative (STORI) loaned me some fancy audio recording equipment, and on Friday, March 8, 2019, in her historical society office on the grounds of Sloss Furnaces, I got the following story.[6]

Gleanings from an Oral History

Marjorie was a Romance language graduate student at Yale when she met her future husband. They married and moved to Birmingham in 1968. She taught French (which, she remembers, more locals could speak back then, so many people having come back from a tour in Vietnam) at the University of Alabama at Birmingham (UAB) and Miles College. In both college and graduate school she'd sat in on some art history classes, but other than that she had no formal training in history. Thinking that our mid-1970s weekend New Horizons in History class at Samford might have inspired her to become a historian herself, I asked her about it. She said that she and two of her friends—all with young children—had decided to take the class just out of intellectual curiosity, but had dropped out after two weekends because, she laughed while letting me down gently, there were just "too many new horizons in history." It turned out that her early history education and guidance really came at the hands of her husband, a lawyer, who had been a serious history major in his undergraduate days at Princeton.

In Birmingham Marjorie had worked at getting grants for the Museum of Art, and had also worked up slide programs to illustrate art history. She was soon struck by how classes of students really awoke when faced with a local example of some national or even international trend or school. On the eve of the US bicentennial year, coincidentally around the time that I first met her in that unconventional weekend history class, Marjorie's husband was asked to take on and revive the Birmingham

Historical Society, founded back in 1942 but dormant for a decade. He said, "I'm too busy, take Marjorie; she'd enjoy that." And so she got her new occupation for the next forty-some years and counting.

Her first goal—as a thirty-two-year-old with three little children not yet even in school—was to write a guidebook on Birmingham and start a historical preservation movement. She'd read about that in the National Trust magazines. Too, she'd had a great experience with local history tours in Paris in her junior year abroad in her Romance languages program. Her "defining education," she says, was in going on every single local tour in a Michelin guidebook, tours that always seemed to end, delightfully, in pastry shops. Raised in Pittsburgh, Chicago, and New Orleans, she probably found the city of Birmingham into which she had married about as foreign to her as Paris, maybe more so for a Romance language student: so why not write a guidebook on Birmingham, she thought, getting to know her new city in the process? That work saw print in 1977 as *Downtown Birmingham: Architectural and Historical Walking Tour Guide*.[7] On the positive side, it sold ten thousand copies and was used as a guide to restoring many downtown buildings later. On the negative side, Marjorie said, since First National Bank (later AmSouth) underwrote the publication, distributed it in the bank's fifty-seven branch locations, and deposited the money to the historical society's account, she mistakenly got the idea that publication was easy. Only later did she realize that there weren't many bank presidents such as Newton DeBardeleben out there whose family histories were tied up in local industry and who were therefore willing to sponsor such things! That work on the downtown led naturally enough to work on Southside. It started out focusing on architectural heritage but gradually shifted more and more into social history.

Next there was a six-year-long exploration of Birmingham industrial development (presented in book form in 1981 as *The Birmingham District: An Industrial History and Guide*).[8] It was helped along by some decidedly unorthodox connections. As Marjorie remembers it, she'd be at the swimming pool on summer mornings, working on the project while her three children practiced for the swim team. Afternoons she'd pile the kids in the car and go exploring. The swim team coach soon learned what she was doing, and said to Marjorie, "I want to go with you; that's where my family made their money that is sending me to college." Marjorie forthwith added her to the afternoon car explorations. The swim coach's father turned out to have "tons of documentation" and was more than willing to share it. One of the most extraordinary people Marjorie met, early on in this project, was James Baird. He'd been manager of the Tennessee Coal and Iron Company's (TCI, the local subsidiary of US Steel) mining and furnace villages. Her first inventory of the villages came when Baird just sketched them out for her. Marjorie says that her historian husband, a sort of éminence grise of her early work, dictated the book's table of contents in what she calls "very classical form—geology, geography, pioneers," and so on, a logical, chronological flow. The heart of the work was on the histories of the companies that created the industrial engine that had powered the city for a hundred years, and Marjorie was keen to see all the sites she was reading about.

Her next ten years after that were spent mainly in research into civil rights sites, principally churches involved in the movement: there had been meetings every Monday night in those civil rights struggle years in some sixty churches, mainly in African American working-class districts. And then she had always had an interest in city planning, but in particular it was the planning for parks, and with it the concept of cultural landscapes, that came next.

TAPPING THE RESOURCES OF THE NATIONAL PARK SERVICE

Early on in this process, from that first major work on downtown buildings, Marjorie began to draw on the resources of the Historic American Buildings Survey (HABS), the Historic American Engineering Record (HAER), and, later, the Historic American Landscapes Survey (HALS), all of which are documentation divisions of the National Park Service and keep their records in the Library of Congress. A native Alabamian, Eric DeLony, born in Dothan, was her first contact. He was with HAER (later he would be its head) when he came to town in 1976, the same year that Marjorie first started working with the Birmingham Historical Society. He came to document the Sloss Furnaces site, which led to its listing as a national landmark and to its preservation. In a subsequent letter to Marjorie, he talked about the pattern of historical sites scattered through the industrial communities of Birmingham. "And I think that may have been the germ that sent us off," she reminisces, into a thorough research and documentation of the whole industrial district.

It was in the research aimed at helping save Birmingham's Vulcan statue (the largest cast-iron statue in the world) and make a quality park and historical museum out of the site that another connection clicked in. As Marjorie was walking around the grounds of Vulcan Park with the current chief of HABS, Bob Kapsch, she says, he "blew his top," saying to her, "We do not document parks; you need Richard!"

Richard Anderson, that turned out to be, of HAER and formerly its chief. Marjorie remembers him as being "totally brilliant." He had written the rule book for HAER documentation, and had consulted with people all over the United States on complicated engineering projects including the Golden Gate Bridge. "And so of course we fell in love with Richard," she says. He came back to do many projects in the Birmingham area, including the historical documentation first for Vulcan Park and then for Turkey Creek Preserve and various other projects, and he would always stay at Marjorie's house when he came to town.

She thinks that Richard Anderson's first visit to Birmingham was in or about 1994. His next-to-last major project hereabouts was to document the planning for the residential subdivision that eventually became Mountain Brook. Richard brought his great friend Paul Dolinsky, formerly chief of HABS and at that point chief of the newly formed HALS, and the three of them worked out a map-heavy project. When Paul came down, he introduced Marjorie to Birgit Kibelka, a German-trained landscape architect who had already had a varied career in the United States, and who—as with Marjorie—had come with her husband to Birmingham. Maybe as early as 2008, and certainly by 2010, as Marjorie remembers it, Birgit, with her landscape architecture Weltanschauung and particularly her map-making skills, was an integral part of most Birmingham Historical Society research teams.

And usually accompanying Richard Anderson to town, or at least following in his footsteps, was HAER's industrial photographer Jet Lowe, with his large-format camera, making the official photographs of the sites under study for HAER to put in the Prints and Photographs Division of the Library of Congress. It takes roughly thirty minutes from setup through exposure and takedown to make a single such photograph. From the end of 1993 to the end of the 1990s, Jet came back periodically. Over that time, with Marjorie as driver and local guide, they went out and made over eight hundred such large-format photos in a five-county area centered on Birmingham. And there they are in the Library of Congress, all in the public domain, available to anyone who wants to order a copy. Some are digitized and so can be viewed online.[9]

Richard Anderson's Last Project

All this history goes far toward explaining how fast and how well Marjorie and company were able to document the Ross Creek culvert, although initially she had no thought of doing so! She and colleagues were working on their history of Shades Creek and the communities along it, and, as she says, "we had no intention of getting lost on the Ross Bridge!" But Richard, it turned out, was terminally ill with cancer, and Dolinsky asked Birgit whether she could come up with one last good, interesting project for him. Coincidentally, it was about this time that I'd led Birgit and Marjorie around the Ross Creek culvert, and so there was their made-to-order last project for Richard. Richard said, sure, he'd come and do the drawings (computerized, CAD, these days), and Jet Lowe said he'd love to come do the photography (not computerized or digital, strangely enough, these days). But when Richard came and looked at it, he said, "Well, we have to have a history." And as Marjorie remembers it, she and Birgit looked at each other and thought, "Hmm, this is very complicated: because no one [among academic historians, I think they meant] will pronounce what the locals all think and feel, [which] is that this is Civil War era, slave built, as told by all the old-timers."

Marjorie expanded the research team to include other veteran coworkers of hers: Katie Tipton, researcher and professional publications editor; Julius Linn Jr., professional medical editor; and Carol Slaughter, geologist, two of the three of whom I would meet on that February 2017 field day. But even for such a research team it was still a daunting project. At this point Marjorie's husband, who was active with the Public Affairs Research Council of Alabama (PARCA, an independent organization housed at Samford University), suggested they add Gerry Waters, one of PARCA's key research assistants, to the team. She was a civil engineer who could help obtain and explain the deeds, and who moreover was up to speed on the new digital databases that were revolutionizing historical research. Marjorie remembers being floored by what Gerry came up with: ". . . newspaper images! We had to go to ads, ads! . . . newspaper ads for how many slaves they had and what they were going to be requiring them to do. You know, laying track, you know, grading . . . building culverts?"

THE MAIN STORY

That June 2017 Birmingham Historical Society *Newsletter*, "'Ross Bridge' Goes On the Record," is—with the addition of an introductory explanation of the time line of the research and a page or two of acknowledgments at the end—generally a compressed version of the official HAER report. The newsletter is beautifully done and, if you're interested in the subject, is what you ought to read first, especially because it liberally incorporates photographs both historical and modern. But the HAER report was most interesting to me as it was footnoted paragraph by paragraph, sometimes sentence by sentence, so I could trace the historical sleuth work that had gone on.[10] Here's the gist of the title page of the HAER report, as presented on the Library of Congress website:

HISTORIC AMERICAN ENGINEERING RECORD
ROSS CREEK CULVERT
(Ross Bridge)
HAER No. AL-214

Location:	[gives latitude and longitude and its location relative to current roads]
Dates of Construction:	1863 or 1864
Engineers:	Chief Engineer John Turner Milner (1826–1898), Bartholomew Boyle (1826–1875), Richard Hamlin Kelly (1832–1878)
Builder:	Red Mountain Iron & Coal Company
Original Owner and Use:	South & North Railroad
Present Owner and Use:	Ross Bridge Master Association; central feature of the Historic Park at Ross Bridge
Significance:	The Ross Creek Culvert is a rare surviving remnant of Civil War–era railroad construction serving a nascent iron industry prior to the founding of Birmingham, Alabama, in 1871. It was built by the South & North Alabama Railroad (chartered in 1854, completed in 1871, and since 1872 a part of the Louisville & Nashville Railroad, today's CSX system). The culvert conducted Ross Creek under the embankment for the railroad mainline from 1871 to 1908; the route served as a spur line to the Oxmoor Furnaces from 1908 to 1927.
Historians:	Marjorie L. White, Gerry Waters, Katherine M. Tipton, 2017
Project Information:	. . . The Ross Creek Culvert Recording Project was completed to HAER Level 1 standards and guidelines by Richard K. Anderson Jr., Principal Investigator. . . . Anderson took the measurements and prepared the data in anticipation of completing the measured and interpretive drawings, which were field checked and completed by landscape architect Birgit Kibelka . . . following Anderson's death in June 2017. Marjorie White, Birmingham Historical Society, wrote the historical report with research and editorial assistance from Birgit Kibelka, Katherine Tipton, and Gerry Waters. Jet Lowe, Baltimore, Maryland, completed the large-format photography.

Reading that was the first I knew about Richard Anderson's death, just a few short months after the field day with him when we cleaned, measured, and photographed the structure. Marjorie told me later that some of Richard's coworkers rescued the CAD version of the digital reconstruction of the Ross Creek culvert from his personal computer, and it showed a noticeable settling of the downstream arch's side, where some of the corner wall blocks are missing. The HAER report, of course, has a long and technical architectural description of the structure (among the terms I had to look up were "ashlar masonry," "spring stones," and "dressed voussoirs"). But then comes the rich, rich history, which was of course ordered up by Richard—all in all a wonderful "one last project for Richard" as requested from Birgit by his old friend Paul Dolinsky.

Southerners Building a Railroad

In Marjorie's phrase, it's "a story of southerners building, or trying to build, a railroad," of which Ross Creek culvert was one small but important and very interesting piece. The South and North Alabama (S&N) Railroad was chartered by the Alabama legislature in early 1854. There were railroads from the Gulf up to Montgomery on the south bank of the Alabama River, and from Nashville and Louisville and points north down to Decatur on the north bank of the Tennessee River. The aim here was to fill in the missing link between Montgomery and Decatur, with the difficult ridge and valley topography between them, and to bridge the Cahaba and the two main branches of the Warrior River roughly midways, and the two big rivers— the Tennessee and the Alabama—at either end.

Although according to the HAER report the early money behind the venture came from Montgomery cotton merchants, accessing the iron ore and the coal along the line gradually became a more important motivation. In 1858 the state's governor appointed J. T. Milner, a thirty-two-year-old Georgia railroad engineer and son of a railroad engineer, to survey a through route that would also maximize access to those minerals. Milner produced the survey later that year, estimating the cost of the 121-mile-long missing link at $2.8 million. Forty-five percent of the estimated cost was for the initial grading, masonry, and bridging for the line. One interesting detail for our purposes was that "box culvert" (a smallish rectangular stone drainage way) was the cheapest masonry work, estimated at $350 per cubic yard; "arch masonry" was twice that at $700 per cubic yard; and "bridge masonry" was the most expensive at $1,200 per cubic yard. Although this was not included in the final report, the researchers discovered that standard figures for acreage of watershed to be drained dictated whether box, arch, or bridge masonry should be used, and how large each should be. In the report Milner also said he preferred "negro" workers: "I have long since learned that negro slave labor is more reliable and cheaper for any business connected with the construction of a railroad than white."

Ross Creek was named for James Taylor Ross. Painstaking research in Bureau of Land Management records, local histories, and genealogical records turned up the facts that in 1858 Ross bought 120 acres along Montevallo Road where it crossed Ross Creek, site of the future culvert, to go with 120 more nearby that he had bought back in 1854. The family—father, mother, and four sons—lived in Jonesboro (near present-day Bessemer) but worked that southern acreage productively: federal census records from 1860 have the six of them (who did not have enslaved laborers) producing fifty bushels of "Indian corn," three bales of cotton, thirty pounds of spun wool from their sixteen sheep, and two hundred pounds of butter churned from the cream of their four milk cows. In addition, James Ross owned a horse, two mules, two oxen, and forty pigs.

Physical work on the S&N Railroad appears to have been set in motion by January 1859, when Milner placed a "Notice to Contractors" for grading and masonry in Montgomery's *Daily Confederation* newspaper. An article in that same paper the following September reported the "glorious news" that work had begun, "85 negroes" having been delivered to Bartley Boyle (Irish-born railroad contractor living in Wetumpka at least as early as 1860, then age thirty-five; by his death in 1875 Boyle would acquire two thousand acres of mineral lands in the north Birmingham area, including the area still known as Boyle's Gap). In 1860 the Alabama legislature officially adopted Milner's route and plans for construction, and floated the S&N Railroad a loan of some $663,000.

In January 1861 the whole complexion of work on the S&N changed when Alabama seceded from the Union: both pace and resources available picked up sharply. Shortly thereafter the state established an Alabama Arms Manufacturing Company to mine ore and manufacture iron needed for the Confederate Army's ordnance. Frank Gilmer, the Montgomery cotton merchant who had been the chief backer of the idea of the railroad back in the mid-1850s, and J. T. Milner were involved in the enterprise. Between May 1861 and October 1862, railroad contractor Boyle and chief engineer Milner bought the land where the S&N was to cross Shades Mountain and Shades Creek at its northern base, including its tributary Ross Creek. Pinckney Brock sold them about three hundred acres in and around what is still today Brock's Gap, the low place in Shades Mountain chosen for the future rail route. With three of their four sons off serving in the military, James Ross and his wife sold about 490 acres of land in the area of Ross Creek to J. T. Milner for the railroad for $1,500. That land deed, which researchers found in the Jefferson County Deed Book, was witnessed by one R. H. Kelly—proof that Irish-born railroad engineer Richard Hamlin Kelly was already in Alabama and working with the railroad. He brought considerable experience to bear: among other things, he is supposed to have designed the 1856 Rock Island railroad bridge at Davenport, Iowa, the first bridge to span the Mississippi River. He was certainly qualified, available, on the job, and in the vicinity (and since that June 2017 newsletter came out, a document proving his involvement in the building of the Ross Creek culvert has indeed been located, Marjorie tells me).

On April 11, 1862, the Confederate government set up the Nitre and Mining Bureau to produce war materials for its arsenals: iron was needed for shot, shell, and warships. The new bureau provided for thirteen new blast furnaces in Alabama alone, with funds for establishing them of up to $100,000 each. Money was also provided for railroads to haul the iron they produced to the arsenal at Selma. In late 1862 J. T. Milner and Frank Gilmer went to Richmond and got a contract from the Confederate government to build a furnace and rolling mills and a railroad to them. On November 5, 1862, these two men and twenty-three others, including industrialist Daniel Pratt, incorporated the Red Mountain Iron and Coal Company, successor to the Alabama Arms Manufacturing Company. To quote the HAER report directly: "It was capitalized with an astonishing $1.25 million in stock options. Thus, the demand for Confederate armament prompted formation of Jefferson County's first iron manufactory and iron ore mines."

In December 1862 and January 1863, ads for "600 negroes" and then "800 negroes" appeared in the papers of Mobile, Selma, and Vicksburg. One of these specifically mentioned the work locale as being "near Elyton [near the heart of today's downtown Birmingham] and Montevallo." Such workers were to live in camps of ten with room and board supplied by the railroad, each gang of ten to have its "woman" (cook) and "boy" (errand boy).

By March 21, 1863, all the land for the route of the railroad north over Shades Mountain to the site of Oxmoor Furnace had been acquired. The furnace itself was "blown in" sometime in October or November 1863, and began producing a minimum of five or six tons of iron a day. The railroad coming up from Selma had reached the coal mines and coke ovens just south of Shades Mountain. Teamsters from the furnace drove oxcarts, each loaded with three to four tons of the pig iron, south down Montevallo Road, up and over Shades Mountain through Brock's Gap, and down to the railhead that connected to the Selma arsenal. When the heavy oxcarts tore up that stretch of Montevallo Road, it was repaired with slag from the furnaces (that same glassy slag that you can see today that is a major component of the causeway over Ross Creek culvert).

The Birmingham Historical Society research team paid particular attention to the financial records remaining from the Confederacy but never could find any specific documentation for the Ross Creek culvert. But the Red Mountain Iron and Coal Company owned the Ross Creek site by January 1863, and hundreds of workers were assigned to the railroad "near Elyton and Montevallo" for 1863 and 1864, with the labor advertisement for getting ties, laying tracks, and building bridges and culverts. And so, the HAER report reasons, "it seems highly probable that the well-capitalized Red Mountain Iron & Coal Company built the Ross Creek Culvert under John Milner's and Richard Kelly's supervision." Tracks weren't laid on the finished grade, and no train ran over the causeway over the culvert until November 11, 1871, when the cut through Brock's Gap was finally finished, more than six years after the end of the war. Heavy oxcarts of pig iron, however, surely did run over the causeway atop the culvert from whenever it was finished in 1863–64 until Wilson's Raiders of the Union Army wrecked the Oxmoor Furnace on March 28, 1865.

In researching the construction techniques of such an arched culvert, the research team found in an online database a tantalizing contemporary parallel, an arched stone railroad culvert built in 1864 in Pennsylvania. This discovery was both revelatory and a bit frustrating to the research team because unlike for the Ross Creek culvert, all the records of finance and construction of the Pennsylvania culvert were available. There were even photographs of the culvert under construction that clearly show the semicylindrical wooden support framework that came first, and the timber cranes that lifted and swung the stones into place. For all their efforts, the Ross Creek culvert researchers could never find the exact date or the exact transfer of money to their project. But here, as a consolation prize, was their answer to the puzzle of why such a magnificent structure was out in such an isolated place in the piney woods. As stone structure researcher James Gage wrote about the equally remote Pennsylvania culvert: "The standard practice of 19th century railroads was to reserve the best quality construction work for bridges and culverts in the most remote areas. The logic being that the most remote and difficult-to-access structures needed to be built to minimize maintenance and repairs."[11]

SAM CURREN AND THE QUARRY

In 1992 Madge Barefield, described by Marjorie White as an extraordinary local historian (and she should know because Barefield worked for the Birmingham Historical Society full time for many years), wrote a history of Hoover.[12] In it Barefield identified a Robert Curren, who had some papers or some sort of write-up on his family's history in the region. The Hoover Historical Society sent out a request for cooperation on its Facebook page, and one of the Curren relatives emailed a response. Eventually Marjorie figured out that the Sam Curren to whom they directed her was the actual Robert Curren who had the papers and whose family had owned the quarry from which the blocks of stone were cut. When she was actually able to talk to Sam, he had all these wonderful family stories about how the quarry had operated. He knew a lot about the Ross Creek culvert, too, relating a story handed down in the family that when Wilson's Raiders came through, the old men and boys remaining hereabouts fired a single formal shot and then surrendered the culvert. Marjorie figures that Wilson could have destroyed the culvert if he had wished to, but since it wasn't his target he quickly went on. I missed the day Marjorie, Birgit, and others toured the quarry under Curren's guidance. It's located just below Shades Crest Road, not far from where the road goes under high-voltage power lines today. From the quarry there is a steep slope to Shades Creek three hundred feet lower down, close to the mouth of Ross Creek. From there it's less than two miles to the Ross Creek culvert site. The same hard sandstone the culvert walls are built of was reputedly used to construct the Oxmoor Furnace a few miles up Shades Creek, which stood until 1929.

After the Civil War, according to Sam Curren, one formerly enslaved laborer stayed on with this Curren family quarry, driving the blocks of stone ("he drove the dray," said Curren) wherever they needed to go. This really resonated with me, because there was one African American family up on Rock Crusher Mountain near Livingston, Tennessee, where my wife grew up, that were originally stonemasons. They were there because they had helped open the quarry that gave the mountain its name. And they were obviously talented stonemasons. Originally, when I thought of enslaved people, a group of undifferentiated agricultural laborers and domestic workers came to mind, and I had to recalibrate to think of enslaved African Americans as specialists in stonework, or music performance, or a whole range of other specialties—a fact that of course now seems obvious to me. One problem with poaching in academic fields in which you have little or no training is that your education is that of the autodidact, with peaks of enthusiasm where you know things worth knowing, but great valleys of ignorance. Trained American historians, I belatedly discovered, already know that there's a whole literature on the skills of those enslaved—from newly arrived ones who were trafficked because they were woodworkers or ironworkers, to the one out of four enslaved plantation laborers who fell into the "skilled" category, which included stonemasons. So all of a sudden the creation of a sophisticated stone structure, with enslaved labor, became more understandable for me. These enslaved workers had received on-the-job training and sometimes even learned their skills from those Irish engineers and masons who dominated railroad construction in the mid-nineteenth-century United States.

WHERE TO GO FROM HERE?

When Marjorie and Birgit made their first presentations of these new findings to the Ross Bridge community, they found considerable interest from the audience but also some misinformation, probably mostly traceable to real estate company conjecture: that Ross was an Irish aristocrat by origin; that he and his sons were great Confederates (Marjorie had learned that one son fought for the Union!); that Ross had offered up this "bridge" to the Confederacy (it wasn't built until after he sold his land to the railroad); that the Yankees blew it up, which is why there are blocks fallen from it . . . The presentations seemed to generate a new and better-informed local interest, including the possibility of the Ross Bridge community and the city of Hoover stabilizing the structure by taking out some big trees growing on the slopes of the causeway (which if uprooted by storms or floods could damage the viaduct) and reconstructing the two corners where stones have fallen out or perhaps been removed. And as Marjorie said to me in our interview: "Which leads us to the point that we have succeeded in raising an appreciation of the structure, and Birgit and I look at each other and say, 'Oh dear, where do we find the technical consultant to help on this one?' (laughter) I mean, that's a great engineering challenge. So I guess that will be on the docket sometime soon."

I retired from full-time teaching in 2016 and have been going half speed at best ever since. I'm guessing Marjorie White and I are roughly the same age, but she's still going full blast, to use a steel city metaphor. I've been a small link in some interesting local institutions and happenings in Birmingham and Alabama in general, the whole point of this book, but in and around Birmingham Marjorie is surrounded by a cloud of witnesses of her life's work.

The appreciation of Birmingham's original architecture, her first project in the late 1970s, undoubtedly has played a major role in the revitalization of downtown. The civil rights struggle in Birmingham, as of the 1990s, was poorly remembered and hardly memorialized; the Civil Rights District probably wouldn't be there without Marjorie's work, certainly its major sites not registered with and celebrated by the National Park Service. Now Bethel Baptist (Rev. Fred Shuttlesworth's church), Sixteenth Street Baptist, and Dexter Avenue Baptist Churches are all on the US World Heritage Tentative List (for possible nomination to UNESCO), thanks to a Birmingham Historical Society project in 2007. Vulcan Park, with its most interesting interpretive center, might not exist and certainly would only be a shadow of its present self without Marjorie's work. Turkey Creek would probably not be a preserve and would have a large prison right on its bank. I think what Marjorie remembers most about the past forty and more years of leading the Birmingham Historical Society are the talented folks she recruited to work on these projects, and she is proud of maintaining their interest and friendship over the years. Marjorie told me in our interview that she led the efforts to document the history of the Ross Creek culvert the way she tried to do all her projects: with a "willingness to explore every route; no conceived understanding of necessarily where we're going until we've explored enough, and then worked with other very wise, knowledgeable people to edit, organize, and define."

And the historical facts turned up were almost always more interesting than anything one could have imagined, Marjorie summed up. All of this, of course, was underlaid by her efforts to get the necessary funding for all this work, most often in the form of grants from private and public sources but, when those weren't forthcoming, from her own family budget. I suspect that last was the case with much of the work on Ross Creek culvert as well, though she wouldn't come right out and say so. I quoted to her the old adage that "he who tooteth not his own horn, the same shall not be tooted," but she's just not comfortable doing that. I've tried to do a little of that for her!

chapter four

Foxfire, Folk Crafts, and Folkcenter South

Discovering *Foxfire*, the Magazine and the Books

In the summer of 1973 my wife and I and our two small children tried to get a camping spot at Cades Cove in the Great Smoky Mountains National Park, but we found it full. We spent the night in a motel outside the park and were back at half past six the next morning to become the third vehicle in line to get a camping spot when the gates opened at seven.

The pickup truck ahead of us had a Rabun County, Georgia, license plate, I noted with interest. A few years before this some of my wife's relatives attending graduate school at the University of Tennessee had told me about the *Foxfire* project from a high school in Rabun County of northeast Georgia, a student-written magazine that took as its primary subject matter the folk culture of the Southern Appalachians. I'd gotten hold of the first book compilation, which had come out in 1972, the marvelously titled *The Foxfire Book: Hog Dressing, Log Cabin Building, Mountain Crafts and Foods, Planting by the Signs, Snake Lore, Hunting Tales, Faith Healing, Moonshining, and Other Affairs of Plain Living*.[1] Both the subject matter and the teaching technique as expounded in the introduction by the teacher who sponsored it at the Rabun Gap-Nacoochee School, Eliot Wigginton, were fascinating to me (and a lot of the rest of the country, judging by the quick sales of hundreds of thousands of copies of the book). So with half an hour to kill anyway, I struck up a conversation with the couple in the truck and found out they were Bob Bennett, who taught at the same school, and his wife, Margie, who actually worked there on the *Foxfire* project with Wigginton.[2] It was a link that opened some future doors.

Folklore, I now think, was my bridge to American culture. In the craziness of the sixties, I'd been drawn away from my natural inclination toward science and math into the social sciences, and then into the study of things further and further from American culture, just to get some perspective on it all. To quote Gulf Coast balladeer Jimmy Buffett, "He went to Paris, looking for answers, to questions that bothered him so." I chose Russian history because it was the most exotic subject Tennessee Tech offered; if it had had a major in Urdu, I'd probably have taken that. Then in European history classes in graduate school at Vanderbilt I'd come across the Brothers Grimm, not as avuncular tellers of stories to children, but as high-powered multilingual scholars. Under the pressure of the Napoleonic occupation of the Germanies, they consciously tried to uncover the past of the German "nation" (and unconsciously invented some of it). They were out collecting folktales for the bits and pieces of the ancient culture they thought were preserved in them. They believed, in the heart of this Romantic age, that if Germans could just revive their original patterns of behavior from way back in "the form-giving period," they would be free, unified, and strong again.

Samford had invented an optional January term "mini-mester" shortly before I'd gotten to campus. In it, said the authorities, a professor could experiment with creative content or delivery without having to provide a full-blown exposition or get the Curriculum Committee's approval, at least for the first time or two. I did my first one during my second year at Samford, in January 1973, on German history from the Grimms' celebration of Germanic folklore to Hitler's perversion of it. This newfound insight into German Romanticism and my attempt to teach it were both in the academic world, of course, but it wasn't just an "academic" matter to me. I had always felt a strength and a dignity in the small-town and rural world of my father's and mother's relatives. In my late teens I had fled the racism and ignorance of the outside world that I had found there, too, but in light of Wigginton and his students' *Foxfire* publications and the Grimms' scholarly works, I could see a new path back to Southern culture, especially rural culture.

Wigginton was just a couple of years older than I was, and he'd had an interesting introduction to teaching. In 1966, with a freshly minted master's in literature, he took a teaching job at a private high school in Rabun County, that northeasternmost of Georgia counties. It was a rough year for him. Shakespeare seemed about as relevant to his students, he said, as Dior fashion, and three courses of action seemed open to him: quit, crack down as a harsh taskmaster, or come up with a new teaching approach. He said he came close to choosing one of the first two paths, but he finally decided to have students write, print, and sell a magazine. His working hypothesis was that they'd be much more interested if they were doing something real—writing for an adult audience—instead of just "practicing" papers on themes that teachers assigned them, to be graded, returned, and thrown away.

The first issue focused on a car chase with the high sheriff after some local moonshiners. But gradually the students began prospecting folkloric topics relating to that last generation of self-sufficient Appalachian pioneers in the area. The Rabun Gap-Nacoochee School was private, but in these years it was also entertaining the nearby public school students because the public school building had burned down, and it was taking some time to build a new one. For a time, then, Wigginton had the unusual combination of well-heeled private school students with such things as Jeeps and tape recorders, and less-well-heeled locals who knew everybody for miles around and were related to lots of them. It made for a fruitful partnership. For Wigginton, of course, students were the whole focus: if they came up with the things to be written about and did the writing and photography themselves, they'd really be engaged. To start with, it was students who came up with the name of their projected magazine: the phosphorescence sometimes seen in a rotting log in the woods, "foxfire," suggested a glimmering of something way off. They did their own interviews, transcriptions, articles, and photography, including their own darkroom developing. But it was mostly the subject matter of the magazine that caught fire with the reading public. Soon subscriptions were coming in from New York and other faraway places. That 1972 compendium of *Foxfire*, with substantial editing from Wigginton, presented the best of six years' worth of such student cultural journalism.

I'd been interested in handicrafts since I was a fifteen-year-old assistant in the crafts tent at a Boy Scout camp in Middle Tennessee. The idea of incorporating traditional folk crafts in an attractive teaching approach, plus the new vistas into folk crafts appearing to me in rural Alabama, changed my classes and my life.

"Mr. Henry," White Oak Basketmaker from White Plains

In January 1974, less than a year after my discovery of that first *Foxfire* book and subsequent encounter with Margie and Bob Bennett, I was browsing in a little hippie-run crafts shop down in the eastern regions of Birmingham's Southside. For sale there was a little strap-handled, round, flat-bottomed white oak basket. The sales tag claimed that it had been made in Alabama and gave the maker's name. When

I bought the basket the proprietor was kind enough to give me the phone number of the maker, one Henry Upchurch of White Plains, a crossroads said to be somewhere on the far side of Anniston. After I got back home, I called him up and asked whether I could come out some Saturday to watch how he made his baskets and maybe learn how to make one myself. He said sure, I could come along that coming Saturday if I was free. I said I could be there by midmorning. According to my old field notes it was January 26, 1974.

This was back when the speed limit on Alabama's main interstate highways was seventy-five miles per hour and most of us drove eighty, and I went bombing eastward at least that fast on I-20. Several miles past Anniston, I turned north on Highway 9 toward Piedmont, heading up a road that I still think is one of the prettiest drives in the state. I found White Plains and the Upchurch trailer home without too much trouble, got out of the car, and walked up to where Mr. Upchurch, in a straw hat with one of those little green visors built into the front of the brim, was already talking to a customer. We all shook hands, and I stepped back to let them finish their transaction. But the conversation ran on about various and sundry, including squirrel hunting, of which Mr. Upchurch allowed that he was now too old "to pull the hills" so he'd given it up. I was standing first on one foot and then the other, impatient for the other guy to get through so I could learn how to make a basket in one hour, two max. They finally got down to business: the customer said he'd been misguided enough to buy an off-the-shelf ax handle, and "it split out on me." Thereupon Mr. Upchurch brought out a hickory handle he'd hewn out of a straight-grained piece, the piece first rough sawn to a cardboard pattern he kept hanging on the barn wall and then finished off with a drawknife. Then a little money changed hands, and the customer drove off.

The Flat-Bottomed, Round, Strap-Handled Alabama Basket

Mr. Upchurch then turned his attention to me. I remember that he had the brightest blue eyes, a sweet smile, and—especially when he wanted to ensure that you were giving proper consideration to his last remark—a sort of quizzical look with a tilt of his head. He took me over to a scrap woodpile where he'd put all the white oak pieces necessary for making a basket, and began laying the ribs down in a sunburst pattern. After he'd crossed eight pieces, making sixteen ends, the first set of ribs of the eventual basket, he added a half piece as a single rib, to make the weaving "dodge," as he said. Then he took a thin split (a splint or weaver) and, in a spiral pattern, went over one rib and under the next, the thin split on each round going over the same rib it had gone under on the round before because the extra rib made for an odd number of ribs (seventeen) sticking out in that radial pattern. When he'd made three or four rounds he had firmly locked everything together. The spaces between ribs had also widened enough, with the widening radius of the bottom, so that he could add eight more pieces atop the original eight plus one half, making sixteen more ends—thirty-three ends in all now—and then he locked this new set of ribs in place by continuing to weave his flat, spiral bottom. If you come across any flat-bottomed, circular, strap-handled basket in Alabama, count the ribs: if it has more or fewer than thirty-three, it's a wild original.

It looked easy enough, and I was itching to get my hands on the basket and try it myself, but Mr. Henry, as I called him from that day forward, knew better. Once he'd locked in the second set of ribs, he "broke them up," bending each rib sharply upward toward ninety degrees and slightly cracking the outside of each one as he did so. He continued the spiral weave from the flat bottom on up the side, simply over-lapping a new split atop the end of the old one for two or three inches when the old one ran out. When the basket weave had grown a couple of inches up the side and he judged the whole thing to be stabilized, he handed it to me. I began weaving, and the basket grew rapidly—and I thought, "I'm a real basketmaker now." Only later did I understand that Mr. Henry had given the very easiest, most rewarding, part of it all to me. When the sides of the basket had grown to seven or eight inches in height, he took it back. He tapered the last of the weaving splits and tucked it in beside the one below, making a fairly smooth top edge on which to build the rim. Then he cut each of the thirty-three vertical ribs off with two vigorous pulls of the knife, so that each now stuck up about three inches above the top edge of the weaving, each sharply pointed, sharp enough in the thick white oak ribs to bring the blood from those who handled it carelessly. Next—and I learned later that this took real hand strength—he bent each of those short and thick white oak rib points over the top weaver and slid it down alongside the same rib, inside the lower rounds of weavers. He did all thirty-three, which took a while, and then he had a recognizable but rather floppy-topped basket.

At this point Mr. Henry took a piece of white oak somewhat thicker than the ribs and fashioned it into a rough handle. He pointed the two ends to slide them down opposite ribs on the outside of the basket. Now he said that he needed two more thick pieces for rims, an inner and an outer one, to lash around the top split in

Figure 4.1.
*Sunburst-style
basket bottom
construction*

The smaller circle (*top*) shows how using a spiral weaver locks in the first eight-and-a-half ribs, making for seventeen radial ends; the larger circle (*bottom*) shows the locking in atop that of eight more ribs, sixteen more ends, for a total of thirty-three ends.

the weaving. He asked me whether I knew how he measured them for length. I said I guessed that he would roll the basket exactly one revolution along a piece of white oak to get the right length. He said, well, a person might do it that way, but he always just laid the rough straight piece for the rims across the mouth of the basket "three times plus a little." I'd once been an engineering major, still came out of college with a math minor, and had at one time memorized pi to the tenth decimal point (five of which still come back today, 3.14159 . . .), but I'd never have thought of that trick. And I wondered later whether he'd been having fun with me, because he said, "You know, it works that way with most any circle," and gave me that quizzical look with one eye crinkled.

He cut the piece he'd measured to length and split (rived) it in half. He sharpened one end of each, and poked one sharpened end under a rib on the outside top of the basket, and the sharpened end of the other piece under a rib on the inside top of the basket. Next he proceeded to lash the inner and outer rims together with the top weaver sandwiched between them. He'd feed the lashing split between the vertical ribs as it came under the rims, and then come over the top of each rib where it had

Figure 4.2.
Henry Upchurch
baskets

The top basket is the original one the author bought that Saturday in 1974.

been bent down alongside itself. He went all the way around the basket one way, and then he did it the other way, leaving an X-pattern all around the top, and a basket no longer floppy but heavy duty indeed. For security of the handle he put a nail through the rims and handle at the juncture on each side, bending the point over to clench it on the inside of the basket.

Mr. Upchurch's Growing Local Fame

My field notes say I stayed from a quarter to ten in the morning until four in the afternoon. I hadn't meant to stay so long, and at noon (despite my weak and easily dismissed protest) he and his kindly wife had me in for lunch. Some of the conversation was on Mr. Upchurch's reaction to his own growing popularity. He showed me an article from the *Anniston Star* from the month before, dated December 23, 1973, about his white oak basketmaking (the article said he was seventy-six years old, I noted with interest). Professors from nearby Jacksonville State University had come to see him, and there'd been a squib about him on Huntsville TV. It seemed to me that he wasn't trying to be famous, and he wasn't overly impressed that he *was* becoming locally famous; he was just fascinated by this unexpected development so late in his life. He made some curio miniature ox yokes for sale, but he mostly stuck to functional white oak split work: chair bottoms, flat-bottomed round baskets, larger laundry baskets. The first job he could remember doing, growing up on the farm, was helping his daddy at such basketmaking, pulling long splits through ribs.

I left at four, having stayed much longer than I'd intended. I paid Mr. Henry for a basket, to his great amusement choosing not the basket I'd worked on but one that was all his workmanship. I still have it today. And I remember driving back at the speed limit or less, the slowness or calmness of Mr. Henry's approach to life having seeped in a little. It only gradually dawned on me that the sociable conversation about other aspects of life was important to all concerned, too, maybe as important as the ax handle or basket.

Zen and the Art of Basketry?

About this same time I was talking to some Japanese friends, about my age, who were taking English as a second language with me on Monday evenings at a downtown church. They had explained many of the Zen Buddhist activities such as flower arranging (*ka-do*), archery (*kyu-do*), fencing (*ken-do*), and a whole range of martial arts (*ju-do*, *aki-do*, *karate-do*, and such), where the Japanese *do* comes from the Chinese *dao* (earlier transliteration *tao*) and translates as "The Way," a spiritual path to enlightenment. And now they said they didn't believe such cultural behavior was all that uniquely Japanese or even Zen, that it must be a generally human thing, it was so basic to life. I ventured an analogy that when I went out basketmaking with Mr. Henry, I heard the accents of my great-uncles from my childhood, partly instructing and partly teasing me, and that for a while after the basketmaking session everything slowed down a little for me, a sort of quiet contentment. "Ah," they said, "basket-do." Maybe so.

I went back many times, often with family and friends, and rarely came back without some gift of vegetables pressed on us by Mr. Henry and his sweet wife. My older children still remember the black widow spiders they found under some watermelons in their patch, and the bunches of yellow and red peppers that I told my son were carrots and allowed him to eat, for which my family has never forgiven me.

Learning the Finer Points: Picking a Tree

Over subsequent visits Mr. Henry took me through the whole process, from choosing the tree in the woods to finishing off the basket. He had access to woodlands with second-growth white oak, which is what you want: fast-growing, straight, small trees of six to eight inches in diameter. Another reason to harvest small trees is that only the sapwood—the outer inch, maybe inch and a half—"works up" correctly (described further along). He taught me how to look for straight grain in the bark, which has a smooth, granular feel; curvy and rough was a telltale of crooked grain in the wood underneath. When in doubt about the grain he'd cut a little chip out of one side near the bottom, split a narrow piece out of it, and then bend it double to see when it cracked. Those that cracked too soon, he said, were brash, meaning brittle—and suddenly it seemed probable to me that "brash" as a description for human behavior so stubborn or rigid that the person breaks instead of gracefully bending to superior force must have come from the botanical world. Such "brash" white oaks he would leave for "saw logs," because the little chipped place would heal over and the tree grow until fit for the sawyer and lumber. But from the suitable trees for basketmaking he would cut a trunk of six, eight, or even ten feet in length, if the grain seemed smooth enough that far up and there weren't too many little limbs that convoluted the grain.

I was a willing but unskilled chopper of trees. When Mr. Henry picked one for us to harvest, I volunteered to cut it down and went round and round it as I chopped. "You cut a tree down like a beaver," he laughed, and showed me how to notch it from one side and then the other so as to fell it in a chosen direction. That first day out in the woods gathering timber, he was already in his late seventies and I was in my early thirties—but he came out of the woods with a white oak log on each shoulder, and I could only manage one. Later I saw him hewing dough trays out of tulip poplar, a two-foot section of a foot-thick trunk having been split in half and red lines drawn on the flat side where an ax should hit to begin hollowing it out. He'd steady the half log with his left hand, hold a heavy poleax choked up in his right, come down with the bit at an angle on that red line, and seemingly hit it every time.

The Fine Art of Riving

"To rive" is an archaic verb meaning to split along the grain. "Lightning-riven oak" and Tolkien's "Rivendell" are about all that's left to us of it in English today, but it was a word most everybody knew a century or two ago when most construction materials were botanical. Some woods will split easily along the grain; others won't. Beech, for example, is almost impossible to rive. My oldest brother-in-law, who used to cut enough of his own firewood to make it through a Tennessee winter, joked that the beech was named when somebody misunderstood the person trying to split it. But white oak is the champion when it comes to ease of riving, and swamp white oak is the best of the best.

Using an ax to start the splitting and then leapfrogging a couple of sourwood wedges down the growing split, Mr. Henry would divide the little tree trunk into halves and then quarters. A quarter round would have bark on one side, an inch or so of white sapwood under it, and then maybe two to four inches of dark brown heartwood—the whole thing looking in cross section like a quarter piece of pie. With a sizable pocketknife, he'd strip off the bark. Then, to weaken the thicker heartwood, he'd use a small ax or machete to chop the point of the pie off, along the whole length of the piece. With a pocketknife (and with a leather pad on his thigh), Mr. Henry would trim the sides of the piece straight and level. He taught me that instead of moving the knife away from you with your right hand, you should hold the knife rigidly in place, at a shallow angle with the wood, firmly over the leather pad on your thigh—then pull the whole wooden piece toward you with your left hand. This "basketmaker's lick" gives you much more control over the knife.

At this point he had a piece of white oak almost rectangular in cross section (rounded a bit on the side where the bark used to be), and about half white sapwood and half brown heartwood. This is where the "froe" (sometimes also spelled "frow") came in. The iron blade is maybe a foot long, with a handle about the same length coming up from one end of the blade at a right angle. "Dull as a froe" is an old country expression, because a froe is supposed to be dull: it's for separating fibers, not cutting them. With a hickory mallet—smaller sibling of the big hickory maul used on the ax head and the sourwood wedges—you drive the dull blade of the froe down into one end of the piece so it generally separates the sapwood half from the heartwood half. Pound the froe in until the mallet can't make it go any farther, and then lever the handle of the froe back and forth, causing the split to go deeper along the piece (origin of "to and fro"?). Then—and this is the real trick to riving—if one side of the split wood gets thicker than the other, which is almost sure to happen—you must force the thick side to bend by pulling the handle of the froe, and thus the top of the blade of the froe, *toward that side*. Then as the piece splits further, the split opening should run back toward the middle, nicely bisecting the piece.

Mr. Henry just kept halving the pieces, switching from froe to knife when the pieces got small enough. He'd twist the knife blade backward and forward, using it just like a little froe, to open the split. Mr. Henry said that most people thought you'd have needed "a fine-bladed knife and keen" to make basket splits with, but you didn't; you needed a knife big and stout that could work part-time as a miniature froe. To give a final polish to his finished splits, or weavers, he'd hold his knife blade across the flat side of the split and pull the wood under the knife. For this polishing, the plane of the knife blade needed to be nearly but not quite vertical to the split. The knife stayed centered on top of the leather pad as he pulled the split under it. Good riving wood under a sharp knife will send up as pretty a curl as any wood plane does, that way.

So anything the pioneers needed a strong strap of wood for, they used white oak—for the arched bands that supported the canvas tops of covered wagons, for the grooved outer band of the great spoked spinning wheel, for blanks for carving net needles of uniform thickness, for shakes to shingle a cabin roof with . . . ax, maul and wedges, froe and mallet, stout knife, and leather pad for the thigh (plus a little know-how and a lot of elbow grease) was all it took.

Figure 4.3.
*White oak
basketmaking
tools*

Hickory maul and mallet, sourwood wedges, and froe: just add a poleax and a stout pocket-knife, and that's all you need to turn a small white oak tree into a white oak basket.

"Cooperage" is the general term for making containers from staves: buckets, kegs, barrels, casks, hogsheads, and such. "Tight cooperage" means watertight. Not only does white oak split beautifully into barrel staves, it is the only oak and one of the only trees that produces watertight dried wood. When it's growing, little balloon-like processes called tyloses slowly fill up the vessels in the xylem and block them off, and gradually get incorporated into the wood of the growing tree. Barrels made of white oak staves became a particular favorite of the whiskey-aging business. Not only were they strong and watertight, but if they were charred inside before the raw whiskey was poured in to age, they gave bourbon, for example, its typical color and some of its taste.

BLOUNT COUNTY HERITAGE

Sometime in or about these same early to mid-1970s I discovered the 1972 book *Heritage of Blount County*. I can't remember who put me onto it, probably one of my friends in Special Collection at the Samford University Library. Opal Adams, an elderly woman, seemed to be the principal force behind the book, and so I got her address and drove up and talked to her about local folklore for an hour or so. She had the most tightly woven white oak basket I had ever seen, flat-bottomed and rectangular, with an unusual central handle made of two straps instead of one. It was so tightly woven it looked as if it would hold water. She told me she had bought it from a nearby African American artisan, and she refused to entertain any cash offer I made for it. On a second visit, though, she showed me what had happened to the basket: she had set it on top of her car and forgotten to load it, and when she backed up it had slipped off and she ran over it. She gave me the ruins, since I thought I could still copy it. I've got the pieces, now mostly two-dimensional, all these years later, but have probably never tried to copy it because I've lacked the confidence to think I could ever match it.

The *Heritage of Blount County* was not professionally put together—no pagination, no overall editorial attribution—but oh, the parts. My favorite was a two-page passage in the folklore section late in the book called "The Old Mill," attributed to one Daisy Ingram, a listed member of the Blount County Historical Society committee that had produced the book. The passage is about a water-driven mill in the Clear Springs community that was both gristmill and sawmill. It was also the communal swimming hole and social center. The men would give one another haircuts there on

Figure 4.4.
*The ruins of
the basket*

Fragments of that remarkedly tightly woven rectangular Blount County basket.

Saturdays. Sunday afternoons the children and teenagers would rally for games there. Several local women kept their big looms up in the spacious room above the working mill floor, turning the usually solitary loom weaving into a running women's social. One part that most struck me was a description of the annual Independence Day fish drive and fish fry there, but I'll save that for the fishtrap chapter still to come.[3]

It was also in or about 1974 that I began visiting with former commercial fisherfolk on the Coosa River. An army vet in my classes those years was also a part-time preacher in a church in Cropwell. He had old-timers in his congregation who had been commercial fishermen on the Coosa River long before it was dammed up. More on this, too, in the fishtrap chapter, but suffice it to say here I learned to hand-tie fishnets with net needle and mesh pin.

Looking back, within two or three years after I came to Alabama I was out rubbing elbows with some of "the folk," particularly handicraft-making folk, and introducing it to students in a folklore class I was beginning to teach every year or so. Which brings me to Folkcenter South.

The Brief, Mostly Happy Life of Folkcenter South

November 20, 1976, was a cold and sometimes rainy Saturday at Tannehill State Park's pioneer farm.[4] Despite the weather, somewhere between two hundred and three hundred people came out to watch ten carefully chosen traditional craftspeople work their trades for the day. Though the crowd was thin because of the weather, most people there came away fascinated by the experience. Spectators were introduced to craftspeople generally through a booklet and then individually by college student "cultural interpreters" assigned to the craftspeople. An "apprenticeship" program in place for the day enabled many onlookers and a few more-serious students to try their hand under the tutelage of de facto masters of country crafts. Sparks flew at the forge all day, for example, and a blacksmith urged an arm-weary apprentice to hammer faster while the iron was still hot and malleable: "Blacksmiths only go to hell for two reasons, son: charging too little and whipping cold iron!" It may have been Alabama's first real "publicly supported" (meaning by government dollars) folklife celebration.

It was almost all the work of a handful of Samford students who won a $7,500 Youthgrant from the National Endowment for the Humanities (NEH) to study folk craft survival in ten counties around and a bit east of Birmingham—Blount, Calhoun, Chilton, Clay, Coosa, Cullman, Jefferson, Shelby, St. Clair, and Talladega. This late November Saturday was the last phase of the students' ambitious four-step plan: do a comprehensive survey of surviving folk crafts in the ten counties, identify the superior or unusual craftspersons, do oral histories and photographic essays on these, and assemble the most interesting ten for a final folk craft celebration.

I was one faculty sponsor for the Youthgrant; Wayne Flynt was the other. We two had recently cobbled together a folklore minor (drawing from Wayne's longtime interests in oral history and grassroots culture in the South, from my newer interests in the European folk consciousness behind nationalism, and from both our interests in traditional crafts, music, and even fishing techniques).

The real key to this folk craft celebration, however, was a particular group of students in our history classes at Samford in 1974 and 1975. Every teacher knows that individual classes and years of students have their own personalities. The personality of this one at Samford, looking back, was some special interface between the spirit of the times and a handful of really interesting students. The zeitgeist was that by the mid-1970s some of the late 1960s ferment and questioning abroad in the country at large had percolated even into this conservative Baptist school in the heart of Dixie.

The two key student personalities were Mark Gooch and Cathy Hanby. Mark's interests were in the social sciences generally (he eventually transferred to the University of Alabama at Birmingham, UAB, to major in anthropology) but preeminently in photography. Even in his student years at Samford his photography was unusual and insightful, already elevated to a sort of Walker Evans/Dorothea Lange Farm Security Administration–style visual sociology. Cathy was an extremely bright history major with great energy and enough interest in folklore to propel her to eventual graduate degrees in it.

As I remember it all these years later, Mark and Cathy had caught some of my fascination with Mr. Henry Upchurch and other folk craft practitioners I'd met, including the Coosa River fisherfolk. Mark, who was from Mississippi, had already made contact and spent some time with the folklorists at the University of Mississippi (Ole Miss), and had hoped to get a job with them in photography and oral history. They weren't hiring, unfortunately for him, but someone there told him about the NEH Youthgrant program. When he came to Samford, then, he started work on just that. Such a grant required faculty sponsors, and of course I was pleased to be asked to be one. Mark and Cathy commandeered the living room in my house as a place in which to write it, despite the wanderings-through of small children, at least one of them once "nekkid as a jaybird." They then recruited a dozen or more enthusiastic fellow students and began serious self-preparation for the grant even before knowing one was awarded. They engaged Professor Flynt to instruct them in the practicalities of oral history. Mark had occasion to travel through Bloomington, Indiana, and took advantage of it to ask the advice of Professor Richard Dorson, noted historian and folklorist in Indiana University's doctoral folklore program (then one of only four such in the country). Mark and Cathy together visited the folklore archives at Western Kentucky University (WKU) and interviewed Professor Lynwood Montell, chair of the Center for Intercultural and Folk Studies there. They corresponded with Jane Rozier of the Tennessee Arts Commission, and spoke with publishing experts at Oxmoor House and exhibition experts at the Birmingham Museum of Art. By the time they won the grant in January 1976, they had developed a thoughtful strategy for combing the ten-county area.

Then came major setbacks. First, the actual grant money was slower to come in than expected. Then a few key members of the student team graduated in May, and one very active member of the group had a personal tragedy that took her away from the project. Membership dwindled until by summertime there were fewer active students than counties to be covered. Mark Gooch took on three counties, and I was promoted from faculty sponsor to honorary student for Blount County. In my old manila folder on the project, on top of the pile is a much-worn Blount County road map. All the tactics we had thought of to pursue folk craft survival—using the public schools, retirement homes, local newspaper columnists, and so forth—turned out to be less effective than simply driving and asking, which we shortened to D&A. I drove every paved road in Blount County at least once, and a lot that weren't paved. I worked Blount County from Rosa to Royal and was intrigued by its beauty—the parts that hadn't been strip-mined, at any rate. I got to know Highways 75 and 79, the two main arteries leading from Birmingham into the heart of the county, like old friends.

Highlights of the year are still fresh in my memory, such as when student William Whitten and I got leads on and then found eighty-five-year-old Homer Rigsby on the porch of his house, a newly made white oak basket in his hands. I spent a delightful afternoon interviewing Flora and Gordon Ballew of Rosa, and although I've long since lost the tape recording I've still got the transcript (which notes it was September 21, 1976). Gordon talked about growing up in a basketmaking family, claiming to have been able to make as good a basket as his father by age fourteen. "Would it be any imposition if I asked you when you were born?" I queried. Flora, laughing, said "February 1." Gordon allowed that it was 1909, and by 1925 his family had moved to the same general area they were in now. He reminisced about how when times were desperate in the Depression, his older sister Savannah and her husband, with nothing but an old butcher knife and an ax, made some white oak baskets to sell. Said Gordon, "They looked awful rough to me, but now they got 'em up something to eat right that way now." Flora said the doctor had warned Gordon not to get out and get too hot, but that she just couldn't keep him in. He said "you just get a fever of it" and have to go:

> Gordon: Now in the spring when the sap begins to rise I'll get out and hunt me a
>   pole timber and I'll make a basket or two. And I made a whole bunch up here

one time and Flora says [mimicking her] "what you want to keep making them baskets for"; says, "you won't never sell 'em." And I'm a son of a gun . . .

Flora: Back last fall . . .

Gordon: They was gone—before anytime. Just one and another coming in and buying 'em.

The Ballews guessed they'd sold between 300 and 350 baskets, from whole bushel to very small ones, during the past year.

I'm sure as many miles were driven and questions asked in the other nine counties as in "my" Blount County. Meanwhile, Mark and Cathy and a few others kept it all organized. They incorporated as Folkcenter South, even designing a logo, thinking this might become a permanent enterprise. Although that was not to be, Samford provided a spare office for the year, telephone included, and Mark held weekly progress meetings there. Every newspaper in the ten-county area got news releases from Folkcenter South, and a large ad was placed in the biggest daily paper in the area, the *Birmingham News*. Mark and Cathy were regular guests on talk shows and at service club luncheons, and they occasionally appeared on the Country Boy Eddie early-morning TV show. Mark's photography skills, I recently learned from him, got a real boost during this project, because Samford also gave him a key to a fully equipped darkroom in the School of Pharmacy building (it had been set up by a pharmacy professor who had passed away, and nobody else used it). Mark said he learned print developing by trial and error in what amounted to his own private darkroom. For a break he'd go down to the pharmacy student lounge; it had a low, soft couch that usually had enough lost coins under the cushions—courtesy of reclining pharmacy students—for him to buy a Coke from the vending machine there.

Results of the crafts survey, in brief: Too many quilters to get a handle on (although the decision to drop this craft from our search meant that traditionally male crafts predominated in the final list). Forty traditional white oak basketmakers still active, an average of four a county. A dozen blacksmiths who, if not still all practicing, at least still had shops and tools. Five traditional woodworkers of various traditional sorts; four makers of fishnets of various sorts, including hoop nets. One true folk potter; one corn-shuck chair bottomer; two folk musical instrument makers. No household in the ten-county area, as far as we could tell, had both a working spinning wheel and a working loom, most having perished in house fires over the years and no new ones made in replacement (which also left women underrepresented in our study). We found no cooperage of any kind, watertight or otherwise.

By early fall, Mark, Cathy, Mary Thompson, and others were focused on the November Saturday celebration. Some three hundred offset-printed color posters were made and posted, and a huge private correspondence was kept up with interested individuals who'd been met throughout the year.

The Venue, Tannehill State Park

Tannehill State Park, about halfway between Birmingham and Tuscaloosa, celebrates the beginnings of ironworking in Alabama. I was one of the hundreds of spectators at the September 16, 1976, bicentennial year refiring of one of the old furnaces there—for the first time since Wilson's Raiders had put them out of commission near the end of the Civil War. Tannehill became the venue for lots of this early celebration of folklore activity in Alabama, not just for Folkcenter South's crafts celebration day.

Unlike almost all the other state parks in Alabama, Tannehill was not a Civilian Conservation Corps (CCC) Depression-era creation. Everett Smith (brother-in-law of my colleague Wayne Flynt and, back when I first knew him, second-in-command at the Alabama State Geology offices) told me that in 1969 he was exploring the old furnace ruins deep in the piney woods there and could still smell the smoke where vandals had blown off a corner of one of the huge rock furnaces. He got local people interested in preserving the ruins, and within two years they had a park up and running with its own board of directors. Jim Bennett (formerly a Birmingham newspaperman and latterly Alabama secretary of state), one of those founding board members, was from Homewood and a passionate amateur historian; as I remember it I got interested in the park from him.[5] The board's best move was probably the hiring of Ed Nelson as park manager. Capable, enthusiastic, and tireless, he presided over the careful transference or reconstruction of historical buildings to the park, plank by board by log—a church, a gristmill, a store, lots and lots of cabins. Eliot Wigginton would later try to hire him away to do the same with *Foxfire*'s growing hillside of historical reconstructions in Rabun County, but Ed was Alabamian through and through and not moving that far away.

So that was the venue. Then came the run-up for the actual crafts celebration day, the flurry of organizing the pioneer farm at Tannehill for it, arranging transportation (rental van) and materials for the artists (potter's wheel, forge, etc.), setting up the information booth, hosting the few press representatives and the NEH representative, ordering lunch for participants, and raffling off a quilt and basket that were door prizes for the day.

Jack Vice was from northern Calhoun County and, as of the festival, was still living on the old family homestead. He still made baskets under the same oak tree where his father taught him. On this day he was mainly a blacksmith. The other blacksmith was Roscoe Simpson of the Sanie community in St. Clair County. He spent many a year as a blacksmith in the mines run by Alabama Fuel, shoeing mules. He'd learned the craft from his father and still had many of his father's tools.

George Keahey, from Clay County, grew up in Bulls Gap, and as of the festival lived in Piedmont. A keen fisherman since his childhood, he wanted to learn how to tie nets, but none of those locals who knew wanted to teach potential competitors. So he sat for two entire days watching two older women tie nets for their fishing husbands to rig up. He "got it in his head" without asking a question. Claude Hayes, our other traditional net tier, grew up in a fishing family on the Coosa River between Talladega and St. Clair Counties; he'd been a commercial fisherman all his life, and was both an expert tier of fishnets and a builder of red oak fish boxes.

Our folk potter for the day was Norman "Jug" Smith. He was born in Perry County, but in 1932 he built his current log house and kiln in western Chilton County. He first saw pottery done when his dad fired a couple of small pieces in their woodstove. A potter all his adult life, he specialized in two-foot churns, flowerpots, and jugs that he speculated were used for liquids not to be named . . .

Beatrice Wills of Clay County had made honeysuckle baskets for sixty years, boiling the honeysuckle to remove the bark and sometimes dyeing the resulting weavers. She did practical work (as for egg baskets) and ornate designs (as for flower girl baskets for weddings). Our second basketmaker was Homer Rigsby from northern Blount County, east of Wynnville across Whippoorwill Creek. At age eighty-five, he was still weaving fish baskets and baby cradles out of "split timber," the local name for the useful white oak. And last but not least there was Mr. Henry Upchurch, the white oak basketmaker you've already met in this chapter, a favorite craftsman of mine and by this time also a favorite of many of the student participants.

A. M. Moon, from Holly Pond on the eastern edge of Cullman County, was a maker of fiddles, guitars, and especially banjos. He'd made his first banjo as a child with a possum hide, and he was known far and wide for his Red Barn, a noncommercial country music and dancing spot. The tenth craftsperson was Jess Willet, a retired steelworker from Birmingham, who made dough trays from orthodox woods such as tulip poplar and experimented with unusual woods such as cedar.

When the folk craft celebration ended late in the afternoon, there was transportation home for those who required it, the whole process ending well after midnight for some . . . a long but satisfying day that still radiates a warmth to me over all the years since.

At the end of the final report to the NEH on the Folkcenter South Youthgrant, written in August 1977, its director, Mark Gooch, added a personal note:

> Looking back over the past two years and my work with this grant, I see a period of my life which I will always remember with fondest memories. Too many times we rush through life overlooking much of the world around us. Youthgrants has given me the opportunity to step back and focus. During the grant period I had the pleasure of talking with hundreds of people throughout the state. Being able to talk with so many different people has had a great impact on me. Each person revealed in a different way what was important in his or her life. Drawing from this experience I am able to weigh the values I have placed on my life and translate this in my daily living. People taught me many new ways of looking at life's situations. I found myself listening, letting everyone teach me. Most of the people I encountered were travelers of another time. They carried with them a wealth of experience. I could see it in their hands as they worked and in the words of wisdom which they spoke. Worries about a life in the world of tomorrow were comforted by caring eyes which looked at me and said, "Live a good life; there's so much to be experienced."

IN RETROSPECT

In 2003 or so (in the process of writing an article about Folkcenter South for *Tributaries*, the Alabama Folklife Association's journal) I called Mark at his photography business in Birmingham and read him his words of a quarter century before. He responded that never in any of the talks he had with any of those folk craft people he got to know best did they ever break off a conversation because they had to go do something else. It hit me then, and even more today, that most every extended conversation I have is ended exactly because one of us has to go do something else.

In general, I have the same fond memories of the year, along with some wistful thinking about how nice it would be now if we had been able to finish oral histories and photographic essays on all these people. Looking back, I see that the sort of survival definition we had of folk crafts was a bit old-fashioned and romantic, but there was a power to it nonetheless. We experienced the same sort of magic that ballad hunters in the high Appalachians did in the 1920s, or that central European folktale collectors did in the nineteenth century. Specialized craft research opened out into dramatic stories and broader life patterns in a rural culture largely unknown to students (and then-young professors).

I still can't put my finger on all the parts of this kind of association that made for improved mental health among the collectors. There were lessons in human resilience from times harder than we had ever known. There was country humor and wisdom woven into turns of phrase in the language. There was the contact with age-old, close-to-the-earth crafts still very much alive and flourishing in forgotten corners of the region. Mark Gooch probably had it right in his final report: it was a fascination with "travelers of another time," and my time machine for this bicentennial year was a blue 1965 Chevy II with a four-year-old son or a seven-year-old daughter sometimes riding shotgun.

O my son

chapter five

What Wondrous Love Is This

Sacred Harp Singing

If you're a regular in the Sacred Harp singing world, you won't need to read this chapter. In fact, I'd rather you didn't, because you'd probably point out sins of omission and commission for me to correct. But if you know about Sacred Harp only casually or not at all, let me introduce you to one of the most interesting cultural traditions of the Piedmont South, the center of gravity of which is surely north and central Alabama.

CLOSE ENCOUNTER

In 1974 I went to my first "fasola" singing—an "all-day singing and dinner on the grounds" of the four-shape-note variety. I'd been in the state three years by this time, and several friends who knew of my folkloric interests had urged me to go. I was reluctant to go hear what I figured would be hokey backwoods music in a dour and fundamentalist setting. But a couple of faculty friends had never been to one either, so we marshaled our collective courage and picked the closest scheduled singing we could find. It was at the Hopewell Primitive Baptist Church a few miles south of Oneonta, Blount County, Alabama. Just go and get it over with so I could say I'd tried it: that was my less-than-positive mood for the day.

Before we could even see the church building, we found cars parked bumper to bumper on both sides of the two-lane country blacktop. We found a place to park ours and began to walk toward the little one-room church. The singing had already started, and as we got closer to the building you could feel the pulse of the song—incredible volume coming out of that little wooden church building. I was first of the three of us up the front steps, and when I opened the church door, I was caught in waves of sound as if I were standing in a surf. I just froze for a minute. They were singing in a haunting minor key, throats open in full volume. They sang with no tremolo or vibrato to speak of, but with perfect chords from a piercing high harmony to the deepest bass section I ever heard outside a Russian Orthodox church.

In front of us there was a short center aisle, and on the left and right a few rows of pews facing the pulpit, or the spot where the pulpit would have been in an ordinary church service. In the front half or more of the church, though, the main aisle was blocked. There the pews and chairs were arranged on four sides, all facing the center, where the leader of each song stood; you could only get in on the corners of the square. There were a couple of folks near the front right corner of the church who were in charge of calling on singers to lead—apparently only one song per leader, since the church was full. Often the leaders who got up would say they wanted to sing such and such a number in memory of older relatives or friends, those too sick to attend or those who had already passed on, whose favorite song that had been. Some specialist in the middle of the front row would pitch or "key" the song (there are no musical instruments in this tradition). The song leader would bring a right hand down to start the music, and off they'd go. Everyone had a hardcover songbook wider than it was tall, but it was obvious that not many needed theirs: they knew their parts of the songs by heart, sometimes all five or more verses.

We stayed through the noon-hour dinner on the grounds, and then on through the two hour-long sessions after lunch. At the end of that second hour after lunch the chooser of leaders asked us all to stand and then called on "Uncle Jimmy," apparently the oldest man present, to conclude with prayer. He came slowly and haltingly up to the front and began by allowing that this could be his last singing there ever (looking at him, I thought the chances of that were quite good). Then he began to pray, soon getting into that backcountry sermon and prayer rhythm in which every phrase ends in a powerful "hah" or "ah," with a pause before the next phrase. He really got wound up, and the prayer went on and on. But then something unusual happened that I later learned was called "singing the preacher down." Somewhere in the middle of the church someone started softly humming a hymn. The humming gradually spread, and then the words began to be used, and as the volume of the singers rose the volume of Uncle Jimmy's prayer dwindled and he brought it to a close. Then, still singing, the members of the congregation began leaving the church, hugging everybody close to them on the way out. There weren't many dry eyes, including mine, and I didn't even know these people. That was 60 percent of my lifetime ago, a lifetime stretching now beyond the biblical norm of three score and ten, and I still remember it as if it were last week.

CARL CARMER'S TAKE ON IT, FORTY YEARS EARLIER

I guess if I had to choose one ten-page essay on fasola singing to give someone who'd never seen it or even heard of it, I'd choose the "All-Day Singing" chapter in *Stars Fell on Alabama*, first published in 1934. Despite the chintzy title, it's one of the most insightful books ever written on Alabama. The author, Carl Carmer, was an upstate New Yorker with a master's degree from Harvard. He taught English at the University of Alabama from 1927 to 1933, and from his base in Tuscaloosa he ranged all over the state—from "conjure and Cajun" country way down south, to Birmingham, and then up into the mountains in the northeast. He even attended a Ku Klux Klan cross burning and was frighteningly, sickeningly close to a race riot and lynching.

In the "All-Day Singing" chapter, he describes going to a singing on Sand Mountain sometime around 1930, riding in a Ford with a politician out to get votes and with a local supporter and his family. After a steep climb up Sand Mountain, on the plateau they came to an unpainted one-room church with an unfinished spire. They parked amid the many cars, horses, mules, and wagons, and went in. A tall man who was leading things had the trebles on the right (as viewed from the entrance, looking toward the front of the church), the basses on the left, and the tenors in the center, the main part of the congregation. When Carmer asked his friends what about the altos, they said not to mention the word; many considered it a newfangled affectation. The music "perfesser" asked a woman in the trebles to hit her highest note, and a bullfrog of a man in the basses to hit his lowest, and then he sang a note somewhere between them:

> "That'll be the pitch," he said. "We'll sing the music first. Are you ready?" He raised his arm, pencil in hand, and brought it down.
>
> Tom and Henry took in great breaths and let out staccato yells. So did everyone else except Knox and me. A fearsome hodgepodge of sound arose. They were singing an outlandish gibberish—great sharp bursts of sound. Knox shouted in my ear:
>
> "They're singing the notes."
>
> I did not understand, but gradually, as I listened, I made out a tune, a wailing

minor, and I discovered that Henry and Tom were singing *mi, fa, sol, la*. I looked at the book and for the first time saw that the notes, though placed on the familiar scale, were printed in different shapes. *Mi* was a diamond, and I found by careful comparison of the book and the singing: *fa* was triangular; *sol* was round, *la* was square. Weeks later by study of the book I learned how these notes are repeated in the scale.[1]

The church was crammed full, and clusters of latecomers were singing at every window opening. Carmer estimated the crowd at two thousand people, at what they had told him earlier was a "right small meetin' at a bad time o' year." He watched the boys and girls begin pairing off at lunch, disappearing during the afternoon sessions, and loitering in the grove after it was over. Then came the last song:

> A haunting melody rose, minor and plangent, a tune that lent itself in some strange way to the reedy, metallic quality of this strange chorus. The words were peculiarly distinct.

> > I've a long time heard that the sun will be darkened
> > That the sun will be darkened in that day,
> > O sinner, where will you stand in that day?

There was a long pause and then the song lifted again:

> > I've a long time heard that the moon will be bleeding

On it went.

> > I've a long time heard that the stars will be falling—
> > I've a long time heard that the earth will be burning . . .

As the last stanza started the singers, still singing, began moving to the door. When the last note died the church was empty.[2]

George Pullen Jackson's Scholarship

It's a truism with historians that by studying how something came into being, one can learn things about it that can't be gleaned from any other approach. So the reflexive response of any historian to something fascinating but puzzling, of course, is to go read about how it got to be that way. Within a matter of weeks of that first singing I ever attended, this habit led me to the works of George Pullen Jackson. He was born in 1874 in Maine, in what he, a great phrasemaker, called "The Deep North." In 1887, when he was just thirteen, his father, a manufacturer, moved the family south to a new and booming industrial city, Birmingham. He spent only his teen years here, moving on to Vanderbilt to college when he was nineteen, and then going to Dresden to study both classical music and German language. He wound up back at Vanderbilt as head of the German department there, retiring in 1943, and dying ten years later. But the passion of his life (which undoubtedly took energy away from his German studies, it is comforting for me now to realize), was fasola music. Ironically enough, he apparently never heard any while he lived in Birmingham, which is about as close to the modern geographic heart of the tradition as you can get; it was a friend in Nashville later who introduced him to it. Of all he wrote on the subject, my favorite work is still his first major book on it, the 1933 *White Spirituals from the Southern Uplands: The Story of the Fasola Folk, Their Songs, Singings, and "Buckwheat Notes."*[3]

Although this shape-note tradition is primarily an American thing, it has roots deep in the Protestant Reformation in northern Europe. That was in part a rebellion against the theater of the Catholic Church—increasingly ornate church buildings, bright and richly gilded decoration, elaborate music and costume, and the elite's exclusive access to the Bible in Latin. I knew that early Protestant services generally were held by plainly dressed folk listening to a preacher at the centrally located pulpit (symbolizing the centrality of the Word, a Word in the vernacular so everybody could understand it), in services that tended to go long. But early on in this same Protestantism, psalms began to be chanted and then set to tunes, lined out by a song leader at the pulpit. Later, on the theory that the Devil shouldn't get all the pretty music, these musically starved congregations—especially the Dissident congregations in Britain, which were estranged from the official Anglican Church about as much as from Catholicism—began to send parties out to the "pot and public houses" to collect beautiful tunes to which they could put the message of their religious faith.

The first result was what are called "parody songs," secular songs transparently adapted to a Christian theme. "How tedious and tasteless the hours, / when Jesus no longer I see; / sweet prospects, sweet birds and sweet flowers, / have all lost their sweetness to me. / The midsummer sun shines but dim; / the fields strive in vain to look gay; / but when I am happy in Him, / September's as pleasant as May," is a verse from one such hymn ("Greenfields") in English. I'd bet money that "sweet prospects, sweet birds and sweet flowers" was a phrase in the original, secular version, a Robert Burns–style celebration of nature and probably wine, carnal love, and song. Key phrases have just been reversed to change the message. One of the most interesting parts of *White Spirituals from the Southern Uplands* is the section where Professor Jackson takes the melody (tenor) lines from the eighty most popular shape-note songs and convincingly traces most of them back to fiddle tunes and sea chanties ("Fisher's Hornpipe" and "Rosin the Bow"), ballads ("Barbry Allen" and "Lord Lovell"), and other secular songs ("The Old Oaken Bucket" and "Robin Adair"). The melody of what had become from my first minute of hearing it my favorite Sacred Harp song, "Wondrous Love," for example, is pretty clearly based on that of the popular "Ballad of Captain Kidd" (the ballad appeared very soon after Kidd was hanged in 1701, perhaps even being printed and sold in the crowd gathered for the hanging itself).

The basic musical tradition came across the Atlantic first to New England. It was not yet written in shape notes, but it already had an a cappella three-part or four-part harmony with a melody line that was not the treble (soprano) but next to the lowest, the tenor part. The basses were usually all men, the trebles all women, but the one or later two middle parts were mixed, with the women's voices usually an octave above the men's—so really as much as a six-part harmony.

Many songs were pentatonic, using the ancient five-note scale instead of the more modern seven-note one. The homely country phrase for the scholarly "pentatonic" is a "gap-tune" scale, because if you've got an ear that is accustomed to the seven-note scale, it feels as if there are gaps, a couple of notes that are rarely or never used. And the music is also often modal, doing stranger things than just major and minor keys. Here, with apologies to real musicians, is a rough explanation of modal. If someone was to play just the white keys on the piano, starting with middle C and going up an octave, to the ear it would probably sound at least superficially as if every step were equal. But they're not, mathematically speaking: the interval from first to second white keys is a whole step (there is a black key between them), and the same from second to third, but from third to fourth is just a half step, with no black key to skip. So if we start on any other note but C and play an octave's worth of just the white notes, the two half-step intervals occur at different places in the scale. Melodies played on such scales, for folks not from that tradition, tend to go in unexpected directions. Music that tends to be both pentatonic and modal, to the suburban ear (my ear in 1974, for one), has an archaic and wild flavor to it.

In terms of how such music was written, as early as in Elizabethan England folks were using solmization, or giving monosyllabic names to particular notes of the scale: *fa-sol-la-fa-sol-la-mi*. Jackson found a songbook from 1721 in Boston that used the first letters of the *fa-so-la-fa-sol-la-mi* scale, placed on a five-line staff: the letter F (without a period after it) was a quarter note, and F. (with the period) was a half note. Most of a century later, in 1802, also in Boston, came the first book he could find with a triangle for *fa*, a circle for *sol*, a square for *la*, and a diamond for *mi*.

This basic musical idiom from old England and this new notation from New England then percolated down through the valleys of eastern Pennsylvania, and then down the Great Valley of Virginia and the foothills of the eastern slopes of the Appalachians, "into the hilly outrunners of the Appalachians to the south," to use Jackson's phrase. Close behind it came the newer European musical traditions, including the more modern seven-note scale, which replaced the pentatonic one and gave the melody line of hymns to the highest, soprano part, and therefore almost exclusively to women. But the older tradition survived and even flourished, not so much in the high Southern Appalachians where the ballads thrived, but rather in "the southern uplands": starting in hilly northwestern South Carolina and northern Georgia, finding its center of gravity in the northern two-thirds of Alabama, and diminishing on through northern Mississippi, eastern Louisiana, and a discontinuous patch in East Texas.

William Walker and B. F. White, Brothers-in-Law

William ("Singing Billy") Walker of Spartanburg County, South Carolina, born in 1809, published the initially very popular *Southern Harmony* in four-shape notation in 1835. His brother-in-law Benjamin Franklin White (they had married the wonderfully named Golightly sisters) had been a joint compiler of the book, but when Singing Billy took it up to Philadelphia to have it printed, no mention was made of B. F. White, much less authorship given to him. The brothers-in-law apparently never spoke again, and B. F. White moved from South Carolina to rural Harris County on the far side of Georgia, just north of Columbus and adjoining Alabama. There in 1844 he published *The Sacred Harp* (presumably referring to the human voice, since this music had no instruments). Either by the book's appeal, or by the tireless teaching of singing schools that B. F. White did, his book generally outdid Billy Walker's, even though Walker would eventually expand his system, releasing a seven-shape notation songbook titled *Christian Harmony* in 1867.

The oldest yearly Sacred Harp singings Jackson could find in Alabama dated to 1873 and 1874. It took deep root, though: by 1909 the Alabama State Sacred Harp Musical Association began holding three-day singings in the county courthouse in Birmingham. A 1911 revision of *The Sacred Harp*, although still headquartered in Georgia, showed a shift westward, with twenty-eight new songs from Alabama and only six from Georgia, and with S. M. Denson from Alabama as the obvious driving force behind it all.

The Logic of the Shapes

In the Sacred Harp tradition, as Carl Carmer figured out at his first singing, the printed music runs the seven-note scale—even though many of the songs just use five of the notes!—beginning with a *fa* (triangle), continuing through *sol* (circle), *la* (square), *fa* (triangle), *sol* (circle), *la* (square), and *mi* (diamond), and then starting the next-higher scale with a *fa* (triangle) again. If you already know how to read music, the shapes seem like an unnecessary complication: you already know the note, musically, but have to add to that the pronunciation of the note. But if you don't know how to read music, it's much easier to learn to read it using shape notes. I've had more than one veteran Sacred Harp singer brag to me about how good they were, by saying with pride that they could read "round notes" too.

Back when Cincinnati and Nashville were country towns and Birmingham was just being dreamed up, singing school teachers would often use shape notes to make it easier for their students. The scale of seven different shapes still used by the Christian Harmony folks is one surviving relic of the era. There was even one small music school that used different farm animals for the heads of the notes—shaped notes with a vengeance. Whatever the shapes, it really does work. In the four-shape tradition, for example, students would start without written music, singing the bottom note of the scale (*fa*), then the note above it (*sol*), and then *fa* again. Then they would sing the first three notes of the rising scale (*fa, sol, la*), drop back to *fa*, go back up to *la*, and then drop down to *fa* again, just to get the interval in their heads. And they'd work up the whole scale that way. Only then would they be shown the written music and be told that the lowest triangle-headed note was that original, first note of the scale (*fa*), that the circle above it was *sol*, that the square above that was *la*, and so on. At a typical singing the whole crowd sings the shapes before they ever sing the poetry, the way they were taught when they were young.

A typical summer singing school of a week or two would be held after the crops were laid by and before the harvest, when there was a lull in the agricultural work of the growing season. For a modest fee children and young people within walking distance of a church, more often than not a Primitive Baptist church, would get instruction at the hands of a traveling music "perfesser." Years ago, back in 1980–81 while researching the Life Histories of the Depression-era Federal Writers' Project (FWP) in the state archives in Montgomery, I came across a short oral history written by Nettie S. MacDonald of the Birmingham-based Editorial Department, titled "A Singing School." Sometime in 1938 she had interviewed a Mrs. Fannie Kelley of 1016 South Sixteenth Street, Birmingham, asking particularly about a singing school that Mrs. Kelley had attended more than sixty years earlier, in 1877, somewhere in the countryside at one of the many churches named Shiloh. The summer singing school wasn't of the four-shape Sacred Harp variety that I had learned, but rather in the closely allied seven-shape Christian Harmony, though I'd guess the singing schools of both traditions worked about the same way. Here's the bulk of the text. I don't think it's ever been printed before:

> Let me see now; it was about the first of July, in 1877 (I can remember the date because John was six years old) that word went around through the country that a singing master would be at Shiloh church to start a singing school in two weeks. It would cost one dollar and a half for the ten-day class if there was just one from a family, but if more than one came, it would be just a dollar.
>
> When the opening day came, everybody from all over that country came. We lived two and a half miles from the church; I know it was that far at least, some said it was at least three miles. There wasn't much of a path; we mostly walked along and made our own path. You wouldn't dare do that now; it's too dangerous. Back there we weren't afraid of anything.
>
> . . . [The church] was just a big square building with posts to hold it up. The rain had washed the dirt away so bad that it looked like it wouldn't take much of a wind to blow it away. We had a door in the side and one in the front, but it sat in the prettiest grove of oak trees you ever did see. The boys had plenty of room to hitch their mules and horses.
>
> When we got inside the church that day Mr. Fagot was there and all ready to

begin. He was a big tall man with light hair. I guess he weighed over two hundred pounds. He brought his wife with him. He passed out the books, but we didn't have enough books to go around. You want to know if the boys and girls looked on together? No sir, they didn't. The boys sat on one side of the church and the girls sat on the other. I can remember the first time that I saw girls and boys sitting together; I thought it was terrible. It almost seemed disgraceful.

Every single day of the whole singing school, the singing master would open the class with a prayer. We didn't pray then like you do now—just pray any way you want to—but every one got down on his knees.

After the prayer was over, the singing master would call out a number and we would all start in to singing. You seem mighty anxious about those shaped notes. Well, I'll tell you one thing; they're not half as hard to learn as the way you sing. Every note had a different shape. One shape stood for a note. Some of the shapes looked almost alike but if you looked right close you'd see that one was curved a little different. The singing teacher would sing a little bit at a time and then we would go over it just like he did. We went over and over the songs after him, until we learned all the notes. Then we could sing any song we wanted to.

After we sang four or five songs, then we would have a recess. Now that's when the boys and girls go together. Some boy would ask a girl if she didn't want a drink of water and then another boy would ask another girl the same thing. Pretty soon they were pretty well paired off and then we would all go down to the spring. We had a big gourd down at the spring and when the gourd was filled, we drank and passed it around, in fact we didn't dip up more water until we drank it all. And it didn't hurt anybody either.

After recess, we came back into the church and sang until dinner time. We all brought our lunch and we'd spread it out and have a regular picnic lunch. Those lunches did taste good. We had an hour for dinner, so you see we had plenty of time to go to the spring some more. It wasn't long before the boys started claiming the girls and then we'd pair off the same way nearly every time. When dinner was over, then we'd go back in and sing 'til three o'clock. One of the prettiest songs in our book was "O bear me away on your snowy wings to my eternal home." You see we all had favorites and Mr. Fagot would let us pick out the ones we liked best and take turn about having ours sung.

Every day when we were through singing and ready to go home, Mr. Fagot would say, "Now turn to page two hundred in your *Christian Harmonies* and let's sing *Parting Hand*." I don't know why in the world he told us to turn to it, for we knew every word of it by heart. When we came to that part that says "Cords around my heart," the boys would look over at us girls and put their hands over their hearts and smile for dear life.

Here are some of the words of that song and it sure was pretty:

Dear friends, farewell I say,
Since you and I must part.
Your company's sweet, your union dear
Your words delightful to my ear.
Yet when I see that we must part,
You draw like cords around my heart

The singing school lasted for ten days and if I do say so myself we all left that class pretty good singers.[4]

Although Mrs. Kelley didn't comment on this, usually on the last day of such traditional summertime shape-note singing schools the whole community was invited to come participate. Some of the terminology of today's singings obviously comes from those mid to late nineteenth-century and early twentieth-century singing schools—for example, calling any given day's singing a "class," and the song or two chosen by any given leader a "lesson."

The Densons

On the lawn of the Winston County courthouse in Double Springs, about seventy miles northwest of Birmingham, stands a tombstone-like memorial to the Denson brothers, Seaborn (1854–1936) and Thomas (1863–1935). It was erected in 1944, the centennial of the publication of B. F. White's *Sacred Harp* hymnal, in honor of the 1936 "Denson Revision" of the book. The text says that the stone was put there in summer 1944 by family members, pupils of their many singing schools, and legions of singers and friends. A line toward the bottom reads, "While 'Uncle Seab' and 'Uncle Tom' sing on," and then comes a staff of music, shape notes and all, and below that appear the matching words of the dying phrase of a hymn, "way o-ver in the promis'd land," the answer from an old camp meeting song to its question,

"Where now are the Hebrew children?" At the very bottom of the stone appear the names of those on the three-person committee in charge of the stone's placement, including one "Dr. George P. Jackson." On my trips from Birmingham to hike in the Sipsey Wilderness, when driving up through Double Springs I'd always give it a glance and sometimes park and walk up to the stone memorial, wondering at the power of this slowly evolving Sacred Harp tradition. I'd felt some of its pull myself.

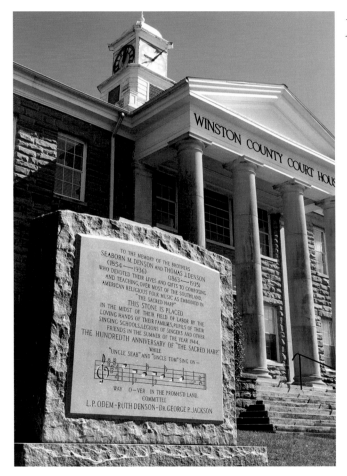

Figure 5.1. Denson Memorial

A monument to the Denson brothers erected in 1944, the centennial of the publication of B. F. White's original *Sacred Harp*. The stone is prominently located on the lawn of the Winston County courthouse in Double Springs.

The exact title of the Densons' 1936 book was *Original Sacred Harp*. "Original" hints that it was something of a conservative reaction to the 1902 "Cooper book" from Dothan, Alabama. The Cooper book uses the same four-shape solmization as the general *Sacred Harp*, but it had become more popular in the southern parts of Alabama and northern Florida by incorporating some more modern hymn practice. By this time, however, conservative or not, the Densons had almost fully adopted the "newfangled" alto fourth part: the majority of the songs say "Alto added by S. Denson." There were future modifications, other "Denson Revisions," published in 1960, 1967, and 1971.

This last edition—*Original Sacred Harp (Denson Revision 1971)*—is where I came into the tradition. Over the years I've bought or been given the latest edition, but I have kept that first one. It's dog eared and scribbled on, and it still stirs up lots of memories. Sometime back in those first years I took it up to the yearly singing at County Line, north of Birmingham, and we sang "Antioch" (p. 277). One reason I like Sacred Harp so much is that you can almost always count on the bass part to be as lively as any other, and it is certainly so in "Antioch." The two-line first verse goes "I know that my Redeemer lives, Glory, Hallelujah! / What comfort this sweet sentence gives, Glory, Hallelujah!" Then there's a half measure of silence and this rousing chorus: "Shout on, pray on, we're gaining ground, Glory, Hallelujah! / The dead's alive and the lost is found, Glory, Hallelujah!" When the song ended I was still swaying to the beat. My neighbor—I found out at the next break he was Frank Miller—on seeing how much I had enjoyed the song, leaned over to me and whispered that his granddaddy off in the Civil War hadn't been heard from in six months and was presumed dead. But the soldier's father, Frank Miller's great-grandfather, saw a familiar figure walking over the field toward the house, and he recognized his son. With his arms wide he went toward the youth singing that chorus from "Antioch." I've still got the story scribbled down on the back page of the songbook.

For years, beginning in the mid-1970s, I attended the Labor Day Shoal Creek Church singing in the Talladega National Forest. My white oak basketmaking teacher Mr. Henry Upchurch, who lived just west of the national forest, had introduced it to me. Apparently when the national forest was created in the late 1930s, many landowners were bought out and had to leave. But the old church building was left standing, and once a year they still spruce it up, weed the graveyard and strew it with white sand, and have a reunion of sorts with an all-day Sacred Harp singing and dinner on the grounds at that church, now deep in the forest.

At the singings I attended there, it was customary for an offering plate or maybe just a hat to be passed around. When I first started going, it seemed to be expected that adult men would contribute a dollar or so. The fees paid for the singing's page in the annual Minutes publication recording Sacred Harp singings in Alabama: who opened the session, who led what song, who led the prayer at the start or at lunch or at close. My two favorite songs, when I was brave enough to lead, were "Wondrous Love" (p. 159), which was so old there was no authorship for it claimed in the hymn-book, and "David's Lamentation" (p. 268), a William Billings song from Boston in the late 1700s about King David's grief over having killed his son Absalom. I don't think I was ever listed in a Minutes book leading any other number.

REVISITING THE 1971 DENSON REVISION

In the process of my writing all this up, it dawned on me that as much as I had used the 1971 Denson Revision book, I'd never systematically gone through it. So one afternoon in January 2017 I spent a couple of hours leafing through it, pausing on the sweet six-page historical summary by Ruth Denson Edwards, and making at least a cursory glance at all 573 hymns. Dozens of them use the lyrics of Isaac Watts, the star of that first Dissident Protestant generation in England to go beyond just setting scriptural passages to music. This late 1700s to early 1800s New England foundation is evident in the tunes, many of which have lively rounds, or in the fugues ("fleeing" songs, because the parts seem to chase or repeat one another) from William Billings and Jeremiah Ingalls of Massachusetts and John Read of Connecticut. Bursts of new songs were dedicated for the big revisions, especially in Georgia for the 1850 revision of the B. F. White book (its first revision) and in Alabama for the 1936 Denson Revision. Toward the end of the book there are some newer songs, composed as late as 1959 and 1960, including a couple of my toe-tapping favorites, "Redemption" (p. 480) and "Jacob's Vision" (p. 551-b); it was obviously still a living, breathing, creative tradition, at least as of 1971. I found a note I'd penciled in at the bottom of page 378, that as of the year 1852 B. F. White had a newspaper called the *Organ*, in which other singers could put their own songs to be tried out to see whether they were good enough for regular use. My note ended in a parenthesis, "according to Hugh McGraw, Nov. 5, 1987," who was talking to me between hymns. What seems to have happened was that when a print run of songbooks ran low, they'd take the opportunity to take out a few little-used songs and put a few promising new ones in before they did another print run, thus the "revision" title. Hugh McGraw's own edition, *The Sacred Harp, 1991 Revision*, would in turn dominate the next couple of decades (more on Hugh shortly, as a central figure in this generation of singers).

I loved the curious titles: "The Last Words of Copernicus," for example, and the songs named after American states but also, without explanation, "Cuba" and "Russia." I'd forgotten the simpler strain of patriotism from earlier in our country's history found in many of these songs, patriotism both optimistic and pessimistic. "Murillo's Lesson" (p. 358), a favorite in the singing schools, was supposedly written by a veteran of the Continental Army in 1777 or so. In the first verse the author talks about leaving "war's dread confusion" and walking down a valley under the cedars where everything got quiet. Then comes the first chorus:

> Perfumes as of Eden flowed sweetly along
> A voice as of angels enchantingly sung
> Columbia, Columbia, to glory arise,
> The queen of the world and the child of the skies

The second verse and chorus continue:

> Fair science her gate to thy sons shall unbar,
> And the east see thy morn hide the beams of her star
> New bards and new sages unrivall'd shall soar
> To fame unextinguished, when time is no more.

> To the last refuge of virtue designed,
> Shall fly from all nations, the best of mankind . . .

"Mount Vernon" (p. 110) is a dirge on the death of George Washington in 1799. Here are some of the words:

> What solemn sound the ear invades,
> What wraps the land in sorrow's shade
> From heaven the awful mandate flies,
> The Father of his country dies.

Where shall our nation turn its eye,
What help remains beneath the sky?
Our friend, protector, strength and trust,
Lies low and moul'ring in the dust.

On the mantelpiece in our living room today, on a display stand, is a metal plate formerly used to print "The Christian's Hope" (p. 134, a William Walker tune of about
1832, alto by S. Denson). Some years ago word was sent around that the printers
were breaking up the old lead-backed copper-faced printing plate collection of my
beloved 1971 Denson Revision book, and the plates could be ordered for ten dollars
each, though you couldn't specify which one. I just wish I could have gotten "Wondrous Love" or "David's Lamentation." If the owner of one of those should happen to
read this and be willing to swap, I'd come up with substantial boot.

Figure 5.2.
Sacred Harp
hymnal and
printing plate

On the display stand on the mantelpiece is one of the metal plates used to print the 1971 Denson revision of *Original Sacred Harp*. Author's copy of the same edition is next to it, open to
"Wondrous Love."

The National Sacred Harp Singing Convention has met in the Birmingham area in the middle of June since its inception in 1980. It's a big affair, held in recent years in a large suburban church down south of town on Valleydale Road, then for 2017 and later moved to Fultondale, just north of Birmingham proper—but they've all been in the general vicinity of Birmingham. It got its start on Samford University campus in Homewood, in 1980, and the original plans were for it to be held the next year at the University of Texas at Austin and the year after that at the University of North Carolina at Chapel Hill. Singers from outside the region, however, protested that they'd rather keep coming to the geographic heart of the tradition, where there would presumably always be lots of those old heads who grew up in the tradition. Recently it's more than just national, but going on international: one year my wife and I housed a woman and her daughter from Oxford, England, here for the convention, who came out of the kindred "West Gallery" tradition in England.

Because the very first "national" convention met on Samford's campus, I was in on it—one of the few Samford faculty members outside the music faculty to have gotten interested in the tradition. The dean of our school of music, Claude Rhea, had linked up with Hugh McGraw of Bremen, Georgia. Hugh was already the single most influential person in the Sacred Harp world. With his draw, and with the spaces and finances available to a dean of music at a college, the two made it happen. I've still got a stick-and-paper fan from the occasion with Hugh pictured on it, posed as if leading a song, book in left hand, right hand raised. The convention was held in the main auditorium of the Wright Fine Arts Center on campus, with the singers all up on the stage as if it was performance music. This arrangement was a little awkward because it's not performance music; it's participatory music. And the veteran singers will tell you that you only get the full blast of it when leading a song yourself, in the middle of that hollow square, high-volume music coming at you from four directions, giving a whole new meaning to quadraphonic sound.

Much to my surprise, making a late entrance one morning of that first four-day-long convention in 1980 was an African American group from Ozark, a town down toward the southeast corner of the state. At that time I'd never seen a single African American participate in these "white spiritual" gatherings, and here was a whole delegation, saying they were representing the Wiregrass Singers. They weren't new converts to fasola: although primary users of the Cooper book, they had produced their own *Colored Sacred Harp* back in 1934, and it had gone through a couple of editions since. The original author and publisher was Judge Jackson, and his son was one of the delegation at Samford in 1980. The greatest singer of the bunch I met in 1980 was probably Dewey Williams, who, as a Samford music faculty member remarked to me in awe, could vocally etch his initials on the front of the balcony in this big auditorium. It was the same four-shape note and four-part harmony, with the melody on the tenor line, as in all other Sacred Harp, but in performance it had obviously imbibed some flavoring from African American musical traditions too. Of all the songs I heard them sing, my favorite was from *The Colored Sacred Harp*, titled "Florida Storm," composed by Judge Jackson himself in 1928 about a September 1926 hurricane. The chorus goes:

> The people cried mercy in the storm,
> The people cried mercy in the storm,
> The colored and the white stay'd awake all the night,
> Crying Lord have mercy in the storm.[5]

Twenty-five years ago I thought Sacred Harp was dying out, on its last legs. At the few singings I tried to go to regularly there was an increased presence of intellectuals—musicologists, historians, sociologists, and so forth—from big university towns such as Boston or Ann Arbor, but there seemed to be fewer and fewer of the old heads. Although I tried not to show it, I resented the dilution of the old tradition by these outlanders (conveniently ignoring the fact that I was from almost as far outside the tradition, though I lived in Alabama). It always seemed to me that these nonsouthern urban and urbane intellectuals came initially to observe the unique musical tradition, but came back at least as much to experience again the warmth of the traditional rural community gathered in a worship service in which the theology was sung, not delivered by an individual preacher. It seemed to me that none of them—Jewish, agnostic, New Age, about anything other than mainstream Primitive Baptist—had every really experienced that before.

THE OLIVERS OF PINE GROVE

For decades, on a given weekend in May, I've taught folklore and natural history classes at the Alabama Audubon Society's Mountain Workshop, held at Alpine

Camp, adjoining DeSoto State Park (the workshop is the subject of a later chapter in this book). On May 20, 1994, I took a class of a dozen adults from the workshop to the porch and front yard of Pauline and Milton Oliver, down Lookout Mountain a little south of Collinsville and not far from the Pine Grove Primitive Baptist Church, where singings were (and are still) held twice a year. Pauline had married into the tradition, but Milton had grown up in it: he and his cousin Bud Oliver had gone to a one-room school in the Pine Grove church building as well, and they were the stalwarts of keeping the two annual singings, late summer and spring, alive. Pauline and Milton were as sweet a couple as ever drew breath. The class sat up on the shady porch with her, while Milton and I sat out in the yard in a couple of lawn chairs facing them. Mr. Oliver reminisced about the role of Sacred Harp in his life and occasionally suggested something for us to sing, him the tenor (melody) and me trying to follow along on bass. Here, too, though the musical tradition seemed to fascinate the class, the hospitality and friendliness of the Olivers likely overshadowed the topic at hand.

I got some hints here of at least minor points of friction with or inside the fasola group. For one, I asked Mr. Oliver about some preachers' criticism of regular Sacred Harp singers for rarely being in their home church for Sunday morning services—because they were off on the road attending a singing somewhere else. Mr. Oliver quoted an outspoken friend who had replied to his own preacher to the effect that when he (the preacher) came up with something as good as Sacred Harp for Sunday morning, he (the singer) would attend. And then there were what seemed to me, an outsider, to be minor doctrinal differences. "Throughout eternity" is a phrase I'd have thought unobjectionable, but to some it apparently implied that eternity would have an end. Those so convinced would either sing different words—"through all eternity"—or not want a hymn that had the phrase in it sung at all, grumbling to those who picked it to sing. But overall you could tell that the Olivers found great satisfaction in the generally warm Sacred Harp fellowship, one of the focal points of their lives. A recording of the class can be streamed from Samford University's STORI oral history collection.[6]

The University of Mississippi keeps up with the calendar for Sacred Harp singings; as of this writing, at least, the calendar is accessible directly on the internet.[7] Singings are listed by Sunday (or Saturday) of the month. The singings are now truly worldwide, but it's still easy to tell the originals. Here, for example, is the list for the first Sunday in January 2017 (which for 2017 was also New Year's Day):

January 1—Cincinnati New Years Day Singing—Harriet Beecher Stowe
House, 2950 Gilbert Avenue, Cincinnati OH . . .

January 1—New Years Day Singing—First Christian Church, 2723 King St.,
Alexandria VA . . .

January 1—New Years Day Singing—Mapperley Village Parish Church, Mapperley, Derbyshire, England. Info: Helen Brown.

January 1—New Years Day Singing—Hollingsworth home, Commerce
GA . . .

January 1—Dominic Ciavonne Ziegler Memorial Singing—Old Felta
Schoolhouse, Healdsburg CA . . .

First Sunday—Shady Grove Church, Hway 195, 3 miles north of Double
Springs AL.

If you wanted to pick one of these to get a feel for the tradition, my advice—even if travel to Ohio or California or Derbyshire happened to be free and instantaneous—would be to visit Shady Grove Church in Winston County. In 1983 we had a new university president who'd come to Samford from Indiana by way of a few years in Kentucky and then North Carolina. Early in his tenure here, to help introduce him and his wife to Alabama, my wife and I took them to a singing here. It's been over a third of a century, but by location and tradition I would guess that the Shady Grove singing is still the real deal.

Custodians of the Tradition: Buell Cobb and David Ivey

If you'd like to explore this tradition in more detail, the great modern Alabama writer on it is Buell Cobb. Back in the early 1980s, a friend of mine who worked at South Central Bell—a friend I'd dragged to the annual Labor Day Sacred Harp singing at Shoal Creek Church in the Talladega Forest—told me he had a coworker knowledgeable about the Sacred Harp tradition. When I subsequently met Buell, I realized "knowledgeable" was an understatement. He'd been bitten hard by the Sacred Harp bug as early as graduate school. At Auburn, where he got his master's, he was in a quartet that fairly exclusively sang Sacred Harp, and he wrote his master's thesis on the tradition. He was subsequently an English professor for seven years at West Georgia College (today the University of West Georgia), and he fleshed out the master's thesis into a substantial book on fasola that focused on the mainstream Denson

Revision book singings; it is titled *The Sacred Harp: A Tradition and Its Music* and was published by the University of Georgia Press in 1978.[8]

West Georgia College was in Carrollton, Georgia, just ten miles south of Bremen, Georgia, where Hugh McGraw, then the executive secretary of the Sacred Harp Publishing Company and an indefatigable teacher of singing schools, lived—and Buell fell into his orbit, at least musically speaking. For years Buell was his unofficial corresponding secretary, and for years Hugh took him around to singings. Here's a little of what Buell had to say about Hugh in his 1978 book: "Now in his late forties, McGraw somehow passed his early life on the periphery of this tradition without being fully exposed to it. Then in 1953 he walked into his first Sacred Harp singing and immediately 'felt a shiver' at the sound he heard. When the class sang the plangent fuguing tune *Alabama*, he knew he had come home: 'I thought that was the prettiest thing I'd ever heard.' That night he called 'Uncle Bud' McGraw, his second cousin and a well-known singing-school teacher, and asked to be taught to sing that music. With the help of his mentor, Hugh McGraw took up a study of the song book very likely unparalleled in thoroughness and intensity."[9]

At that first national singing, held at Samford in 1980, a couple of years after the above was written, I heard Hugh challenge the conventional wisdom that said Sacred Harp was dying out: "It'll not die out in my lifetime," he said only half-humorously. As Buell said of him in his 1978 book, "The present and immediate future of the tradition depend obviously on his continued energies and service."[10]

In the first week of June 2017, in preparation for the national singing coming up midmonth, I finally got around to reading Buell Cobb's newest book on Sacred Harp. It came out in 2013 (thirty-five years after his first one) and was titled *Like Cords around My Heart: A Sacred Harp Memoir*.[11] The title is a phrase from that old singing school favorite "Parting Hand." A singer from outside the tradition, from Maryland, had bought copies of Buell's 1978 book for himself and friends. He later told Buell that he'd thoroughly enjoyed it, but he'd have liked more on the personalities. As Buell says in the preface to the new book, the critique ate at him until he decided to do something about it. And there are indeed personalities, and adventures—performances at the Smithsonian Institution's Festival of American Folklife in 1970 and 1976 and the Montreal World Expo in 1971; recording sessions in Henagar in the northeast corner of Alabama for part of the soundtrack to the 2003 film *Cold Mountain* and a subsequent performance with Alison Krauss and others at the 2004 Academy Awards presentation . . .

I'd have enjoyed the book even if I'd never done any fasola singing, but some of the accounts awakened memories. One of the personality sketches in it is of Bud Oliver, stalwart of the Pine Grove singings that I tried to get to regularly, and a man that is just as vividly alive in my mind all these years after his death as could be. Although Buell says he never met Frank Miller himself, he got that same Civil War story from the family about his great-grandfather singing "Antioch"—"The dead's alive and the lost is found"—as he walked to meet his miraculously living son home from the war, a story I'd heard decades earlier. And he had a great description of a June 14, 1998, singing at Hopewell Primitive Baptist Church near Oneonta, the same church where I'd first heard Sacred Harp being sung way back in June 1974.

So on the afternoon of June 8, 2017, I called Buell to tell him how much I'd enjoyed the book. We're the same age, both born in the centennial year of the 1844 publication of the original *Sacred Harp*. I knew he'd be busy getting ready for the national convention the following week, but he'd been busier than I knew. He'd given the eulogy at Hugh McGraw's funeral just a week before, and I hadn't even heard about Hugh's passing. There'd been a falling-out earlier, probably mainly about Hugh's "genial but dictatorial" managerial style with the publishing company board, and maybe also about some other personal problems, but there'd been substantial reconciliation later too. Buell told me the move of the national convention to Fultondale was to get better acoustics—a little smaller hall with a lower ceiling—hopefully to satisfy singers who claimed they weren't getting a "return" on their voices in high-ceilinged auditoriums.

One other indispensable person in the evolution of Sacred Harp over the past quarter century is David Ivey. He's from one of those two great singing families from Alabama—the Iveys and the Woottens—each of which can field a sizable class of Sacred Harp singers just of family members. They're from the northeast corner of the state, up on Sand Mountain, which, like Lookout Mountain to its east, is a long, narrow plateau running southwest deep into Alabama before dwindling out. David is from Henagar, born in 1955. He was the youngest member of the editing committee of Hugh McGraw's 1991 revision of the book. He worked with the group that did the Sacred Harp music for the *Cold Mountain* movie. I knew him from the Pine Grove twice-a-year singings I tried to attend. There he regularly keyed songs—sitting front and center in the tenor section, sounding the notes of the first chord of music of each hymn so members of the class in each part knew what tone to start on.

Even twenty years ago David was working hard toward a revival of Sacred Harp.

I thought it was impossible to do, and I was wrong. Perhaps the key institution David and friends built was Camp Fasola. Starting in 2003, it was an updated version of the old frontier singing schools. By now there's an adult camp usually meeting the second week of June, held at the Episcopal Church Camp McDowell not far from Double Springs, and a youth camp the first week of July, held at Camp Lee, a Methodist retreat center near Anniston. David has led cultural forays into places as far afield as Ireland and England, sparking yearly Sacred Harp singings there. One of the most interesting episodes of state folklorist Joey Brackner's *Journey Proud* series with Alabama Public Television, on aspects of Alabama folklife, is just called "Camp Fasola," and features David. Like all the *Journey Proud* episodes it is freely available for viewing online.[12]

Baklava at Dinner on the Grounds?

I drop in and out of the fasola world, but I seem to need a regular fix, a dose of the vibrant musical and spiritual tradition that calibrates some sort of reset in my behavior and activities. So on June 15 and 16, 2017, Thursday and Friday morning, I made it to a couple of sessions of the national convention, being held that year in Fultondale. I sat in the back row of the bass section. On the first morning the fellow to my left was from Burlington, Vermont; the fellow to my right was from Decatur, Georgia, and had come straight from Camp Fasola; and the fellow in front of me—also a Brown, Ted Brown—was from Derby, England. When a woman named Brown was introduced to lead a song, and introduced it with an English accent, I tapped Ted on the shoulder and asked whether they were related. "She's me wife," said he. I assume this is the Helen Brown named as point of contact for the Mapperley Village Parish Church, Mapperley, Derbyshire, in the 2017 Sacred Harp listings. She'd introduced Ted to the tradition around twenty years before; apparently folk music–themed radio stations in Britain lump Sacred Harp in with American folk music in general.

There were some decidedly modern touches in this iteration of the old rural tradition I'd first encountered forty-three years before in a one-room wooden church building without electricity or modern plumbing, with wooden shutters instead of glazed windows, and with dirt dauber nests up in the corners of the ceiling. Now there were cell phones going off with exotic ringtones in the pockets and purses of some who'd forgotten to mute theirs. The chairman read text off an iPhone about the medical condition of a woman who'd fallen off a golf cart at the singing the day before. And the chairman thanked whomever it was who'd brought the tray of baklava for the coffee

*Figure 5.3.
Dinner on
the grounds,
Pine Grove*

The well-stocked table and a hungry crowd of singers at a typical noon-hour dinner on the grounds of the Pine Grove church, on Lookout Mountain south of Collinsville. Samford folklore student Chase Trautwein is documenting the same scene from the far end. (Photo courtesy of Jonathan Bass.)

and dessert tables outside the main hall. I immediately tried to envision baklava on the dinner-on-the-grounds table at the Pine Grove church singings and couldn't do it. But the music was essentially true to its roots, enchanting all the singers, who—as one veteran singer once put it to me—sing not for an audience, but for the other singers.

The fellowship was just as warm and caring as always. On the way back to the car I passed a woman running to grab something out of her car to take back inside, apparently trying to lock it and failing in her hurry, and then just slamming the door without taking time to lock it. We looked at each other and laughed and each said something about not having to worry about locking your car at a Sacred Harp singing. What wondrous love is this.

chapter six

Telescoping Time

Landscape Architecture, Historical Geography, and Greenways

By luck of the draw, Samford's history department back when I came to campus in 1971 was housed on the ground floor of the School of Business building. This threw me into almost daily contact with Fred Hendon, at that time the school's only economist. From my admittedly biased point of view as a former arts and sciences faculty member, economics really should be housed in arts and sciences; it partakes generously of history, math, and even psychology and sociology. One reason that it usually isn't in arts and sciences is probably the generally higher pay scale for business faculty, which economics professors don't need a PhD to understand.

On most issues Fred was a conservative Republican, the true son of a DuPont executive, and I was a yellow dog Democrat from college professor and librarian stock; but he'd spent his army years in Germany and brought home a Dutch bride, so from the very beginning we had lots of European topics to discuss. For decades he was one of my best friends at Samford, and I miss him greatly. The salient point for this chapter is that early in our acquaintance he introduced me to some key books that profoundly affected my point of view, showing me more where the field of history fit in the broader intellectual world. Among them was E. F. Schumacher's *Small Is Beautiful*, which came out in 1973. I still remember how struck I was by the chapter titled "Buddhist Economics," and the idea that whole subconscious worldviews underlie supposedly rational economic systems.[1]

In terms of my developing worldview, though, the most important book Fred put me onto was Ian McHarg's *Design with Nature*, published in 1969. More than any other single book it transformed my approach to teaching. Fred and I were discussing it as early as 1974, and by 1978 we wrote (with our political science colleague Dave Gillespie) a series of "land use planning" articles based on it for the *Birmingham News*.[2] The first of my two articles was on Henry David Thoreau's appreciation of wilderness, on George Perkins Marsh's discovery of the importance of reforestation, and on Benton MacKaye's Appalachian Trail idea for building a green dike against East Coast urban sprawl. My second article was just on Ian McHarg.

DESIGN WITH NATURE

McHarg was a prickly, chain-smoking Scot who, at the time I discovered him in the mid-1970s, headed up the landscape architecture department at the University of Pennsylvania. He despised the term "regional planning," but that's really what he did. On his faculty, working on what I came to think of as a "telescoping time" theory, he had geologists, geomorphologists, botanists, zoologists, anthropologists/folklorists, historians, economists, and political scientists. A team of his would come into an area interested in intelligent planning for the future, and the members would scatter, study their particular subjects in detail, reassemble, and compare notes. Then they'd announce something like this to the locals: *We've come up with these land use, water use, population growth, etc., trends. Projecting them out, here's what—barring meteor strikes and other "acts of God"—you're going to look like in fifty years. Conversely, if you don't like that picture, tell us what you do want to look like, and we'll tell you which of these land use, water use, population growth, etc., curves you've got to change to make it happen. Design with Nature* is a summary of many such projects, beautifully illustrated with color maps—much more difficult to make in those days before personal computers. It's probably not just coincidental that Earth Day celebrations began in 1971, just a couple of years after its publication.

Professor McHarg was frustrated by departments of transportation that took physical features into account (slope, floodplain, sinkholes, and such) when planning for new roads but rarely ever considered "human" ones (greenspace value, recreational value, historic value, and such). To integrate the latter into the planning process, he developed a system of stacked transparencies (i.e., overhead projector sheets), with one transparency for each significant variable: black for unsuitable areas, gray shades for varying degrees of suitability, clear for perfectly suitable areas. Then his ideal department of transportation could stack them all up, shine a light through from below, and watch as the optimal route(s) for a new road lit up. Many scholars see that system as the original inspiration for modern computerized geographic information systems (GIS) such as Google Earth or the Environmental Systems Research Institute's ArcGIS suite, with their stacked layers of (digital) transparencies.

Speaking of GIS, decades later, in my last ten years of teaching before retiring in 2016, I integrated GIS presentations into almost all of my history lectures. I worked up a Google Earth–based presentation of McHarg's early life and conversion to landscape architecture: it seemed only fitting that it be illustrated by a GIS program that he had distantly inspired. In the first and shortest chapter of *Design with Nature*, titled "City and Countryside," McHarg outlines his own earlier life. Since that short chapter goes far toward explaining his view of the world and eventual approach to planning, I would read the chapter aloud while simultaneously using Google Earth to frame sites and embed appropriate photos to show exactly what he was describing—how the hills called the Paps of Jura appeared from a distance, for instance, or what Ayrshire cattle look like. But the presentation usually focused on three distinct turning points in his life as summed up in that first chapter.[3]

KEY PASSAGES IN IAN McHARG'S LIFE

Born in 1920, he grew up about ten miles north of Glasgow, a city that was, in his words, "a memorial to an inordinate capacity to create ugliness, a sandstone excretion cemented with smoke and grime." In the opposite direction lay the beautiful Black Woods, no more than a mile away from his house, then the farmlands of the Old Kilpatrick Hills and the Campsies, and way off the "final wilderness" of the Western Highlands and Islands. Every year as he grew up, he says, he went a little farther both toward Glasgow and away from it.

He discovered landscape architecture as a potential career field by age sixteen, but World War II postponed his formal education and in fact nearly ended it. In 1943 and spring 1944 he was with a British parachute brigade in the Allies' northward advance up the Italian peninsula. It ground to a halt for a while at the feet of the Gustav Line, held by the Germans with their fearsome 88-millimeter artillery on the high ground including Monte Cassino. As McHarg remembered it: "Day after week after month it continued, no sleep by day, engagements by night, cold, wet and muddy, living in one and then another hole; the attrition became serious, 'bomb happy' was a normal malaise, the ranks thinned, the time would surely come, it was ridiculous to expect to survive."

Then came two weeks' leave for rest and recuperation, and McHarg's first important turning point. He decided to spend it not in the big city of Naples, where many of his mates would go for a hedonistic blowout, but in a rural hotel in Ravello, high on the Sorrento Peninsula: "Here was peace absolute, the only noises were the sound of footsteps on the stone floors, the whispering of servants, the ringing of church bells, the calls of the street vendor. The smells were of baked bread, garlic and pasta. Near to the piazza was a garden. From this, perched on cliff edge, could be seen the glittering bay and Capri, the road snaking down the mountain to the coast." It was the Italian equivalent of the Scottish woods and farmland opposite Glasgow: "Here was equanimity and health."

After the war it was four years at Harvard studying landscape architecture, and then back to Scotland to practice what he had learned. Nostalgic for scenes of his childhood and youth, he went to see the Black Woods with its little creek ("burn") with small trout and redbreasted minnows, wildflowers including a native orchid, stands of pine, larch, beech, thorns, and laburnum, grouse and other wild birds, foxes, red squirrels, weasels, hedgehogs, and, in the very heart of the Black Woods, the Peel Glen, transformed in spring with its carpet of bluebells. Unfortunately, however, this was to be McHarg's second important turning point. McHarg says he returned home expecting to see the natural landscape shrunken but not obliterated. Instead, it had all been replaced with mind-numbingly uniform four-story apartment buildings: "seventy feet face to face, seventy feet back to back, fifteen feet from gable to gable. The fronts were divided by an asphalt street lined with gaunt sodium lamps, the backs were stamped soil defined by drunken chestnut paling; drying green poles supported the sodden laundry." Housing was surely needed, but this kind of housing had just bulldozed the land flat and destroyed everything that had made the Black Woods a marvel; just a little intelligent design, with nature, could have made it a wonderful place to live.

The third turning point in his life came because he had also come back from America with tuberculosis. It worsened, and he was sent to a converted house near Edinburgh that was a "colony for consumptives." The windows were propped open year round, even when snow came in. Rooms were swept in a cloud of dust. Here's McHarg's eloquent condemnation: "The spirit of the place was acrid; the doctors lived in mutual dislike under a despotic chief, the staff were sad emblems of the nursing profession, filled with sullen animosity. There were enough patients in the place who had been there for a decade or more to infuse the sick with a quiet resignation. The sun never shone, the food was tepid and tasteless, there was little laughter and less hope." Six months there reduced him, he said, to "a miserable, thin, sweating rag." But by chance he learned that there were beds in a Swiss sanatorium reserved for British parachutists, so he made his escape. On the train trip to London, Calais, and Lausanne, he rediscovered sun and food. And then he went up to the summit at Leysin with the hotel where he was to stay: "The Dents du Midi shone, their peaks supported on cloud . . . for six lovely months I walked and climbed . . . past the jangling cows to the summit, lying on shelves watching the eagles sail below, finding gentian and edelweiss, equanimity and health."

Ian McHarg wasn't anti-city—he loved parts of Edinburgh and New York and even Glasgow—but his burning idea as a landscape architect became how to keep enough nature in the city to add that "equanimity and health" to the vibrant economic, intellectual, and arts activity usually only found in cities.

My Own Predilection for Maps

Part of the attraction of McHarg's work for me, back in the mid-1970s, was how wonderfully illustrated it was by maps: I've always loved a map because of what it reveals about the course of history.

In January 1974, to illustrate, when I taught the Brothers Grimm to Hitler minimester course for the second time, I had the bright idea of making a film of what's usually called in English the Barbarian Migrations that destroyed the western Roman Empire. Since "migration" implies that people knew where they were going, it's a misnomer, and the German *Völkerwanderung*, a Folkswandering, is probably more accurate. We made an outline map of Europe on a poster board and laid it on the floor of the garage in my rental home a few minutes' walk from the Samford campus. We nailed a wooden framework to the exposed rafters to hold the family eight-millimeter movie camera, with its attached light that got to approximately the surface temperature of the sun. Then we moved piles of glitter around the map, aiming to represent people's movements from 200 BC to AD 500 or so—gold for the Romans, red for the Celts, blue for the Germanic tribes, black for the Huns . . . Students in charge of each group would have to research their whereabouts over time and negotiate interfaces with other students who might have come up with slightly different times and locations for their groups. Since the camera filmed at twenty-four frames to the second, we'd try for eight movements a second (moving the glitter, then clicking the camera three times), and do five years to the second or a century in twenty seconds.

I've still got a copy of the old film, converted to digital format now. It worked pretty well, early on: you can see the blue bulge of the original Germanic tribal pressure coming south toward Roman Republic holdings around 100 BC, and Caesar's successful invasion of Gaul in the 50s BC is a quick spear of gold, but the camera light half-failed soon thereafter, and the rest is very dim. We only made it to AD 200, so there's no dramatic Hunnish invasion about AD 375 coming from the east like a cue ball about to break a rack of Germanic tribes, sending them flying around the European pool table. And it got really sloppy toward the end, a flash of an occasional hand photographed still trying to move glitter piles. It was one of those "reach exceeds the grasp" projects, but I'm still proud of the reach. In 2006, a third of a century later, when Samford's GIS specialist from the geography department and I were invited to demonstrate our "history through ArcGIS-style mapping" approach to the arts and sciences faculty of Ohio State University, I used that film as introduction (though partly for comic relief; technology had progressed so far beyond it).

Another reason McHarg's telescoping time approach immediately resonated with me was that back in graduate school I'd been introduced to Fernand Braudel's 1949 *The Mediterranean and the Mediterranean World in the Age of Philip II*, which covers roughly the second half of the 1500s.[4] The book would be a strong contender in a "most influential history book of the last century" contest. It was a massive 1,200 pages in two volumes, and it only got to standard political and military history about page 900. It started off with geology, botany, and zoology, and it spent a good deal of time on the trilogy of grape, wheat, and olive and the seasonal "transhumance" nomadic lifestyle of rocking back and forth from grasslands in the rainy season to wells in the dry season. When I finally came to it, the Spanish Armada of 1588 appeared as a military ripple on a political wave on an underlying swell of population growth and land use, modulated by epidemics of disease.

THE APPEAL OF CARL SAUER'S "HISTORICAL GEOGRAPHY"

Soon after Fred Hendon introduced me to Ian McHarg's work, I also discovered Carl Sauer, the dean of the first generation of academic geographers in the United States, most particularly his 1966 book *The Early Spanish Main*.[5] Sauer's early life and education had been in Missouri, Michigan, and Illinois, but as a still fairly young scholar in his early thirties he was hired at Berkeley to create a geography program. In California he was fascinated from the first with two very different zones of culture, Hispanic American and Anglo-American, that existed across the same mountain ridges and valleys.

He spent much of his first decade there working up a kind of geographic approach that leaned heavily on history and anthropology, focusing on northwest Mexico. Tracing the roots of that culture back in time and eastward in space, he wound up looking attentively at the creation of that Hispanic American culture in the first twenty-five to thirty years after Columbus's initial contact, and in particular on the island of Española (Hispaniola, today's Haiti and Dominican Republic), site of the first major Spanish settlements. Here, for example, the villa-pueblo pattern of Hispanic life was invented: a town or even a manor house mainly lived in by those of European ancestry, surrounded by villages mainly lived in by those of Native American ancestry, a labor pool for the villas. Sauer was very interested in food supplies, noting the South American–style root crop agriculture that extended up the West Indies, sharply distinct from the maize-based diet just across the Florida Straits that was representative of Central and North America. A careful student of the Spanish destruction and replacement of the population of the West Indies, he was a fierce critic of environmental determinism, toward which I had been leaning. He was the real inventor of a "historical geography" that drew heavily on history and anthropology, and I was thinking I could edge that way with a "geographic history" that drew heavily on geography and folklore.

With all three—McHarg in landscape architecture, Braudel in history, and Sauer in geography—I could see that same general telescoping of time approach beginning with geology and soils. It belatedly dawned on me that virtually every field in the humanities and the social sciences had "invented" its own such telescoping time model as it recognized its place in the larger chronological pattern.

But Ian McHarg's work was the catalyst for all this. In my old folder on him is a copy of an article from the *Atlantic Monthly* titled "Land Politics: Ian McHarg." It was from January 1974, by which time I'd obviously taken note of his work.

THE BIRMINGHAM REGIONAL PLANNING COMMISSION'S MCHARG-INSPIRED STUDIES

In these same mid-1970s I discovered that the Birmingham Regional Planning Commission (BRPC, covering Walker, Blount, St. Clair, Jefferson, Shelby, and Chilton

Counties) was producing a series of county studies consciously modeled on McHarg's principles.[6] As I understand the genesis of the regional planning commissions (or regional councils, as they are generally known today), the whole country had been divided up into such districts as a way for the federal government to check that the same project didn't get funded two or more times by various federal agencies. Gradually, however, as one of the few local institutions to have a broad overview of what was going on in a region (or area), they logically enough took on a positive role in planning, in coordinating the efforts of those looking ahead.

Going to See McHarg

In fall 1976 I took some of those McHarg-inspired BRPC county studies up to show Professor McHarg himself. It was a busy fall. One weekend in August we'd had an intensive organizing committee meeting for a Tannehill-based experiential education seminar (discussed later in this book). One Thursday in September I'd spent at Tannehill for the refiring of the old Civil War–era furnace. The Folkcenter South students and I were gearing up for their Saturday, November 20, crafts celebration day, again at Tannehill (I talked about these last two back in chapter 4). But the weekend before that crafts day celebration, the American Folklore Society was having its annual meeting in Philadelphia—a fitting place in the bicentennial year—and McHarg just happened to be at the University of Pennsylvania just over on the west side of town.

So, amazingly enough to me all these years later, my folklore students Mark Gooch and Cathy Hanby and I took off the long weekend before the Saturday folk craft celebration, driving up to Philadelphia and back. We went in Mark's old Audi, which nearly didn't make the round trip. It was all on a financial shoestring; back then there was almost no travel money for Samford faculty members, and we even had to have permission from the office of the vice president of academic affairs to make a single long-distance phone call. I paid for the gas. We drove to Philadelphia on one long, long day, and we crashed the first night with some of Mark's friends in a dormitory in another college on out the Main Line, west of the University of Pennsylvania. Coming back home late Saturday night through Virginia, down Interstate 81 and Highway 11 at about one in the morning, groggy from lack of sleep, we pitched a tent on the snow near where the Appalachian Trail crossed the roads. With sleeping bags but no decent sleeping pads, we got four hours of fitful sleep, and we broke camp before dawn at five in the morning. We left behind three melted person-sized holes in the snow and undoubtedly some bent if not broken Samford rules for teacher/student interaction in the process. But the trip was worth it all just for the hour that Professor McHarg spent with us.

As I remember it Professor McHarg was pleased to see a regional planning commission using his approach but was a bit disappointed in the basic geology maps that started the BRPC county studies. He was even more disappointed by the fact that the introductions to the studies pointedly said that the McHarg approach had been criticized for not giving enough weight to existing businesses, and that these Alabama studies would rectify that. The result was that the massive property holdings of US Steel and the various timber and mining companies tended to dominate these county studies by the BRPC; the studies, as a result, may have been predictive but weren't really planning documents. McHarg spent a full hour with us, and he seemed to appreciate the breadth of approach that Mark, Cathy, and the others in Folkcenter South had adopted, and that I was increasingly using in my history courses, nestling history in among other disciplines in that telescoping time pattern he had developed so well. We all came back more confident in our approach because of his benediction.

The 1977 Environmental History of Alabama Seminar

Given my interests in the natural world and folklore—which helped with several layers of that telescoping time model—I had already begun designing some courses that embedded history in this broader framework. The main drawbacks were that I began poaching widely in fields in which I had little or no training, and that I was poorly defended from the accusation that I was designing my classes to incorporate all my hobbies. One offsetting advantage was that I could present some innovative teaching techniques as justification for this unorthodoxy.

By this time I'd taken several graduate-level biology courses with Bob Stiles, and we'd begun socializing and fishing on the side. Given our sometimes overlapping, sometimes complementary interests, it was probably inevitable that we would team-teach some classes integrating biology and history. It helped that Bob was a passionate amateur historian, especially interested in the moving American wave of European culture and its interfacing with Native American culture, from the times when it came through his native Kentucky and then rolled on west to the Rockies with the mountain men. Bob had little interest in botany, and I used to tease him that he only knew pines from hardwoods and that his only interest in aquatic plants was as locators for certain kinds of fish. He'd respond by asking me something about American history, about which I was generally ignorant. But between us, what with fishing, arrowhead hunting, archery, and muzzle-loading hunting, and with coastal marine biology, herb lore, folk crafts, and other eclectic reading interests that even included theology (in which Bob had a master's degree from Vanderbilt), we had at least a foot in many levels of that telescoping time model that began with geology and ended with future planning.

Our first team-taught course was in spring 1977. Alabama's ecosystems were the general subject matter: how they'd been changed over time by the changing culture, and how in turn the changed ecosystems set new limits on that culture. We'd at least dabble in basic geology, soil, native botany, native zoology, prehistory, Native American cultures at early contact with Europeans, the lifestyles of those early colonists, and on like that. One of the assigned texts, of course, was McHarg's *Design with Nature*, and we spent a good bit of time with William Bartram's *Travels*, especially his travels in and around 1776 in what is today Alabama.

Students were required to do an oral history with someone who could tell us things about parts of that land use pattern, preferably someone who could enlighten us about lifestyles close to the land a generation or two before. One of the most interesting interviews that resulted was with a game warden in Cullman County who talked about his conflicts with an old farmer who ran an illegal fishtrap on the Mulberry River (discussed later in this book). But the most lasting impact of the course, especially in terms of dozens of interesting things we can see around us in the greater Birmingham area today, may be that the course in general and McHarg's *Design with Nature* in particular convinced one student to drop out of Samford.

Jane Reed Ross and the Greenway

Running along Shades Creek today, passing between Samford University and Homewood High School, is one of the most popular walking/jogging trails in Alabama; just this past year walkers and joggers used it an estimated 180,000 times. This "phase 1" of the Greenway, as it was called, was finished about 2003. It runs from Brookwood Village down along Shades Creek to Columbiana Road, first on the northern bank of the creek and then crossing over to the southern bank at the bridge to the Homewood High School grounds. It is two-and-a-quarter straight-line miles long, and just over two and a half miles as the trail runs. It was named the Greenway because it was meant to be more than just a trail; historically it is the real keystone of the Red Rock Trail System plan for greater Birmingham, a plan for some five hundred miles of such trails and connectors. Landscape architect Jane Reed Ross was its main designer and in fact was the driving force behind it from the beginning.

I got to know her first as Jane Reed, an undergraduate student at Samford who took several of my history classes in and around 1976 and 1977, someone who even considered a possible history major. But then Jane took that 1977 interdisciplinary class that approached Alabama through the model of geology to future planning. She came to it with a positive attitude, she told me recently, because when she was growing up in Huntsville there was a family friend who was a landscape architect. Long story short, the course convinced her that landscape architecture was the career for her. She left Samford and signed up for the closest landscape architecture program, the one at Auburn.

Auburn's was a five-year program, so she was essentially starting college over, but Jane says she thrived on it. She remembers great professors there, particularly Richard Rome, the head of the department. The highlights of her studies, however, were the summer internships she had in Washington, DC. Remarkably, she found cheap lodging there (house-sitting!). She hiked and biked all over the city, getting to know its parks and great public spaces, its summer festivals and its trails, its great mass transit bus and metro systems—in her words, she got to see what a fun, healthy city was like. Faced with all the various specialties covered by the general label "landscape architecture" (which range from golf course design to residential housing development settings), Jane was from the very first interested in working with, as she says, "site-specific public spaces" to create "sustainable and resilient landscapes" that engage people in active lifestyles.

After Auburn, freshly credentialed as a landscape architect, Jane then took a Wanderjahr to backpack around Europe, staying in cheap hostels and marveling at the public places of the major cities. She met her future husband, a genial Aussie named Neil Ross, when they were both working at a ski resort in Austria sometime that year. Her first job back in the States was with a firm in Washington, DC, and she later had one in Huntsville, her old hometown, where Neil for a time had a restaurant. But soon she was commuting to Birmingham, which had a lot more in the way of landscape architecture firms.

Soon the growing family moved to Birmingham, in fact to Homewood (twenty years ago Heath, the older of their two sons, was in my wife's kindergarten class at Edgewood Elementary!). She joined a firm that needed the in-city contacts she could provide, and then from 1993 to 2007 she ran her own firm. She sold it when the family experimented for six months with living in Australia (unluckily picking the absolute low point of the recession in which to try changing housing and moving assets), and she has generally worked with Goodwyn Mills Cawood (GMC) since the family's return to the States in 2008. There are so many visual signatures of her work most of us hereabouts have seen; I can only offer here an incomplete list.[7]

The angled water fountain (or "cannon," I always thought of it) in front of the I. M. Pei–designed Kirklin Clinic was her idea, a sort of "projecting a life force into the community" visual in line with the main entrance. One highlight of her work is that she remembers how much Pei loved the idea when she presented it to him. She worked on the sculpture gardens of the Birmingham Museum of Art, trying to mediate between the dramatically competing visions of two famous artists assigned parts of it. Although much of her landscape design work around Children's Harbor Family Center, attached to Children's Hospital, has been replaced by other buildings, some is left, including the statues of the boy and girl there (Jane's son Heath was the sculptor Cordray Parker's model for the boy). I followed her landscape work of revitalizing Homewood Central Park fairly closely. She took the concrete-ditched, chain-link-fenced Griffin Creek and turned it into a meandering brook complete with local aquatic vegetation, allowing it to flood the low-lying areas of the park after heavy rains so Homewood residents downstream on Griffin Creek no longer had to sandbag their back doors against floods. She was a key designer of the children's part of the Birmingham Zoo, from the wildly popular "splash pad" down to the otter exhibits, and as of 2020 she was working on the Highway 280 entrance and the Asian exhibit. She had a hand in designing Veterans Memorial Park off Interstate 459. Her work on St. Vincent's wellness center on Highway 119 included what is probably the area's first comprehensive "bioretention" system for rainwater, absorbing it in plant beds instead of just funneling it or piping it off-site, where it adds to the flash flooding that erodes so many local riverbanks and creek banks. Her design work on Railroad Park (with landscape architect Tom Leader of Berkeley) had just been completed when the family took off for Australia; lots of the work done there was still to her design. It has to be a source of great satisfaction to her to be surrounded by so many examples of her visionary work. But I still think the crown jewel of it all is the Shades Creek Greenway in Homewood.

Jane had loved the trails through natural settings that she had walked in those Washington, DC, summers—the Chesapeake and Ohio Canal trail, the Sligo Creek trail, the Rock Creek Park trail. Under the tree canopy it always felt ten degrees cooler in the hot summer than elsewhere, and the greenery along the trail just did something for people. Early after her return to Birmingham, she thought, we can do that here. Some cities got into this earlier than others: Boston and Denver, for example. It was all about active lifestyles, healthier communities, alternative transportation to the automobile: it just made a lot of sense and was gathering momentum nationwide. Soon there were federal grants to be had for planning and construction of such trails. The chief problem here, from Jane's point of view, was that almost all the available grants had to come through transportation departments. Departments of transportation (Alabama's included) had always been laser focused on roads for car and truck traffic (because of the demands of we the public) and were more than a little touchy about the federal government telling them what they needed. Walking trails were not on their agenda and were generally not favored even when added to the agenda.

As Jane remembers it, she was working with Mike Lamb of KPS Group, an established architectural firm, when they made their first trails proposal: it was for twenty-four miles from Irondale to Hoover, going through Homewood. It was rejected, by whatever federal agency they'd applied to. The second effort, reducing the scope of the project a bit, was along Shades Creek the three miles from Brookwood Village to Wildwood Shopping Center. It was also rejected. But it turned out that the Regional Planning Commission of Greater Birmingham (what I knew back in the 1970s as the Birmingham Regional Planning Commission, BRPC) took note of these efforts. The RPC folks told Homewood mayor Barry McCulley that if Homewood would fund a master plan for a greenway down along the Homewood stretch of Shades Creek, they thought they could get CMAQ funds to do it (CMAQ being the Congestion Mitigation and Air Quality Improvement Program, which was instituted about a year after the Clean Air Act amendments of 1990). So Mayor McCulley hired Jane's firm to do the master plan. It was accepted, and the initial grant from CMAQ was $6 million.

The initial master plan had three phases: (1) a section from Brookwood Village down along Shades Creek to Columbiana Road, (2) a section from Columbiana Road down Shades Creek to the environmental services complex, and (3) an overpass (over Lakeshore Drive) from Homewood's environmental services to John Carroll High School and thence to West Homewood Park. Looking back, Jane thinks they should have tried all three simultaneously: the money was there. But the mayor, apparently wanting to show quick progress, insisted they focus on phase 1. Jane says that with the Alabama Department of Transportation's traditional concern with roads, getting this trail constructed was one of the hardest things she ever did. But built it was, in 2003, and almost overnight it became extremely popular. Some political leaders locally, back then, were not all that positive about expanding the trail. They worried about the money it would take to maintain extra parks and trails, among other things. It apparently took a while for most everybody to realize that these sorts of green amenities were attractive to young adults deciding where to live, and that the costs of such amenities to a given city government are on average much less than the benefits. Today there's almost no foot-dragging; as of this writing all these years later, phase 2 of the Shades Creek Greenway is finally set to go into motion.

When Jane returned to Birmingham from Australia in 2008, she picked up where she'd left off. One US government response to the recession, created in 2009, was the TIGER grant program (for Transportation Investment Generating Economic Recovery).[8] In 2010, the landscape architecture firm Jane was working with, GMC, asked for $30 million for a greater Birmingham network of trails and won $10 million, still not chopped liver. A master plan of such trails was hammered out over the next two years, with the Freshwater Land Trust taking a lead role because it encompassed the whole area and probably also because it had an environmentally conscious slant. As a result, in something of the way that stimulus money in the Great Depression (funneled through various public works projects) left as a permanent legacy most of the nation's state parks, so the stimulus money committed to healing the 2008 recession (and maybe keep it from becoming a true depression) seems to be leaving as part of its legacy some wonderful public greenways.

THE FUTURE RED ROCK TRAILS

This projected "Red Rock" system of trails, as it has taken shape, is based on six valley trails, each running along or near a creek or river: roughly north to south, they are Turkey Creek, Village Creek, Valley Creek, Five-Mile Creek, Shades Creek, and the Cahaba River. These, and connectors between them, when complete will total over five hundred miles. The main artery of these six, going through the densest of local populations, is to run from Railroad Park west to Red Mountain Park, and from Railroad Park east to Ruffner Mountain. Today, if you're walking or driving on Twentieth Street South a block or so south of the railroad that bisects Birmingham, you'll pass the entrance to one new four-block-long piece of it, the Rotary Trail. The sign where it starts is a replica of the iron-grid sign that welcomed people to Birmingham, "The Magic City," a century ago. It was made tall enough to be visible from Railroad Park and the stadium to the southwest, so as to attract people to the trail and create a visual axis.

Saturday a couple of weeks ago (writing this in September 2019), I went by Jane and Neil's house to drop off a book; he met me at the door and said she was off volunteering at a workday on the Rotary Trail. May her tribe increase.

FIRST SABBATICAL LEAVE: INTERCULTURAL AND FOLK
STUDIES AND MORE "TELESCOPING TIME"

The fall semester after that spring 1977 semester with that team-taught environmental history of Alabama course, I was eligible for my first sabbatical leave. Sabbatical leave is the policy many traditional colleges and universities have of giving teachers a temporary course release so that they can focus on some research or teaching project so as to get back out on the cutting edge of their field. Samford's sabbatical leave policy was that if you could convince the relevant committees that you had a worthy project, you could take one semester off with full pay or two semesters off with half pay, in or after your seventh year at the school. I was coming up on academic year 1977–78 and my first opportunity to apply, and given said pay and the state of family finances, one semester off it was going to be, fall 1977. With the advantage of twenty-twenty hindsight, I can see that this was the watershed moment when I closed the door on being a true Russian history specialist (I could have used this time to polish my dissertation for publication, say, or gone to do research in libraries in the Soviet Union) and opened quite a different one. I decided to spend a semester studying folklore.

The closest graduate program in folklore was at Western Kentucky University (WKU) in Bowling Green. I knew the town because I had a great-uncle and some distant cousins there. In 1970 the head of the folklore department at WKU, Lynwood Montell, had written *The Saga of Coe Ridge*, which I'd read and loved. It was the story of an African American community from around 1865, when the formerly enslaved laborers of a riverside plantation had been given some cheap, hilly land near the Cumberland River for a settlement, to the 1950s, when the settlement finally withered away. Montell had reconstructed the remarkable, vivid life of the community from a few written records but mostly through oral histories, since the courthouse archives of the three surrounding counties had all burned at one time or another.[9]

We tried to find affordable family housing and good elementary schooling for my school-age older daughter in Bowling Green but struck out, so my wife and now three children (nine years, five years, and eighteen months) stayed with my parents in Cookeville, Tennessee. I stayed in a little house owned by some of the cousins, and commuted from there to Cookeville on Thursday nights and back to Bowling Green on Sunday nights. Looking back, I was asking way too much of the family, especially my wife. But the three and a half months I spent on that postgraduate semester in folklore eventually made possible the best teaching I ever did. It was a whole intellectual package that hit me like a ton of bricks and reinforced the "telescoping time" approach to locales and regions.

For one, I had some contact with the Barren River Area Development District (BRADD), a regional planning commission in Kentucky. For another, I had absorbed enough of McHarg to see this new region in a broader way. I interviewed a farmer near Auburn, a little town out west of Bowling Green mainly known for once having had a Shaker community. The interview was mainly about his farming practices, but he was most friendly, and I got to be at least casual friends with him and his wife. She'd been adopted by the Shaker community when she was two and her family fell apart because of her father's alcoholism—though later, un-Shaker-like, she'd married. They even had me over for a Shaker meal, of which unfortunately I can no longer remember the dishes. But every time I hear "'Tis the Gift to Be Simple," the old Shaker anthem from the mid-nineteenth century, it's not just some historical song; it reminds me of this friend in Bowling Green who was raised in a Shaker community.

I had a foothold in folktale scholarship from my studies of the lives and work of the Brothers Grimm to develop a national consciousness. Now in this graduate folklore program I was introduced to a parallel contemporary movement in Denmark led by N. F. S. Grundtvig. By the mid-nineteenth century it produced the Folkehøjskole, or "Folk College" for young adult education, which reinvigorated Danish rural society and was arguably the key institution to ease the country's way from monarchy to vibrant democracy (more in the chapter on experiential education). Now I saw too how that same folktale scholarship developed in Finland late in the century (also in the development of a national consciousness movement there!) into the "historic-geographic" method of dating and tracing the evolution and travels of folktales. Then, in the 1920s, in reaction to that historic-geographic school with its catalogs of "types and motifs" of folktales that made every folktale look distinct, Russian folklorist Vladimir Propp came up with his brilliant method of analysis, in which diagramming of traditional folktales strongly suggested that just one tale was being told, psychologically speaking.

Since I was trained as a historian of modern Europe, and was particularly interested in the development of national consciousness(es), this all fell on fertile ground. But the eclectic nature of the field of folklore also meant that there were all sorts of American parallels and applications for these studies. Stith Thompson, for example, had done a classic Finnish-style historic-geographic study of the widespread Native American folktale type called "the Star Husband tale," working with geographic variants of the tale ranging from the Southeast with the Coushatta (when they still lived in what's today Alabama) to deep into the American West and the Canadian Northeast and Northwest. And there was an interesting class on the evolution of the ballad in its transmission from the Old World to the Americas, on which more will be said in a later chapter.

FOLK TECHNOLOGY: BASKETMAKING
COMMUNITIES NEAR MAMMOTH CAVE

But by far my favorite class was the one on folk technology. I was fresh off the Folkcenter South crafts research and festival, and so I came with a real interest in the topic. The focus of the course this semester was on the basketmaking communities in the vicinity of Mammoth Cave, little communities such as Wax and Cub Run, where white oak basketmaking played a central role from the 1880s (when all the big timber had been cut out) to the 1930s (when automobiles generally replaced horses and farmers no longer needed white oak bushel baskets from which to feed the horses or mules ear corn). Typically, from Monday morning until Friday evening, mother, father, and all the kids in a family in these cutover hill lands would make bow baskets of second-growth white oak saplings. Saturday they'd take them to the local country store to swap for things they couldn't produce themselves—calico, salt, coffee, and such. The country store owners would pile up baskets until they had hundreds, even thousands, and then contract with specialists who did long-distance peddling

*Figure 6.*1.
*Close-up of a
bow basket*

A typical bushel-sized white oak bow basket, the size favored by farmers in north Alabama and points north a century ago to carry ear corn to the stock.

of these—a loop "up through the Bluegrass" through Frankfurt and Lexington; a long oval loop down to Memphis; a shorter loop down through Nashville. The traders went in modified road wagons, with poles set into the frame and the basket handles slipped over the poles.

In 1977 there were a good many older folks left from those basketmaking communities of their younger years, and some of them taught us how to make bow baskets. I already knew how to rive white oak splits, courtesy of Mr. Upchurch, but now I learned the very different construction of the bow basket. It starts with the fastening together of a circular handle and a circular rim by means of an "ear" or "god's eye" of splits woven around the two joints where handle and rims cross. The next step is for flat ribs for the bottom and rounder ribs for the sides, tapered and sharpened on each end, to be poked into those ears. The weaving around them proceeds from each "ear" toward the middle of the basket; when they meet, it's finished. Such bow basketry is a European-style construction technique of great antiquity, and undoubtedly came over with the first European immigrants.

I was lucky enough to find the man who was probably the last surviving long-distance wagon peddler of such baskets, and did a couple of good oral history interviews with him. He was "Rec" Childress, son of the third wife of "'Lijah Tom" Childress, famous basket peddler and local character. In 1918 Rec was fifteen when he first went with his father on one such trip. Almost sixty years later he remembered every single place they spent the night, including the first night, when—to his horror—his father decided to park their two wagons beside what he called a "gypsy encampment." They never sold on Sundays but rather laid over in some convenient livery stable. Rec's Uncle Bob went with them, driving the second wagon so they could

Figure 6.2.
Bow basket
peddling
wagon

A peddling wagon loaded with bow baskets, somewhere between Franklin, Kentucky, and Gallatin, Tennessee, around or about 1930. (Photo courtesy of the Tennessee State Library and Archives.)

split up during the day and so hit twice as many small towns, then meet up again at an agreed-upon larger town for the night. Once Rec had spent the day with his uncle, and they'd gotten to the rendezvous before his father. His uncle was apparently seized with a sudden homesickness, and he left Rec—who had probably never been five miles from Wax or Cub Run in his life and was frightened of the big towns—on his own. His father eventually rolled in, found Rec alone and a bit shaken, and took him out for a fairly new and exciting drink called Coca-Cola and something to eat, by way of making it up to him.[10]

The growing number of automobiles in the late 1920s killed the basket trade in two ways: it became too dangerous to drive a horse- or mule-drawn wagon on the main roads, and cars didn't need to be fed feed corn from bushel baskets. It was remarkable how much of the changing natural environment and social and economic structures in a region could be seen through the lens of this one folk craft, especially as assembled in a couple dozen graduate school research papers on different aspects of it.

BRINGING IT ALL BACK HOME

In the context of that Kentucky basket trade I remembered stories I'd heard back in Alabama of Depression-era jug peddling from wagons, the traveling vendors selling their jugs for a nickel a quart capacity. After that postgraduate semester in folklore, most all of my history classes (not just my own semiregular course in folklore) promised to be much richer. Recently I was looking through my stack of what now seem to be terribly old-fashioned green-backed grade books from those early years, and I found a 1982 interdisciplinary class I was in charge of titled Latin America: From Tectonic Plates to Liberation Theology. The first three sessions were on McHarg and his approach, and the fourth was on the BRPC's local McHarg-inspired county studies. Bob Stiles from biology held forth on Latin American ecosystems; I followed with some anthropology studies (again poaching out of field) and history. The head of the world languages department spent two days hitting the highlight of Latin American literature; Fred Hendon did two sessions on an economist's view of the region, and we brought in a guest speaker for Liberation Theology proper. One of the books I championed for the course was on the Peruvian Amazon, Avencio Villarejo's *Así es la Selva*, roughly "And Such Is the Jungle." Its table of contents was a perfect example of telescoping time, from geology upward—starting with the scientific belief that the Amazon originally flowed westward but that the Andes rose so quickly (geologically speaking) that the Amazon was cut off from the Pacific and made to find an outlet in the Atlantic, leaving a basin of deep silt.[11]

I'd gotten the family back to our home in Birmingham after Thanksgiving. So as to leave my wife with the car I'd taken the train from Birmingham up to Bowling Green for final exams and then came back again the same way. Given the train schedule, I arrived back in town at half past one on an early December morning, everything dark, cold, crisp, and really, really quiet. Instead of having arranged with my wife to wake all three kids and get out at that unholy hour to come get me in the car, I'd told her I'd find a way to get home. I had all my possessions in a duffle bag, so I just put the bag on my shoulder and walked from the midtown train station up Twentieth Street and over Red Mountain, down into downtown Homewood and then our Edgewood neighborhood. I got home at about three in the morning. After all my wife had had to put up with, it was the least I could do.

chapter seven

Herb Doctor Tommie Bass and the Scholars

Tommie Bass, Alabama Herbalist

In my old manila folder on herbal medicine in Alabama is a folded, yellowed, July 14, 1974, newspaper article clipped from the *Gadsden Times*. The article included a grainy photo showing A. L. "Tommie" Bass, herb doctor from near Leesburg, a little town northeast of Gadsden, nestled at the eastern base of Lookout Mountain. He'd have been around sixty-six years old that year. Pictured with Bass was a young folklore fieldworker, Allen Tullos, a native Alabamian who at the time was working on his master's in folklore at the University of North Carolina at Chapel Hill.[1] They're standing in a blooming elderberry patch (or what I guess is technically elderflower when it's in bloom). The article quotes an old herbal medicine book but says nothing about Mr. Bass or even what he thought the medicinal uses of the elderberry were. But obviously I had taken notice of him by then, and within a year or so of that article I began visiting him on a fairly regular basis, singly and later with classes of folklore students. He was most friendly and generous with his time, and I loved visiting with him. More than once he played his harmonica and sang for us, usually "There's More Pretty Girls Than One." A couple of times I went out collecting with him in the woods, him with a pickax for turning up roots. Once I took my wife up to meet him, detouring by there on the way up to our old home places in Tennessee. She was frankly not all that keen on going out of our way to see some rather eccentric bachelor, and threading our way through his junk-strewn yard to the front door didn't improve her mood. But he charmed her from the very first, with a courtly "Come into the house, pretty young girl."

I've still got a paperback titled *The Herbalist* that I bought from Mr. Bass early in my acquaintance with him, still with the little tag glued in, "Distributed By A. L. Bass." The book was first printed in 1918 and then was lightly revised a couple of times over the years. My copy has about three hundred pages, and the medicinal plant use section of the book, alphabetical by the plant's common name, is roughly half of that. The second half of the book is mainly by category of use. The breadth is amazing—examples in time back to classical Greek tracts and in space to China, India, and Africa—but the main cultural stream referenced seems to be from England to early colonial America, with a secondary emphasis on Native American herbal usage. Some of the medicinal claims are made with greater confidence than authors in our more litigious age might venture. Here, for example, are the listed properties

Figure 7.1. Tommie Bass playing his harmonica for visiting students

This photograph was made sometime in the 1980s, on one of the folklore class field trips to Mr. Bass's house.

and usages of adder's tongue (*Erythronium americanum*), known nowadays more commonly as trout lily or dogtooth violet: "It is emetic, emollient, and antiscorbutic when fresh; nutritive when dried. The fresh root simmered in milk, or the fresh leaves bruised and often applied as a poultice, together with a free internal use of an infusion of them, is highly useful in the condition in which such a remedy is indicated. The express juice of the plant, infused in cider, also has been found beneficial."[2]

Tommie himself was a walking encyclopedia of herbal remedies. I don't have good recall (or notes!) of what I learned from him and when, but in my files is a half-page article clipped from the *Birmingham News* in 1978, a sampling of what a couple of reporters got from him in just one visit. It's a good snapshot of how quickly information came at you in a conversation with Mr. Bass; you didn't have time to write it down properly, much less digest what you'd just heard, before he was off on another remedy. I'll summarize some of it here: "Life Everlasting," or rabbit tobacco, he found good for coughs, colds, and clogged sinuses. "Queen of the Meadow," he said, was good for kidney ailments and diabetes: "It's not a cure," Bass said, "but persons taking it can get by with less insulin." It was also good for asthma, with eye-opening instructions for use: take a double handful of the plant, submerge it in scalding water, put a towel over your head and lean down to inhale the steam. Peach tree leaves boiled fifteen minutes made a tea good for the stomach or the kidneys. Inner bark from the wild cucumber tree (bigleaf magnolia, which grows in Little River canyon and smaller ravines thereabouts) helps with rheumatism or arthritis. Preparation: take three ounces of inner bark, boil it in two quarts of water for an hour; store in jars in the refrigerator, and take two tablespoons three times a day. Visitors often asked him for hyssop (wild oregano), mentioned in the Bible. He recommended boneset as an Indian medicine for easing pain. Preparation: boil four ounces of leaves for thirty minutes, add honey or sugar to make a light syrup, and "take a tablespoon of it as often as needed." One of his favorite herbs, because of its many uses, was pennyroyal, with its minty smell. It was good for coughs and colds when made into a tea, and also "good for fleas on dogs and to keep weasels out of seed." And of course sassafras root for tea. Redshank for a baby with colitis. Goldenrod for a tea that "calms the nerves." Ground ivy leaves for a tea that relieves headache.[3]

Unbeknown to me for a long time was that Tommie Bass was being discovered not just by me but by the wider world, thanks initially to the work done on him by Tullos. In the decade of the 1980s Tommie was the main subject of a study of traditional herbal medicine by John K. Crellin, then a professor of medical history at Duke

University (lots more on Dr. Crellin and Mr. Bass later). Among other things in that decade Tommie was profiled on the front page of the *Wall Street Journal*, and he was invited to a panel at the Smithsonian Institution to compare notes on herbs with a Chinese herbalist. In 1993 a short documentary film on Tommie Bass was done by Tullos and Tom Rankin. We'll return to it a little later, but among other things it's got Mr. Bass playing his harmonica and singing "There's More Pretty Girls Than One."[4]

HERBAL MEDICINE ASCENDANT

To a certain extent, in the 1970s and 1980s Tommie Bass was surfing on a popular culture wave of interest in herbal medicine and the more scientific-sounding homeopathic medicine. So, for example, readers were highly interested in the home remedies coming out of the *Foxfire* project talked about in a couple of earlier chapters, beginning with a list of curatives in the very first *The Foxfire Book* (1972). In *Foxfire 9*, which came out in 1986, the book opened with a section titled "Remedies, Herb Doctors, and Healers," based on student research articles going back to the late 1960s. It begins with one of *Foxfire*'s famous personality studies, this time of Flora Youngblood, born in 1906 in White County, Georgia, somewhat southwest of Rabun County, where the *Foxfire* project was based. Her father, crippled with arthritis that Flora believed was caused by his wintertime gold mining in the creeks when young, had been a well-known local herb doctor who rode around in a mule-drawn cart. From the cart he had directed young Flora to go dig herbs he spied, and she in her generational turn had become a person locally known for herbal remedies. Students compiled a list of remedies from Ms. Youngblood and many other interviewees. Some called for incorporating nonherbal substances such as alum, lard, or sulfur, or drinking water from a container with rusty nails, and there were some that just involved reading Bible verses at a certain time or magicking ailments away. One nonherbal "remedy" struck me as so crazy that it just might mess with a person mentally enough to work: "If you could remember the last place you seen a frog that had been run over by a car on the road, it would cure your hiccups." But most of the remedies are indeed herbal:

> For chapped hands, an ointment made of cooked-down persimmon tree bark;
> For chills, strong tea made from pennyroyal leaves;
> For colds, chew the leaves and stems of peppermint, or drink tea of ginger and sugar;

For colic, stew some calamus roots and mix in some catnip tea;

For cooties/lice, wash hair twice a day with a tea made from stems and leaves of larkspur;

and so on for the better part of thirty pages.[5]

DR. JIM DUKE, ETHNOBOTANIST: THE AMAZON CONNECTION

Fast-forward twenty years from that original 1974 *Gadsden Times* newspaper article on Mr. Bass to 1994, when internationally known ethnobotanist Jim Duke expressed an interest to my friend Bob Stiles in meeting this celebrated Alabama herbalist. Drs. Duke and Stiles had originally connected, given the strange ways life works out, down in the Amazon rainforest.

Bob and I had been team-teaching "culture and environment" courses (cross-listed for either biology or history credit) since 1977, as was talked about in the previous chapter. Our general teaching approach was one of telescoping time: begin with looking at the environment from the ground up (starting with geology, that is), then see how human culture had changed the environment and how that had possibly set new limits on the culture. In January 1981 we first took this course model on the road, internationally speaking, leading a class to the Peruvian Amazon. Sometime in 1980 Bob had said to me, "You want to go to the Peruvian Amazon?" and I'd replied something like, "Yeah, and I'd like to see the dark side of the moon, too, which is about as likely." But a former biology professor turned ecotourism director had approached him about the prospect. She said that if we recruited ten students each, our ways would be paid for. We outlined a course, recruited nine history and biology students total from Samford and one adult from a presentation at the local Audubon Society, got permission from our respective spouses to pay the remaining half fare for our participation, and started such a course.

In terms of herbal medicine and home remedies, this was my first direct exposure to folk medicine from another culture. I'd had one indirect experience, with a Japanese friend; he'd been raised by a grandmother in rural Shikoku and could name five herbal remedies for every one I could name. But now I had some direct experiences (albeit through an interpreter) with herbal medicine in another culture. For starters, most of the homes we visited along the rivers had little medicinal gardens next to bigger food gardens. And we heard a lot about *curanderos*, the folk healers of the Spanish American world, including these Spanish-speaking neotropics. Our chief guide was a most personable twenty-eight-year-old man named Eduardo; he spoke English, German, and French fluently just from his association with tourists. His father was a healer from somewhere upriver, he told us. I was curious about how they learned their cures, assuming that they apprenticed with older healers. The key step, however, seemed to be the taking of ayahuasca, a hallucinogenic tea made from a couple of local plants. In the visions induced, according to *curanderos*, the plants with healing properties appeared to the viewer and revealed their own medicinal properties. Hmmm, I thought, trying to delay judgment.

On that first trip to the Amazon rainforest the profusion of life there just blew me away. I hadn't realized what limits frost and drought—though neither were extreme in my corner of the southeastern United States—put on life. In the rainforest, competition between life-forms was almost such that every species had to have its own gimmick, or niche, to live. Most folks know of Darwin's insight into evolution on the 1831–35 voyage of the *Beagle*, supposedly sparked by his viewing of the sparse life-forms of the Galápagos Islands (a few finches, a few giant tortoises, all obviously from the same ancestry but each specific to its own island). But after being stunned by the variety and the niche lifestyles of the rainforest, I wondered whether it hadn't been his earlier landing on that voyage in tropical Brazil that had set that train of thought in motion.

Hoping for a Cure

Eduardo was our guide to all this, and he seemed especially interested in the food and medicinal uses of plants. He showed us a giant tomato-family plant, recognizable as a tomato plant by shape and leaves and fruit but a sturdy ten feet tall with thorns on the bottom of the leaves and with both the fruit and the leaves poisonous. Earlier on that hike Eduardo had collected a particular kind of vine that he said was good for skin rashes; now he broke a little branch off of the monster tomato plant and, with his left forearm turned up to expose the tender skin, began to gently strike it with the tomato plant leaves held in his right hand. In no time—like instant poison ivy—an impressive red rash appeared there. Eduardo showed it off a bit to those of us on the nature walk, and then he spread the sap of the vine on the rash, and we watched it slowly go away.

As it happened on that first trip, folk medicine in Amazonia was not just of armchair academic interest to me: I was seriously ill upon arrival at our base camp. Our flight into Iquitos, Peru, the closest airport to our destination, was from Miami. We'd decided (unwisely, in retrospect) to try to save money by caravanning in cars from Birmingham, overnighting in a hotel in Orlando. At a fast-food restaurant in Homewood, at six o'clock in the morning just before our departure, I ate an egg-and-muffin sandwich, and I am convinced I got food poisoning from it. I spent part of the night in Orlando "kneeling at the porcelain throne." Things seemed to improve a little on the four-hour-long flight from Miami to Iquitos, and during the night spent in a motel there, probably because I was running on adrenaline from all the new sights. But on the six-hour boat ride the next day to base camp—down the Upper Amazon (Ucayali) and up the Napo River on a *colectivo*, a long, thatched-roof riverboat—I spent most of the ride in the little privy perched on the extended gunnels behind the huge outboard motor. That first afternoon and night in camp I was somewhere beyond diarrhea and on into dysentery, which my Imodium was not touching—dehydrated, visibly losing weight, and so weak I couldn't go on the first nature walks. There's nothing quite like being really sick far from home, especially with the closest good hospital twenty-four to thirty-six hours away.

Eduardo himself became concerned. "You've eaten some poison food," he said; "Come with me to the kitchen." So I tottered after him the hundred feet or so to the kitchen and sat and watched him prepare what I was to take. First, he squeezed the juice of six limes into a glass, and my first thought was, "citrus juice on an inflamed stomach?" Then he took manioc roots (which I only knew as the source of tapioca) and grated them into a big metal basin full of water. After letting it settle a bit he decanted off most of the liquid, leaving a gummy white paste in the bottom of the basin. He put three or four big spoonfuls of it in the glass of lime juice, stirred it up into a colloid, and said, "Quick, drink it before it settles." I only hesitated a heartbeat or two; it was desperation time.

I kept supper down that night, was ravenous at breakfast the next morning, and fully participated in the activities of the next day. Two days later I was 100 percent. I told Eduardo it had worked like magic, and that I assumed it was a recipe he'd gotten from his father. No, he said, he'd learned it from someone knowledgeable about plants, someone from Yewkla. My Peruvian geography was still in its rudimentary stages, and I was curious what province or town of the country was Yewkla, so Eduardo had to spell it out for me: a botanist from the University of California, Los Angeles, that is, UCLA. So much for my "local" herbal cure: the gummy white substance was just starch, and apparently the starch coats your stomach lining long enough to give you a fresh start on things. And lime juice turns out to be a classic help for children with diarrhea. It had worked so well for me, in my hour of need, that for years thereafter, when traveling anywhere tropical, I assumed I could always get limes locally but packed a little box of starch. Eventually wiser friends convinced me that traveling with little boxes of white powder was sooner or later going to attract unwonted attention at airports, so I gave it up.

I team-taught the Amazonia course four times during the January mini-mester from 1981 to 1993 and then dropped out for other international travel/study courses. Bob, on the other hand, stayed with it and got deeply involved in environmental education programs in and around Iquitos through the Birmingham-based ecotourism company International Expeditions. This—the last link that finally completes the communication circuit—is where he'd gotten to know Jim Duke.

JIM DUKE'S LIFE AND SCHOLARSHIP

I'd only gotten to know about Jim Duke in 1990, when he and coauthor Steven Foster published *A Field Guide to Medicinal Plants and Herbs of Eastern and Central North America*.[6] Foster was the general botanist for the book, describing the physical features and preferred habitats; Duke was the scholar interested in the medicinal use of plants. At the time, mainly because of Tommie Bass, I was keenly interested in herbal medicine, so I got a copy. I remember being especially struck by one passage from the book, a warning that when coauthor Duke had nibbled on the root, or rhizome, of bloodroot, for a time thereafter he experienced tunnel vision! The tone of the book was set early on in the preface, which was attributed to both authors, though this paragraph seemed more in Dr. Duke's wheelhouse: "We believe that safer natural compounds could be found to replace the synthetic compounds that occur in about 75 percent of our prescription drugs, and that evolution has better equipped us to deal with rational doses of preparations from medicinal plants. But since it costs, in our litigious American society, $125 million to prove a new drug safe and efficacious, we may need to wait for the Japanese to develop these natural medicines for us."[7] This defense of natural medicines sounded reasonable to me.

Then in December 1994, I got to meet the famous Dr. Duke. He came to Birmingham for a major gathering sponsored by International Expeditions. It turned out, interestingly enough, that Jim Duke was not only as unpretentious and down home as an old shoe, but he also had a soft spot for Birmingham: he had been born (in April 1929) and raised here (until age seven, when the family moved away) in the East Lake part of Birmingham. In fact, his botanical interests had really started in those childhood years hereabouts. He told me about an old-timer in his neighborhood who took him up on the woodsy slopes of Red Mountain, showing him herbs and natural foods. Later I found a short paragraph on that very subject in an autobiographical note Jim wrote in 1997: "lonely old Mr. Brooks lived across the street. He had no close friends or family, and he spent most of his time talking to his rabbits in their hutch—and to me. He took me for walks in the nearby woods, and he introduced me to the world of edible wild plants such as chestnuts and watercress. Since that time, I have always had a keen interest in edible plants. And walking in the woods is still my number one therapy for personal rejuvenation."[8]

The Duke family moved to central North Carolina, where Jim's outdoor and botanizing interests only sharpened and matured. He took three degrees in botany from the University of North Carolina at Chapel Hill, and then—feeling he'd been academically a little too inbred—he got himself assigned to botanical work successively in Mexico, Costa Rica, Panama, and Peru. During these years, he says, he fell in love with Latin America and became an ethnobotanist before he ever knew the word. In 1977 he was chosen to head up the US Department of Agriculture's Medicinal Plant Laboratory, the main project of which was to screen plants from all over the world for cancer-fighting properties. Funding for that project dried up a decade later, and then in 1991 came what Jim called "a pivotal event" in his life: an invitation from International Expeditions to teach medicinal plant workshops to ecotourist groups in the Peruvian Amazon. And this is where Jim and Bob Stiles had met and become friends, as faculty members on the same teaching staff there.

Introducing Jim Duke to Tommie Bass

So it was that shortly before he arrived in Birmingham in December 1994, Jim Duke sent word to Bob Stiles that, if possible, he would like to visit with Tommie Bass. Bob said he had a friend who took classes to see Bass every so often, and then he asked me whether I could set up such a visit. I called Tommie to arrange it; he didn't answer the phone, but since that wasn't unusual we decided to chance a visit anyway. On Saturday before Christmas, Bob and I (and Jimmy, Bob's son) drove with Jim Duke up to Leesburg, to Tommie's house. He was indeed home, and welcoming. We threaded our way through piles of magazines and other stuff into his living room, where the only light was the orange glow from a ceramic gas heater.

I've always been proud (probably overly so) of being able to interpret between "the folk" and the intellectuals. It was clear after an exchange or two, however, that Tommie and Jim were on the same wavelength and that anyway Jim could do his own interpretation at least as well as I could. Tommie would talk about some medicinal uses of yellowroot, to treat mouth ulcers, for example, and then Jim would say, yes, we know it's got four alkaloids that evolved to fight off the plant's viral and bacterial enemies, and as medicine they probably have a synergy, adding up to more than the sum of their parts. We were there almost three hours—hours of conversation that really, really should have been recorded but weren't.

We took Tommie out for an early supper. After we'd dropped him off at his house and were headed back to Birmingham, I asked Jim Duke whether anywhere in that three hours of conversation he thought Tommie had been off base, botanically or medicinally speaking. Jim said he thought Tommie had confused devil's walking stick with another small, thorny tree, but he went on to say that even botanists had a hard time telling them apart when they weren't in flower. Other than that, he said, he had found Tommie generally knowledgeable and trustworthy.

Thinking all this might be worth sharing, Bob and I worked up plans to get Jim Duke and Tommie Bass on the same stage at the Birmingham Botanical Gardens. The folks at the gardens were enthusiastic about the idea. We got to work on a grant application to fund it, to pay for the transportation and housing of both principals, and to set up video cameras and a large projection screen to show the audience close-ups of plants Jim and Tommie would be handling. Through other channels Tommie did get down to Birmingham and do one session by himself, which fell fairly flat as a friend of mine who used to work at the gardens remembers (with no Jim Duke as cultural and botanical interpreter!). But before we could get the two of them on a stage together, Tommie had a fall and got caught out in a night rainstorm, and he went downhill quickly. He died in August 1996. I've still got the inscription that Jim wrote on a later trip to Birmingham, opposite the title page of my copy of his *Field Guide to Medicinal Plants*: "To Jim who took me to see Tommie Bass before the end, Jim Duke 2001." I remember too that on the 1994 trip that introduced the two men, Jim had also had some herbal medicine advice for me. When I'd complained about how short my lease on a cup of coffee had gotten, he recommended taking saw palmetto berries for such difficulties associated with an enlarged prostate.

After that day with Tommie Bass and Jim Duke, naturally enough, I had a more positive attitude toward herbal remedies, having seen folk wisdom and academic wisdom seeming to pull in tandem. And then I took an adult group up to see Mr. Bass, a group that included some nurses. On the ride back to Birmingham, the nurses collectively pitched a fit. "This is so wrong," they all agreed; "people play around with peach tree leaf tea for cancer, and then when they come to us it's way too late." And my newfound faith in herbal remedies faded a bit.

TRYING TO GIVE EASE

Another book published in 1990 (the same year as *A Field Guide to Medicinal Plants*), one that I took even longer to find, was by medical historian John Crellin and associate Jane Philpott, titled *Herbal Medicine Past and Present*, volume 1, *Trying to Give Ease*.[9] It was a decade or so old when I finally discovered it—a most serious study of Appalachian herbal medicine using Tommie Bass's life and herbal practice as the prime case study. Over the previous decade the authors had spent hundreds of hours with Tommie (and his customers/patients) in and around Leesburg and had driven Tommie over to Duke University for eight separate one-week-long sessions there. I've professed history for half a century and read biographies and oral histories by the dozens if not hundreds. I don't think I ever read one that so sensitively and succinctly explained a person in his complete social and historical setting as this one (the only other one that comes close is the 1974 *All God's Dangers: The Life of Nate Shaw*, based on author Ted Rosengarten's sixty hours of interviews supplemented by sixty more later). Anybody seriously interested in herbal medicine should find Crellin and Philpott's truly in-depth study of Tommie Bass and his herbal medicines fascinating.

For starters, it is deeply sympathetic with Tommie's attitudes, and those of the general rural culture he served, in a locale where lowland Deep South culture meets Appalachian culture in a ridge-and-valley topography. The last line of the book—a paraphrased quotation from Robert Coles—could stand alone as a great summary of the ethos of the still fairly young field of "popular culture" as of the 1980s: "The lives of ordinary people have their own various ways of struggling for coherence, for a compelling faith, for social vision, for an ethical position, for a sense of historical perspective, for a meaning—a *raison d'être*."[10]

It was that sentence that inspired me when I reread it recently to go back and review the 1993 Tullos/Rankin film on Mr. Bass, which had gotten deeper into his biography than I ever did. Tommie was born in 1908, the oldest son, and was, as he remembered it, continually "bemeaned" by his father (his father could quote the Bible, Tommie said, but had an explosive temper and didn't "live" the Bible; his mother didn't quote it but lived it). He remembered hunting squirrels with a rifle and pretty well doing a man's work on the farm by age seven. Most of the little money the family saw came from timbering in the winter, squaring up logs with broadaxes to make into crossties. On the side they truck-farmed in the growing season, and his father ran a fur trading business in the winter, which Tommie too did in later life.

With the family just scraping by, Tommie never went to school; when he was about four his mother taught him his ABCs from the printing on shotgun shell boxes. He jokes that he did go to school one day, and for that day was the teacher. When he was drafted in 1942, about age thirty-four, they asked for a show of hands from all those who'd never gone to school. Those who raised their hands were put in a room and given a simple pamphlet to see whether any of them were literate to some extent, and Tommie instructed them all on the answers. When the sergeant came back in the room and found out about it, he kicked Tommie out of the literacy test class and back onto labor detail.

In the video, there's footage of Tommie opening mail and identifying the pieces for the camera: a get-rich-quick scheme, a political ad asking for money (Tommie said he'd "talk" for a candidate he liked but wasn't going to "pay his way" into office), something from a local church. There's a part about him getting a haircut and, as a captive audience, a dose of religious philosophy in the form of poetry from the local barber. Some of the footage I found most interesting was of him walking by booths at the Collinsville Trade Day, in the valley on the other side of Lookout Mountain from Tommie's home near Leesburg. If you've never been to Trade Day you ought to go just to people watch, as my wife would say; it involves a whole sprawling hillside a bit south of Collinsville with hundreds of booths and thousands of customers, open every Saturday morning. On the documentary Tommie's local fame is evident as people call out to him or come over to talk. The destination for Tommie's walk this day was an herbal medicine booth that stocked his "angelico" (angelica), yellowroot, salves, and rubs. When the proprietor calls out his wares, "Angelico or boar root makes a young man out of old," Tommie nods and chimes in with verbal approval. Early in the documentary Tommie was musing about mortality; many a time, he said, he'd seen an old pear tree have a huge crop, only to be "graveyard dead" the following spring. I took that to mean that his life at age eighty-five was going surprisingly well, given how it had started, but he was prepared for the end. Toward the last, the film-makers showed Tommie wandering in the cemetery where his best friend in life was buried and where his own plot was. It was the very next year, 1994, that Jim Duke, Bob Stiles, and I came up to interview Mr. Bass. After the interview we drove to a local boat dock to have dinner, and on the way we passed by that same cemetery. Tommie pointed it out to us and was proud of the fact his plot and funeral service were all prepaid and that he'd leave no debts.

Professor Crellin was not only much taken with Tommie Bass as a person; he also admired the wholistic, personal approach Tommie took with his patients, as contrasted with the often aloof and impersonal atmosphere of modern clinical medicine. He particularly appreciated the theme in most of Mr. Bass's life of primarily relying on his own experience—including self-educating himself by adding ideas from almanacs, herb buyers' lists, calendars from drugstores, the radio, and domestic medicine manuals.

Overall, however, most of the substance he found in Tommie Bass's herbal remedies (each of which are treated in detail in the accompanying volume 2, *A Reference Guide to Medicinal Plants*) is of the nature of a placebo effect, especially heightened when his prescription results in some sensation, smell, or visible effect, such as sweating. Crellin worries about possible dangers to patients' health from some of Tommie's practices: patients on insulin might be endangered by drinking Mr. Bass's huckleberry tea without telling their doctors, for example; or, to echo my nurses' earlier concerns on Tommie's treatment of cancer, "his reputation may encourage some laxity toward follow-up examinations and, on occasion, delays in regular medical treatment."[11] In particular, writes Crellin, Tommie encourages spending some time using herbs for prostate problems in men or for cancer in female organs before turning to surgery.

Crellin generally puts Tommie Bass in the "Eclectic" school of folk medicine of the post–Civil War era. This school "accepted many aspects of regular medical practice but maintained a botanical emphasis in treatments" (Meyer's 1918 *Herbalist*, the book I bought from Mr. Bass, is of that same persuasion).[12] But Crellin also says that Tommie's craft was anything but a static relic of the past. He sees in Tommie Bass's medicinal advice "elements of transition, of revision and compromise." There's little of the old medieval "doctrine of signatures," wherein God supposedly gives a visible clue to the use of a plant in some part of its shape; also absent is the ancient notion of a "balance of humors" in the body. Rather, Tommie's overview of the body as a machine, with certain medicines cleaning out vessels like unblocking a gas line to a carburetor, and his insistence on the importance of "filters" (he includes liver and kidneys in this category), Crellin traces to the Industrial Revolution. Crellin's encyclopedic knowledge of the evolution of popular medicine is often frankly over my head, and my eyes have tended to glaze over in those parts, but he is so obviously an expert in the field that I tend to trust his judgment.

WINTERTIME FOR A BACKWOODSMAN

In the process of reviewing all the things about Mr. Bass I'd saved in files over the years, I recently rediscovered a couple of things I'd long forgotten about. One was a copy of a formula for his signature salve, a formula that by age seventy-four (in or around 1982) he was just giving away.

The other item was a twenty-some-page pamphlet dating to 1983 by John Crellin, Jane Philpott, and Allen Tullos titled *Wintertime for a Backwoodsman: Reminiscences of A. L. Tommie Bass of Leesburg, Alabama, "Same address since 1925."* Crellin and Philpott, who had apparently learned about Tommie Bass from Tullos, were at work on their massive two-volume *Herbal Medicine Past and Present*. It wouldn't be published until 1990, but they'd already done hours and hours of recordings, and

Figure 7.2. "Bass Quick Rubb," the recipe

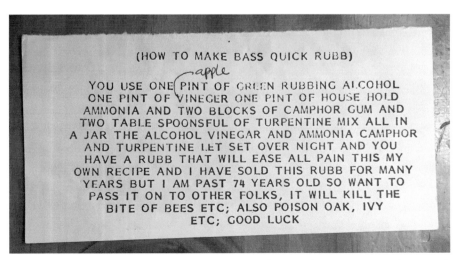

(HOW TO MAKE BASS QUICK RUBB)
~apple
YOU USE ONE PINT OF GREEN RUBBING ALCOHOL ONE PINT OF VINEGER ONE PINT OF HOUSE HOLD AMMONIA AND TWO BLOCKS OF CAMPHOR GUM AND TWO TABLE SPOONSFUL OF TURPENTINE MIX ALL IN A JAR THE ALCOHOL VINEGAR AND AMMONIA CAMPHOR AND TURPENTINE LET SET OVER NIGHT AND YOU HAVE A RUBB THAT WILL EASE ALL PAIN THIS MY OWN RECIPE AND I HAVE SOLD THIS RUBB FOR MANY YEARS BUT I AM PAST 74 YEARS OLD SO WANT TO PASS IT ON TO OTHER FOLKS, IT WILL KILL THE BITE OF BEES ETC; ALSO POISON OAK, IVY ETC; GOOD LUCK

Tommie's generosity extended to giving away perhaps the most famous curative in his arsenal. His "green alcohol" here is probably short for "wintergreen oil," apparently a common additive.

had gotten what they thought were interesting memories on other subjects: "Unfortunately, many of Mr. Bass' reminiscences and thoughts cannot be included in the book. Some, which reflect his life as a countryman and backwoodsman full of native wit and ingenuity, rather than as an herbalist, are brought together in this booklet. They were recorded mostly in 1983." There are reminiscences from boyhood about catching his first muskrat in a trap but having its pelt cheapened by mud turtles who got to it first; of being able to buy a French harp (a harmonica) every Christmas when he was in his teens, after the family's dire poverty let up a little; of planting by the signs (plant anything that grows above ground in the twins, Gemini). My favorite passage was on how closely in late winter he watched for signs of spring, starting with the yellow tassels of the streamside tag alders that bloomed in January and February: "Tag alder makes you think spring is coming, but don't put too much confidence in it." Then the bloodroot bloomed, May apple shoots came up, the lizards began to move around, and the barking tree frogs would be heard . . . You can tell be the way the little pamphlet is written that the researchers had all fallen in love with their subject.[13]

"HERBAL MEDICINE ON SAND MOUNTAIN"

In late winter of early 2017, I watched Alabama state folklorist Joey Brackner's newest *Journey Proud* episode, titled "Herbal Medicine on Sand Mountain."[14] It features Darryl Patton, who apprenticed with Tommie Bass for years and wrote a book about him and his herbal medicines that came out some eight years after Tommie died. Joey asked Darryl the circumstances of his meeting Tommie Bass. It was in 1983, when Darryl was just out of the military and working on a degree in special education, and getting involved in a lot of homesteading activities on the side, that five different people told him he ought to meet Mr. Bass. So he eventually drove to Leesburg and found Tommie repairing his roof but pleased to come down and talk about herbs. Darryl said he had meant to stay twenty minutes but wound up staying three hours and twenty minutes, totally captured by Tommie and his knowledge of plants. On later trips he'd gather roadside plants and bring the whole bag for Tommie to sort through. There'd be a few Mr. Bass didn't recognize, but the great majority he knew and associated with medicinal properties.

In 2004, a bit more than a decade before this *Journey Proud* episode was made, Darryl had written *Mountain Medicine: The Herbal Remedies of Tommie Bass*.[15] I'd found it to be a beautiful volume with some wonderful color photos of medicinal plants that make them especially easy to recognize. Just over half of the book's 240 pages are devoted to the section titled "Roots, Leaves and Bark," which deals with the sixty-odd most important plants used medicinally by Mr. Bass, and is organized—like Meyer's 1918 *Herbalist*—alphabetically by the plant's common name. The rest of the book gathers assorted other material and is heavy on Tommie's own reminiscences of his childhood, remembered cures, and interesting personalities. One little part has the words to his favorite songs. I was pleased to see that it includes "There's More Pretty Girls Than One," with a picture of Tommie on the same page blowing his mouth harp. I'd guess that Darryl Patton spent more time with Tommie Bass than any other person ever did, including even folklorist Allen Tullos and medical historian John Crellin.

By the time the *Journey Proud* episode was being made in 2016, Darryl Patton had his own apprentice. Despite newfangled machinery such as blenders, and Darryl's common use of alcohol to draw chemicals out of plants in the form of a tincture (as opposed to Tommie's usual steeping or boiling in water to make teas), I noticed a lot of continuity. Darryl favors combinations of herbal extracts. He emphasizes the fragrances, implying that they are meaningful in medicine. He seems to love yellow-root, which, like me, he especially associates with Tommie Bass; he said that was the first medicinal plant Mr. Bass showed him. Darryl seems to mean as well as Tommie did, wanting to, in Tommie's words, "give ease" to those who either can't afford or are not helped by modern medicines.

In Darryl Patton one can see the adoption of scientific medical terminology by the herbalist as he prepares a "protocol" for his apprentice, who is said to be still recovering from Rocky Mountain Spotted Fever. Patton speaks confidently and without qualification of the antibiotic properties of the bitter alkaloid berberine, which is found in both goldenseal and yellowroot, and so, watching the episode, I go back and look up both plants in Crellin and Philpott's second volume on herbal medicine as practiced by Tommie Bass. This is where Dr. Crellin discusses each plant and its use as described to him by Tommie ("The Herbalist's Account") and then evaluates those claims in the light of modern scientific information ("Commentary"). Particular emphasis is placed on the results of double-blind experiments, in which neither subject nor researcher knows which group got the placebo and which got the real thing; such experiments, it turns out, have been extremely rarely done with herbal medicines. Crellin couches it all in the politest of terms, and he gives the benefit of the doubt when proper studies haven't been done, but his overall take is clear.

Here is Crellin on Goldenseal: "The use of hydrastis [goldenseal] for treating wounds and skin ailments has been rationalized by the antibiotic action of berberine, but this property has not been tested in controlled clinical situations employing hydrastis extracts. Likewise, the reported effects of berberine on amoebic infections, cholera, tuberculosis, and *Giardia* have not been subjected to close scrutiny, although naturopathic and other physicians often give strong testimony to the use of hydrastis preparations for *Giardia* infections." The footnote that follows this paragraph references D. B. Mowrey's 1986 book *The Scientific Validation of Herbal Medicine*, "a somewhat uncritical report," Crellin gently concludes.[16]

On yellowroot, Crellin writes, "Little physiological evidence exists to suggest any specific activity on ulcers from the presence of the bitter berberine [see goldenseal] or from other alkaloids present." Yellowroot apparently *has* been subjected to scientific scrutiny, with negative results; the footnote that follows cites a peer-reviewed 1963 study.[17]

And so, in these two dense, heavily footnoted volumes, Crellin generally supports the opinion of those nurses who told me decades ago that if you have something serious and go play around with herbal medicine, you are then liable to have waited too late for modern professional treatment to help. And as much as Crellin liked Tommie Bass and respected him, he admitted to a certain amount of disappointment with Tommie's switch, circa 1983, from collecting his own medicinals and dispensing them to being front man for a local commercial herbal pill business—because at that point Tommie began making claims that went beyond his own experience.

I've tried to sort out the pros and cons, the logic or illogic of this whole herbal medicine thing. The logic starts with the fact that many effective medicines were originally herbal remedies: digitalis from foxglove; aspirin from willow bark; quinine from the bark of the cinchona tree; morphine from the opium poppy . . . Even if many of their replacements today are synthetics, it is still the basic compound from nature that is being replicated, or a similar one inspired by that natural one. And the millions of species of plants and animals have collectively evolved uncounted chemical compounds that promote life, at least their own lives.

But the illogic, which seems to trip up even some scientists, may be in the expectation that it should be easy to find new medicinal uses for those compounds that benefit the *human* species. Living in the Birmingham area has thrown me into contact over the years with a good many teachers and researchers from the University of

Alabama at Birmingham's (UAB) medical school, arguably the flagship of higher education in the entire state, drawing in bright minds from countries all over the world. I remember talking, decades ago, with a medical researcher there who was originally from Peru. We discussed the famous 1552 illustrated herbal of "Aztec" (Mexica) remedies that a Franciscan priest had assembled from the area around present-day Mexico City and sent back to the papal library in Rome. That led to talk about the Peruvian doctor's own work all these centuries later with testing herbal medicines. He had been extremely disappointed in the results, I remember.

Professor Crellin himself talks about how on the whole scientists have lost their enthusiasm for plant remedies and their ingredients because of how remarkably few new drugs have been found after years of intensive research.[18]

THE GREEN PHARMACY AND THE PASSIVE VOICE

I liked Jim Duke about as well as I liked Tommie Bass. He was most personable, musically inclined, and respectful—maybe too much so!—of folk cultures everywhere. Jim was a prolific author, and his best-selling book (at least 1.5 million copies sold) was *The Green Pharmacy: New Discoveries in Herbal Remedies for Common Diseases and Conditions from the World's Foremost Authority on Healing Herbs*. It was published in 1997, and I'm sure Jim was already working on it by December 1994, when we went to see Mr. Bass; soon after our visit I got inquiries from Jim to make of Tommie, on exactly what plant was called St. John Conqueror root in our part of the country (Solomon's seal, Tommie told me, and I relayed the knowledge).

When I finally got the book I was immediately interested in a page-long inset just after the yellowroot entry, titled "Folk Wisdom Vindicated Again," where he talked about Tommie Bass's testimony in light of Crellin and Philpott's conclusion that "little physiological evidence exists to suggest any specific activity on ulcers." Jim Duke claimed that their conclusion had been reached before the discovery that most ulcers are caused by bacterial infection, and that, when he checked his database, he found that berberine "had, in fact, been reported to have anti-ulcer effects."[19] He never cited the source that was in his database, and I didn't think it was much "vindication" at all. Although I was much attracted to *The Green Pharmacy* at first reading, on longer acquaintance it seemed almost altogether anecdotal; there was almost nothing in the way of referencing double-blind scientific tests. The clinching argument for me personally in all this was the appearance of an article in the *Journal of the American Medical Association* in 2011 to the effect that—according to strict double-blind tests—there was no difference in results on enlarged prostates between taking saw palmetto berries and a placebo, even with the former given in dosages two or three times higher than recommended.[20] Finally, in reviewing this chapter, I was struck for the first time by the regular use of passive voice and other dodges, similar to what I'd seen in that quotation early in this chapter from Meyer's 1918 *Herbalist* on the uses of trout lily: "has also been found beneficial," "is highly useful in the condition in which such a remedy is indicated," and "is often applied as a poultice." In retrospect, that seems to me to be the common speech of herbal medicine generally.

I'm no scientist, but I've defected to Crellin's camp. I've felt the pull; I'm fascinated by herb lore itself and the idea of herb lore. I loved herb doctor Tommie Bass as did most everybody who met him, and I liked and respected ethnobotanist Jim Duke as well. Looking back, though, for me this herbal medicine thing was 95 percent a cultural seduction, not a rational process. I've concluded that there's almost nothing real here, compared to modern medicine, and I walk away arguably a wiser man but a sadder and duller one too. I think my disappointment, though, may be a real measure of the romantic attraction that the idea of herbal medicine has for most of us.[21]

chapter eight

Experimenting with Experiential Education

From my point of view as a young teacher hungry for teaching approaches that really clicked with students, the *Foxfire* model talked about back in chapter 4 was the first example I came in contact with of what generally came to be called "experiential education." By the next year, 1974, I had discovered not just other examples but a whole movement afoot in that general direction.

EXPERIENCE AND EDUCATION, THE BOOK

Recently I reread the classic that gave the movement its name, philosopher John Dewey's little 1938 book called *Experience and Education*, which is only 116 large-print, small pages in the edition I read. The text of a series of lectures given during the Great Depression, when times were hard and expectations were low, this book held out new hope for improving life by broadening and deepening education.

First, Dewey argued that the traditional method of teaching—in which the teacher hands out all knowledge, and that knowledge is meant to allow students to solve problems at some point in the future—was deeply flawed. He does not hedge his indictment: "How many students . . . were rendered callous to ideas, and how many lost the impetus to learn because of the way in which learning was experienced by them? How many of them acquired special skills by means of automatic drill so that their power of judgment and capacity to act intelligently in new situations was limited? How many came to associate the learning process with ennui and boredom? How many found what they did learn so foreign to the situations of life outside the school as to give them no power of control over the latter? How many came to associate books with dull drudgery . . . ?"[1]

On traditional education, he summed up: "Those to whom the provided conditions were suitable managed to learn. Others got on as best they could."[2] Now I suppose most college and university teachers the world over are survivors of such traditional educational programs, and we all "managed to learn" under those conditions. But looking back, I knew many smarter and more sensitive souls than I who did not survive, and I wonder sometimes whether such traditional education did not limit me in some ways as well.

John Dewey's alternative, of course, was education through experience. You must engage students in the solving of current problems through experiences that arouse curiosity and strengthen initiative, exactly those things he claimed were deadened by traditional education. Look at this final critique and see if it doesn't ring true to you: "We often see persons who have had little schooling and in whose case absence of set schooling proves to be a positive asset. They have at least retained their native common sense and power of judgment, and its exercise in the actual conditions of living has given them the precious gift of ability to learn from the experience they have. What avail is it to win prescribed amounts of information about geography and history, to win ability to read and write, if in the process the individual loses his own soul: loses his appreciation of things worthwhile, of the values to which these things are relative; if he loses desire to apply what he has learned, and above all, loses the ability to extract meaning from his future experiences."[3]

Dewey wanted to turn education into a social process, for him a more natural way of learning. The teacher would give up the role of absolute boss and take on that of leader of group activities, organizing a series of experiences for the students and remaining sensitive to student feedback all the while. Instructors who are "intelligently aware of the capacities, needs, and past experiences" of their students can help student suggestions develop into a learning plan.[4]

I first read this little book decades ago and only dimly understood what Dewey had to say. As I look back now on almost five decades of teaching, however, it seems to me that almost all my memorable successes were those that actively engaged students in problem solving and turned me into more of a guide and fellow learner than a self-proclaimed absolute source of all relevant knowledge.

It was in the 1970s, nationwide, that experiential education really became popular. The high school student-generated *Foxfire* magazine from northeast Georgia was the model for the strand of experiential education that came to be called cultural journalism education. Earlier I talked briefly about my discovery of the *Foxfire* project, hearing about the magazine, which started in 1967, and getting a copy of the first book compilation when it was published in 1972. I was initially interested by the subject matter, the folklore and folk crafts of the Southern Appalachians, but soon my interests came to include it as a teaching approach as well. The teacher, Eliot Wigginton, wrote the introductions to all the *Foxfire* compilation books, and his introduction to *Foxfire 2*, which came out in 1973, was clearly aligned with Dewey's educational philosophy. Wigginton talked about how one of his students got excited about a project in the photography darkroom but ended up late to his next class, which meant that he had to write five hundred times, "I will not be late to class anymore." In my copy of the book I underlined a passage that came a little later: "Too many of us fall short of that love and patience and self-confidence it takes to work with kids as equal partners. We must do better. There is so little joy in the world of most kids. The recognition of worth and accomplishment is so strained and so stingily parceled and our condemnation so freely given that it completely overwhelms the elation of any positive, shared experiences. I find it no mystery at all that kids tune us out. And if you think I'm exaggerating, you're probably part of the problem."[5]

But it turned out that there were many other strains of experiential education, too. One of the minor kinds was to get your students singing their way through history.

SINGING HISTORY

In the family photo archives is a picture of my older (then only) daughter dressed in pioneer-style clothing, bonnet and all, dated October 4, 1974. Andrea had turned six just the day before. The caption on the back of the photo says, "Andrea getting ready to sing with her daddy at the Samford folklore seminar." I remember we sang the old Child ballad "The Devil's Nine Questions," me playing on guitar and singing the devil's part, her responding with the schoolboy's answers:

> Oh, you must answer questions nine, Sing ninety-nine and ninety
> Or you're not God's, you're one of mine, And you are the weavering bonty
>
> Oh what is higher than a tree, Sing ninety-nine . . .
> And what is deeper than the sea, And you are the weavering . . .

Oh heaven's higher than a tree, Sing . . .
And hell is deeper than the sea, And . . .

Oh what is louder than a horn, Sing . . .
And what is sharper than a thorn, And . . .

Oh thunder's louder than a horn, Sing . . .
And death is sharper than a thorn, And . . .

Oh you have answered questions nine, Sing ninety-nine and ninety
You must be God's, you're none of mine, And you are the weavering bonty

This performance was done as part of our graduate seminar New Horizons in History, which four of us on the history department faculty offered in the fall semesters of 1974, 1975, and 1976, and which was talked about a bit back in chapter 3 (as seen through the eyes of Marjorie White: "too many new horizons in history!").

Polly Powell, a most vibrant English professor at Samford (and the faculty member who first encouraged me to go listen to Sacred Harp singing), had brought Laurie Seidman to campus in or around 1973 to demonstrate how to teach history and other subjects through singing folk and traditional songs. An education professor at the C. W. Post campus of Long Island University, Seidman had long done this in his own classes. He came with his just-finished *Once in the Saddle: The Cowboy's Frontier, 1866–1896*, essentially a sing-along through history that was both entertaining and educational.[6] Despite the fact that he had a great voice and I had a mediocre one, I started doing this in some classes. My preface was usually that if I could sing in public with *my* voice, nineteen out of twenty people could do as well or better—so if you were in the nineteen you had no excuse not to try!

One of the first units I worked up was on outlaw ballads. It started with some sociological argument to the effect that almost all outlaws, beginning with Robin Hood, usually emerged where broader national law (the new Norman French rule after 1066, to pursue the Robin Hood theme) differed from local norms (the old Anglo-Saxon ways). Those who bucked the new national law were fed, sheltered, informed, and made into heroes by the local population, who despised new rules. And outlaws, as they grew larger in local lore, stole from the rich and gave to the poor because what does it profit one to steal from the poor, and all that giving to the poor was just the usual poor-person-suddenly-rich liberality with money . . . The great US trove of outlaw ballads in the old Southwest, just back under federal control after the Civil War, involved Charley Quantrell and the James brothers and such. Many of the ballads were transparently reworked from Irish themes and even tunes, such as "Brennan on the Moor." My lecture and sing-along also included one thread of the folk music revival in the United States from the late 1950s, the singing of old ballads, starting with the Kingston Trio's rendition of the old North Carolina ballad "Hang Down Your Head, Tom Dooley," and winding down with one of Alabama's own outlaw ballads, "Railroad Bill."

In the 1960s Joan Baez, especially, popularized many British and American ballads in her work; she was the first person I ever heard sing "Mary Hamilton." It wasn't long before I found a copy of John Jacob Niles's 1961 collection of Appalachian versions of old British ballads, *The Ballad Book*, began learning a few of them, and found myself enjoying the stories of where they'd been collected.[7] When I first discovered him in the early 1970s, Niles was still giving concerts. He repopularized the mountain dulcimer and had a great ear for catchy songs, but in performance I found his voice shrill and overly dramatic, and I turned down a chance to book him at Samford (though Birmingham-Southern College actually booked him about this same time, and I remember wondering whether I'd made a mistake). Eventually all this led me to Evelyn Wells's 1950 history of the ballads from Britain to America, *The Ballad Tree*, and I remember stealing several lectures from it for the folk music third of my evolving folklore class.[8]

The Role of Folklore in Reinvigorating Arts That Have Become Stilted

It seems to me that in virtually every artistic medium I know anything about, there's a tendency over time to overemphasize technique, with artists trying to impress other artists but forgetting about the larger audience—bluegrass banjo players playing fast chromatic riffs, to use a down-home example. When any art gets so stilted, with technicians showing off for one another, it often benefits from an infusion from the folk arts. These arts are cruder, maybe, but they have undeniable life and popular appeal, or they wouldn't have been passed down over the generations.

That's my explanation, at least, for the popularity of Bishop Percy's *Reliques of Ancient English Poetry*, published in England in 1765.[9] Some years before this, Percy, an Anglican clergyman, had been visiting in the great country home of a wealthy family. Up early one morning, he saw the housemaid using yellowed old paper sheets to start a fire. Curious, he looked at some of the paper and saw that it was the words to old country ballads in the handwriting of maybe a century before. He rescued the remains of the pile from the maid, and they became the nucleus of his 1765 book of poetry. Quaint, ungrammatical, and with wildly creative spelling they may have been, but the ballad texts had a life about them that challenged the increasingly ornate literature of his day and struck a chord with the reading public. *Reliques* was the first book Sir Walter Scott, later a most famous author of Romantic novels but at this point just twelve years old and not yet a sir, ever bought, and in a way it set the course for his whole life's work. In a lesser way, ballads were my main doorway into the scholarship of folk music.

Francis James Child's Work with the Old English and Scottish Ballads

The simplest definition of a "ballad" is a song that tells a story. And the so-called Child ballads—like "The Devil's Nine Questions," which I sang with my daughter for Samford students—were not for children, as I had supposed, but were named for the Harvard scholar Francis James Child. Born in 1825, he became an undergraduate at Harvard on a clear science and math trajectory. But then the Revolutions of 1848 in Europe, with all the refugees and notable speakers showing up in Boston and other East Coast cities, shifted his interests to history and the social sciences, I learned with personal interest. So he went to the Germanies and studied with—and this was a real eye-opener for me—the Brothers Grimm. From them he learned that most language groups in Europe had already compiled their late medieval ballads into bound collections, but that this had not happened in the English-speaking world. So Child spent the last decades of his life, back at Harvard, doing just that. He was interested not in the music of the ballads but just in the poetry, and he carried on voluminous correspondence with the Grimms and lots of other European scholars, which was important for his work because most of the old British ballads have their relatives in other European countries.

The final publication, ten books bound in five volumes, came out in 1888 and was titled *English and Scottish Popular Ballads*.[10] It listed 305 ballad "types" (a group of songs telling recognizably the same general story), sometimes with dozens of variants of a single type. The types were numbered, which is why scholars today refer to "Barbry Allen," for example, as Child no. 84. Child's scholarship was so thorough that well over a century later scholars have generally agreed that only one other ballad type—no. 306!—has been turned up. So the first great irony of British ballad scholarship is that it was an American who did the foundational work.

OLIVE DAME CAMPBELL, CECIL SHARP, AND THE MUSIC

The second great irony is that it was a Brit who did the most to collect and save the music of the American versions of the ballads. His name was Cecil Sharp. He was a music teacher who had fallen in love with the last fragments of the ballads in England, and had arranged them for the boys' choirs he was teaching. In 1916, asthmatic and too old to fight in World War I (in his late fifties), he was lecturing in New York about the ballad in Britain, which he declared moribund and on its last legs. A woman in the audience asked to speak with him after a lecture, claiming she had found the old British ballads very much alive in the Appalachians. Disbelieving though he was, he humored her enough to take a look at what she had to show.

The woman was Olive Dame Campbell, who with her husband, John C. Campbell, represented the Russell Sage Foundation in Asheville, North Carolina, then just a mountain village. In her travels in the Southern Appalachians she'd heard little mountain kids who'd never been five miles from home singing forty-verse songs about lords and ladies from London Town, and been enchanted by both the words and the strange-sounding melodies. It had all started in 1908 when she and her husband, on a comprehensive tour of schools in the Southern Appalachians, visited the fairly new (founded in 1902) Hindman Settlement School in the eastern Kentucky mountains. Years later she remembered her reaction when a teacher asked one of the students, a local girl, to sing "Barbry Allen" for the visitors: "Shall I ever forget it? The blazing fire, the young girl on her stool before it, the soft strange strumming of the banjo—different from anything I had heard before—and then the song! I had been used to sing 'Barbara Allen' as a child, but how far from that gentle tune was this—so strange, so remote, so thrilling. I was lost almost from the first note."[11]

She said she couldn't rest until she learned that new melody, with its "subtle" new intervals—her introduction to the "gapped tunes" and modal scales of this archaic English and Scottish music. And then in 1916, in the meeting with her that lecturer Cecil Sharp had reluctantly agreed to, she showed him the words and melodies of dozens and dozens of the old ballads. Sharp was so excited about this that he came down to the Campbells' place in Asheville and used it as a home base for his own collecting. He did this off and on for a total of about a year's time spread over 1916–18. The first results were published in 1917 as *English Folk Songs from the Southern Appalachians*, and of course the music was a feature of the collection every bit as important as the poetry.[12]

The Rage for Collecting Folk Songs, Including in Alabama

Sharp's research helped trigger a massive folk song collecting movement in America. From 1920 to 1950 most every state had its own collection published (Alabama's came in 1950, with Byron Arnold's *Folksongs of Alabama*).[13] And for decades the greatest prize a collector could find was one of the old Child ballads. I still remember my own excitement when one of my folklore students came in with a recording of her grandmother, who lived up on Lookout Mountain above Gadsden, singing a version of "The Wife of Usher's Well" (Child no. 79). The singer said that she had learned it from *her* mother, of whom she said: "Mama knowed every old folk song there was in the country and she sung them every night. We knowed them all." She knew the song as "Three Little Babes":

> I once knew a lady Little babes she had three
> She sent them away to a northern school To learn their grammar and read.
> They hadn't been gone but a very short time, Twelve months and a day,
> 'Til death spread all over the land And swept her babes away.
> She cried to the King of Heaven above Who chose to wear a crown,
> "Pray send to me my three little babes That I may once more see."
> It happened to be about Christmas time When the nights were long and cool.
> The three little babes came running home And in their mother's room.
> She spread the table very fine. Stood upon it bread and wine.
> Saying "Walk up, walk up, my three little babes, And eat and drink of mine."
> "We cannot eat your bread, dear mother, Nor neither drink your wine.
> For yonder stands our Savior dear And unto Him we'll join.
> Green grass grows at our head, dear mother, Cold clay lies at our feet.
> The tears you shed for us, dear mother, Would wash the wandering sheep."

Some of the words seem to have gotten a bit garbled over the years; the last phrase seems to be a misunderstood version of "wash our winding sheets," for example. But the basic theme of the old, old song—the plea of the ghosts of the three children that it's time for their mother to quit mourning and get on with her life because it's disturbing their peace in the afterlife—still rings loud and clear.

Back to Education by Way of Denmark: The Folk High School

Olive and John Campbell, looking for institutions they might adapt to the problem of reviving the depressed Southern Appalachians—especially in the field of education—got very interested in the Danish folk high school, brainchild of one N. F. S. Grundtvig.

Apologies here for once again slipping briefly into European history mode (though I'm probably more to be trusted here!), but in short Denmark got hammered in the first two-thirds of the 1800s. It tried to stay neutral in the Napoleonic Wars, but when the British burned the Danish fleet at anchor near Copenhagen, Denmark reacted by joining the war on Napoleon's side—just in time to lose the war and, in the peace, to lose Norway. In 1864 little Denmark was invaded by large Prussia and Austria, and it lost its two southern provinces to the growing, soon-to-be-unified, new German state. And those are just the highlights of Denmark's sufferings in this period. Grundtvig, born in 1783, became the great Danish scholar of Old Norse antiquity. In this high Romantic era he kept seeing the contrast between the creativity of the old culture and what he saw as the passivity and apathy of the current one. As with most Romantic scholars of the age, including his almost exact contemporaries Jacob and Wilhelm Grimm, he saw the vitality of the old culture as still partially alive in the common people. A brilliant scholar who'd done his university work in Latin, he now championed "servants' hall Danish," and on that foundation he may have done more than any other single person to create the modern Danish language.

And now to the key point: this erudite scholar, the author of dozens of books, now called for a bookless school for mass education. He thought that learned folk had to be few, but that all Danes had to be educated and useful citizens. In his most important book, the 1832 *Mythology of the North*, he first called for a Folkehøjskole, "Folk College," a folk or people's high school. It wouldn't be for students of what we think of as high school age today but rather for young adults, ages eighteen to twenty-five, a time when lives start to jell, with decisions being made about permanent partners and lifetime occupations and such. It would be taught by teachers through oral transmission, not from books—and especially by those teachers who knew something of common life and everyday work, not just academics. In history classes, for example, there was to be no mechanical memorizing of dates and events; to get at the real heart of a nation you ought to teach it through the ballads, folktales, and sagas. Traditional education drew the best and brightest *away* from the farms and small towns where most of the people still lived; this new sort of education was to make their lives more fulfilling in place. It wasn't called "experiential education," but it could have been.

The first such schools were set up in the 1840s, and they spread as the idea caught on. At first only for young men in the winter months (when little farm work was needed), they soon became coeducational. More than one historian has identified this institution as a key in the revival of Denmark. The Danish dairy cooperative movement, which made Denmark the leading dairy producer in the world, grew up in the shadow of the folk schools: an estimated 20 percent of the rural population attended a folk high school, but over 80 percent of the heads of the dairy cooperatives had, for example. During the last half of the century the vote was extended to more and more people, and the folk high school educated a critical mass of the population in the exercise of democracy.

Might that work in the Southern Appalachians? The Campbells wondered as much, and they planned to go tour the folk high schools in Denmark one day. John died in 1919, before that ever happened, but not long after his death Olive recruited a friend (and a Danish American high school student as interpreter) and spent eight months touring the Danish folk high schools. One impressive result was her 1928 book *The Danish Folk School: Its Influence in the Life of Denmark and the North* ("the North" because such schools had spread to other Scandinavian countries).[14] Another was the establishment of the John C. Campbell Folk School in Brasstown, North Carolina, in 1925. It's still there almost a century later, famous among craftspeople and musicians—though, disappointingly, it never multiplied and spread over the countryside the way the folk high school did in Denmark.

But doesn't just going lightly through the history of the folk high school start you rethinking public education? Back in 1974 I asked students in my January minimester folklore class to come up with their own folk high school curriculum on the assumption that they were living in Southside, Birmingham; in my files I still have a most creative one. On the title page is the motto of the principal of the very first folk school, Kristen Kold: "First enliven, then enlighten."

Bob England and *Sparrow Hawk*: Cultural Journalism in Alabama

One student in both the 1974 and 1976 iterations of our New Horizons in History seminar was Bob England, a Samford alumnus and at that point a high school history teacher. He'd graduated in 1970, a year before I'd gotten to Samford, but we had become friends at alumni reunions and state historical association meetings. He had been powerfully affected by the *Foxfire* teaching model, too. After graduation and a couple of years spent working as a city park manager, he had decided to become a teacher. That year was a buyer's market, if you were looking for such a job, and Bob had a choice of teaching positions at two elite private high schools in the Birmingham area or at a more provincial public high school an hour away in a much more rural county. In conversation with Birmingham radical character and bookstore owner Gene Crutcher about his choices, Bob told me, he was referred to two new books: that first volume of *Foxfire* and Pat Conroy's *The Water Is Wide*, both published in 1972. Go, like Conroy, to the place more off the beaten path (in Conroy's case the Sea Islands off mainland South Carolina), advised Crutcher; put your soul into your job, and it will temper and refine your character. Bob took his advice and the job at Bibb County High, in the county seat of a most rural county (much to his parents' consternation, he remembers). From the first he felt a warmth from the Centreville community, a bond that only deepened in the community cleanup after the massive tornadoes of 1973, the ones that nearly wiped the nearby town of Brent off the map.

After reading the first *Foxfire* volume, he'd called and talked to "Wig" (Eliot Wigginton), who wasn't yet so famous that he wasn't answering his own phone. The whole *Foxfire* enterprise was gradually moving to the new consolidated public Rabun County High School, and it was beginning to put out a series of newsletters on how to do such a teaching project in one's own school. At Samford we had actually gotten Wigginton himself to come present a session on *Foxfire* to our New Horizons in History fall seminar, and as he habitually did, he brought two of his students with him to talk about it from their point of view. That was part of his teaching strategy, taking students out into the wider world—students who'd never seen an elevator or left a wake-up call with a hotel desk, and who'd never gotten much in the way of recognition. Here's what Wigginton said about this question of recognition in a twenty-five-year retrospective on *Foxfire*: "It also turned out to be valuable because the recognition that they received was brought back home and shared with other students, and there was an energy there that raised the level of intensity a little as they shared their experiences."[15]

Recently Bob told me that it was that first New Horizons seminar, in fall 1974, that had pushed him into action at his own school. He and a couple of students went over to Rabun Gap and Clayton, Georgia, to talk to Wigginton and see for themselves the whole *Foxfire* setup. By 1975, with the enthusiastic support of the current Bibb County superintendent of education, Bob had the approval and funding to publish a quarterly *Foxfire*-style student-written and student-photographed magazine. The students voted to call it *Sparrow Hawk* after the elfin, elegant American falcon that seemed to be increasingly rare. The first issue—volume 1, number 1—came out in October 1975. As with all future issues, it was about sixty-eight pages long with a print run of seven hundred copies that sold for $1.75 each. It was a major success, in terms of both student education and public reception.

Every Teacher's Worst Nightmare

Then within weeks the worst tragedy any teacher could imagine struck. Two carloads of students and faculty sponsors were on their way to the submarine *Drum* near Mobile, to follow up on an article about submarines that involved the school superintendent from the first volume. The trailing car was involved in a major crash—killing faculty adviser Mary Jimm Roden, the driver, and student Faye Helton. Bob saw it all in his rearview mirror, he related in a retrospective twenty years later called "The Flight of Sparrow Hawk." At that time, and even more later, I was occasionally driving or leading car caravans of students all over the Southeast, and I was always terrified something like this would happen. How would you go on after something like that? Bob offered his resignation upon return to Centreville, but the superintendent refused it with a sort of tough love: "Take a week off," he said, "but if you're not back teaching by the next Monday we'll sue you for breach of contract."[16] Bob remembers the kindness of students' parents over that next month or so—bringing pizzas for faculty and students working late on the second issue, one parent even bringing a banjo for a light break in the work. And so the magazine lived on for several years.

One of the discoveries Bob England and his *Sparrow Hawk* students made got written up in the *Birmingham News*. Bob had heard Samford history professor

Wayne Flynt rehearse an African folktale about a man who came across a talking skull. When the man asked the skull how it got there, the skull replied it was by talking too much. When the excited man ran back to tell everyone about this miracle, he was accused of lying; and when the crowd indeed reached the skull it was silent and inert. The enraged crowd proceeded to kill the liar, as they thought, and after they departed the skull said to the man, see what talking too much gets you? After Bob repeated the story in his class, Deborah Avery, an African American student, said, "My daddy tells that story." The students thereupon did a series of recorded interviews with her father, Chelsie Avery; here's the matching excerpt from one of those interviews: "There was a man named Mr. Charlie and he had a fellow working for him named John. And one day John told him, said, 'It's too wet to work, so I'll go down and kill us a mess of squirrels.' So he told him, said, 'Well, take the gun and go down kill us a mess of squirrels, John.' So John went on down in the swamp. He found an old skull down there, and it spoke to him. So John said to the skull, 'What are you doing here?' and the skull said, 'Tongue brought me here. And if you're not careful, it'll bring you here too.'"[17]

And in the tale of course it did. This and more of Mr. Avery's folktales took up most of two early issues of *Sparrow Hawk*, along with his musings on his ancestors' journey through space from Africa and over time through slavery. This was 1977, the year that the *Roots* miniseries (based on Alex Haley's 1976 book) had aired on television in January. It was also the year that Bob England wrote an interesting pamphlet called *Teaching with Sparrow Hawk*. The personal accounts of many older Bibb County people who were featured in the magazine's articles are sometimes the most vivid reminders of them that their descendants still have. Bob is probably too close to this emotionally to do it, but somebody who was involved in all this really needs to write a book about it, including interviewing former students who worked on it (mostly in their sixties now, they should have great perspective on it!).

But it was also later in 1977 that Bob England resigned to go back to graduate school. He'd gotten a master's in history from Montevallo (while teaching at Centreville, because Montevallo was the only college around that offered a night program). Now he resigned his teaching position in Bibb County and went to the University of Alabama for his doctorate, taking a most unusual PhD in social studies with allied work in education, American studies, and history. The topic of his dissertation was, not surprisingly, a survey of faculty sponsors of *Foxfire*-type projects all over the United States; one list I saw from around these same years had projects in thirty-five states, some states with several each. *Sparrow Hawk* lasted a couple more years and finally expired under a less enthusiastic administration. Bob spent most of his later teaching career at Northwest-Shoals Community College, mainly teaching history survey courses and outdoor leadership courses. This last is especially meaningful for me because Bob was my bridge to two other major sectors of experiential education: adventure-based education and crafts-apprenticing education.

ADVENTURE-BASED EDUCATION: OUTWARD BOUND

The way *Foxfire* was the prototype of cultural journalism education, so Outward Bound was the prototypical adventure-based education program. Brainchild of Kurt Hahn, an innovative educator in Germany in the 1920s and 1930s, it argued for weaving projects of real responsibility into the curriculum of boys' schools. Forced out of Germany because of his outspoken criticism of Hitler, Hahn founded the Gordonstoun School on the western Scottish coast. There, schoolboys were charged with the rescue of folks who were shipwrecked on that rugged coast. After the rescues, the boys were then asked to bring the lessons they'd learned about motivation, organization, and successful completion (or failure) of mission to the rest of their educational experience. Outward Bound got its first American chapter in 1961, eventually with famous venues in North Carolina, Maine, Colorado, and beyond. In terms of education, the basic idea was to face a stern physical test and later sort out what had been done to meet it: students needed to show clear preliminary analysis of what the challenge was, a prioritized list of what had to be done to solve it, and an awareness of their mood and attitude while doing their best work solving it . . . and then they had to go apply all that to other matters in which they needed educating or which they needed to teach!

CRAFTS-APPRENTICING EDUCATION: THE APPRENTICESHOP

The Apprenticeshop program at the Bath Marine Museum in Maine was the early model for crafts-apprenticing education. Lance Lee, its director, a great teacher and communicator (who had also come out of Outward Bound), headed up a project of building small traditional wooden boats with traditional tools. From antique half models a foot or two in length—in modern times, half models are just decorative items on the walls of seafood restaurants in New England, but in earlier eras they were true design tools—they would take the lines off the sides and build a full-scale replica of the boat. Gangways around and over the workshop let visitors to the Marine Museum watch the whole process. Lance would talk about how 150 years before there had not been today's sharp, rather artificial, division between childhood school and adult work; boys would hang around the shop, maybe get adults to bandsaw toys for them, and gradually ease into little jobs, then bigger jobs. The goal of the average Apprenticeshop project was crystal clear: production of an authentic replica of a particular kind of traditional wooden sailing boat. Apprentices worked under master craftsmen who knew—as with instructors in adventure-based education—what needed to be done and in what order, exactly how to do it, and the state of mind needed to produce one's best work.

IDEAS AND ALABAMA'S SUMMER/FALL 1977
WORKSHOP IN EXPERIENTIAL EDUCATION

As of 1970 Murray Durst, a former head of Outward Bound in North Carolina, had begun to see a unity or at least a commonality in all these strands of experiential education. He was executive vice president of the DC-based Institutional Development and Economic Affairs Service (IDEAS). In that year IDEAS hired Eliot Wigginton to develop a plan for replicating *Foxfire* "in other cultural settings" all over the United States. In 1972 IDEAS was funded by the Ford Foundation to the tune of a couple hundred thousand dollars to get a dozen sets of educators from the East Coast to Alaska interested in doing this. The Choctaw community near Philadelphia, Mississippi, incidentally, was the closest of these eleven to us in Alabama, with its *Nanih Wayah* journal named for the Choctaw "origin mound" north of the city.

In the process these teams all traveled to Rabun County, where the *Foxfire* project was located. The next year the process was reversed, with workshop faculty hitting the road and helping set up a dozen more sites. There was another two-year Ford Foundation grant awarded in 1975, and a new thrust from IDEAS to begin work within educational systems and other existing institutions.[18] And somehow in this process—I've never learned exactly how—the folks involved turned up at Tannehill State Park with a proposal to create an experiential learning center there. Bob England says that somebody on the Tannehill board referred the idea to him, and that he listed my name, among others, as somebody who might be interested in such a program.

Then came the tragedy of the car crash involving the *Sparrow Hawk* students and faculty from Centreville High School, November 22, 1975. Murray Durst, probably partly out of sympathy and partly out of a desire to see whether *Sparrow Hawk* would survive to contribute to the Tannehill project, sent IDEAS staffer Ron Gager down to see Bob. Ron, a New Englander, had a master's in experiential education from the University of Colorado, and had worked for Outward Bound for years as a program director. He and Bob hit it off—they still communicate regularly all these decades later—and he encouraged Bob to go take the Colorado Outward Bound course partly to expand his experiential education horizons, but mostly, I think, as an antidote to lingering depression six months after the car crash. And it worked: it's one of Bob's favorite memories of his whole life, and the certificate of completion of that June/July 1976 course hangs on Bob's living room wall to this day. I remember he came back from that course leaner and wide eyed. He told me they were setting up tents in a blowing snowstorm at about 11,000 feet, and that the Outward Bound leader stopped everybody to show them one tent that had been set up "elegantly." And Bob says that in about two seconds he went from "what sort of foolishness is this" to appreciation for what he'd been shown.

So for one long weekend in August of that same bicentennial year, 1976, at Tannehill State Park, IDEAS brought in Eliot Wigginton from *Foxfire*, Ron Gager from Outward Bound, and Lance Lee from the Apprenticeshop, among others, to sit around and brainstorm with a handful of us interested local educators about how to create an experiential education center there, and maybe lead up to it with a model course. Adolph Crew, of the secondary education department at the University of Alabama, was a key person; he brought with him Doug Phillips, working on his doctorate at the time (and of course not yet famous for his *Discovering Alabama* series, which started on Alabama Public Television in 1985). I remember swapping book titles with Doug, one each that the other had never read, *Sand County Almanac* for *Bartram's Travels*.

For my part I was particularly charmed by Lance Lee. I waxed enthusiastic with him about all the new information on local rural craftspeople we'd begun working up for the Folkcenter South project earlier that year. Among other things, Lance and I talked wood and wood grain—New England's preference for brown ash in basket-making (pounded until it loosened along the coarser summer grain line, not rived) versus the South's penchant for riven white oak. The week after his visit I mailed him a sample white oak basket I'd made, and in return he sent me fifteen copies of a wonderful little pamphlet of his from the Apprenticeshop called *Half-Modelling*.[19] It starts with a 1921 photo of a master shipwright sitting on a bench in front of a 124-foot Gloucester fishing schooner, surrounded by an obviously interested gang of boys, with him showing them the two-foot-long half model from which the ship had been built. A dozen pages of history and illustrative photos delve further into such half models. In brief, in colonial days many coastal Americans were smugglers; we had to be faster than the British who policed the seas, and the half model was a

Figure 8.1. Half-Modelling *pamphlet and resulting half model*

Produced by the Apprenticeshop, then located at the Bath Marine Museum, this 1976 pamphlet begins by outlining the history of the half model as a design tool and then offers instructions for making a half model of a twenty-two-foot-long Muscongus Bay sloop.

design tool that helped us be faster! The pamphlet's middle foldout gives the sheer (the hull outline as viewed from the side), the top view (just the left half of it), and five section lines spaced along the hull from stem to stern. By tracing the sheer and top views on a block of wood and bandsawing them out, and then using a half-inch chisel to chisel away everything that doesn't fit the section lines (and fairing things out between them), you can make yourself a nifty thirteen-inch-long half model of a Muscongus Bay sloop. You haven't just seen the complex curves of the side; you've felt them as you created the model.

The Tannehill-Based Workshop in Practice

At the three-day brainstorming session at Tannehill, we outlined a pilot course to be called a Workshop in Experiential Education. We'd offer it for six hours' graduate or undergraduate credit (three in education from the University of Alabama and three in history or folklore from Samford University). It would meet six weekends spread over six months in summer and fall 1977, most of the time at Tannehill State Park. The three themes we'd pursue in the course were experiential learning techniques, local cultural history, and the local environment (this last in the ecological sense). Adolph Crew was the senior local instructor. I was a second. And IDEAS would make available to us as guest instructors such national figures in the experiential education movement as Eliot Wigginton and Lance Lee.

As a historian and a convert to Ian McHarg's telescoping time approach talked about back in chapter 6, I lobbied, and successfully, for a roughly chronological presentation. Weekend 1 was titled "Wilderness: Alabama on the Eve of European Settlement." The experiential learning techniques were adventure based, taking place on a two-day backpacking trip in the Sipsey Wilderness area of the Bankhead National Forest. Doug Phillips was a key instructor in the field for this weekend, spending a lot of time explaining primeval botany there and having us experience it. Activities included an introduction to the forest by a slow, single-file walk, keeping the person in front just in sight at a distance; a blindfolded "trust walk" (learning the local vegetation by feel); a night hike; a map-and-compass exercise; a community bread bake the night before the trip; group packing; and communal meals including natural foods. I tried to contribute with what I'd been learning about Native American use of the land as seen through the eyes of the early European explorers.

Weekends 2 and 3 were back-to-back in August at Tannehill State Park, from nine in the morning on Saturday to half past two in the afternoon on Sunday. The local cultural level was rural settlement from pioneer times. The ecological horizon was the European-style farming of the land. The major experiential learning techniques were oral history and cultural journalism for weekend 2, and crafts apprenticing for weekend 3. Eliot Wigginton came for Saturday of weekend 2. We had in mind to listen to him for half the weekend and try to put out a small cultural journalism project in the other half, based on what the *Foxfire* magazine and books had done with the heritage of northeastern Georgia. Wigginton indeed talked about cultural journalism in a powerful way; one especially memorable phrase he used was "those intricate tricks of self-sufficiency." Better yet, he and two of his high school students conducted a remarkable interview in front of the class with Ray Farabee, the retired engineer who had presided over the refiring of a Tannehill iron furnace the year before (an interview that wound up in *Foxfire 5*, the metallurgy volume).[20] But he cautioned us not to see a magazine as the end-all of experiential learning, and our high-pressure crash course in magazine production evolved into several gentler seminars on photography, oral history, layout, and such, and left some time for other things. I led a class sing-along and history lesson on the mountain ballad and fasola music, particularly Sacred Harp.

We discovered later that Kathryn Tucker Windham, Alabama's premier collector of ghost stories and fine teller of tales herself, had heard of our course and came to sit in on it, only to be turned away by someone who didn't know what she had to offer! Every region tucks its most powerful thoughts away in stories of its strong men and women, tragic love affairs, and supernatural happenings. And in the mid-1970s, those nineteenth-century settlement cultures were only a step or two back in folk memory. One especially nice feature of that second weekend was that Tommie Harrison from Shelby County schools and Bob England from Bibb County schools came to talk about their *Foxfire*-inspired student-produced magazines. Bob brought some of his *Sparrow Hawk* students to talk about their work on the magazine.

Weekend 3 featured Lance Lee. He talked about the mechanics and magic of apprenticing and the values associated with old-time handicrafts. Not only did he discuss good and bad tools, we learned them by touch in carving models. A considerable historian and folklorist of the seafaring community of northern Europe and New England, Lance was quick to point out the Tannehill furnaces as the key to an entire nineteenth-century craft matrix. The iron and soft steel ("soft" here meaning not brittle, easy to sharpen) of woodcraft tools once came from here and similar places. Part of Lance's vision for a future learning center was that Tannehill, as part of an educational process, might once again produce quality "soft" steel tools to replace those antique ones that were gradually disappearing. I brought my newfound knowledge of folk craft artisans from the Folkcenter South project and earlier. We tried to show that some of the same beauty, economy, and strength of Maine wooden boat building could be found in white oak baskets and hand-tied nets from the Deep South. Looking back, we should have done more with the changing landscape under massive new immigration into the state: the great pine and hardwoods falling to the saw, the loss of topsoil, the siltation of rivers that disrupted fisheries. The creeks at Tannehill itself, today blue-green, ran brown and red from the ore pits that fed the furnaces, and the woods for miles around were cut down for charcoal to fire them.

Weekend 4 was on urbanization and industrialization: Alabama in more recent times. The ecological horizon was the massive urbanization of the last century and the accompanying development of industry. The major experiential learning techniques were developed in the context of a two-day adventure in downtown Birmingham, the largest and most industrialized city in the state. Ron Gager set this weekend up, with help from Mark Gooch, who lived downtown. On Saturday morning the class and instructors set off from the Samford campus, walking four blocks to the nearest public bus stop. There followed a morning-long cultural scavenger hunt in Southside, an old and ethnically diverse neighborhood of the city. By early afternoon we moved base camp to Baptist Church of the Covenant on what was then Eighth Avenue South, now University Boulevard, where we spent the night camped out on the floor. We drew a "human interest map" of the area as we gradually explored it, and we listened to the education minister of the church, a dedicated church worker and enthusiastic city dweller, talk about the minuses and pluses of city life. Ron took us through a series of "new games" (games that featured cooperation instead of competition, such as "hand untangle") in the city, fondly remembered in course evaluations later.

The class members were mostly suburban or rural in origin, with a built-in distrust of anybody's inner city, but by the end of the first day, a whole new attitude toward cities and city people was evident. The spark of city life that got struck several thousand years ago in the Near East is still very much alive in Birmingham. All of a sudden the city was recognized as responsible for civilization (museums, zoos, great libraries, etc.), a place of unparalleled social variety and excitement. Having seen the attractions of city life, one had a more balanced view of the social price of late: white flight and inner-city collapse, street crime, and the like. But overall the chief lesson learned was that the city is of fascinating potential as a setting for education.

Weekend 5 was on regional planning: awareness of what is to come. The cultural and ecological level under consideration was the foreseeable future; the experiential learning techniques were ways of community planning. Ron Thomas of Attic and Cellar Studios in Washington, DC, was brought in by IDEAS as our special consultant for the weekend. From him we got a professional's view of participatory design and cognitive mapping, and he presented lots of community planning projects from across the United States. Course evaluations later suggested we spent too much time indoors and not enough in hands-on learning. We preached but forgot to practice our "experiential education" theme.

Weekend 6 was a presentation of student projects. Students had been asked to keep a diary of their reactions to their experiences, and some time was set aside every weekend for students to discuss course experiences with one another.

Writing It Up for the New *Journal of Experiential Education*

Adolph Crew, student Joyce Lackie, and I jointly wrote an article about the course for the brand-new *Journal of Experiential Education* in May 1978.[21] Looking back at it all these years later, I find that what's most interesting are Joyce's remarks on the camaraderie developed by classmates and especially the creative projects they developed with their own classes. I wasn't around for the sixth and last weekend of the course, and I only got to hear about student presentations secondhand; by fall 1977 I was off on my first sabbatical leave, taking that postgraduate Intercultural and Folk Studies semester program at Western Kentucky University (WKU) that I talked about a few chapters ago. I had managed to recruit only one student from Samford for the Tannehill-based course, and although I was approached by IDEAS with offers of playing a role in a permanent experiential education program there, I felt I had lost any mandate to do so. It was essentially a teacher education project, dependent on recruits from schools of education. Adolph Crew diligently stayed with it until his retirement in 1987, developing a learning center there at Tannehill that lasted for years.

I never had another article in the *Journal of Experiential Education* after this cowritten one for the inaugural issue. But this exposure to other themes of the experiential education movement enriched a good many of my future classes, especially my Folklore: From Europe to America class. Because of Lance Lee, especially, for a time in the class half models were the required folk craft, starting by borrowing the bandsaw in the campus's physical plant building. A decade or so later when I took a leading role in Samford's effort to radically reshape its general education curriculum—an eight-year-long experiment called Cornerstone—the humanities-based Cultural Perspectives sequence incorporated such things as wilderness-style backpacking in the Sipsey Wilderness, hands-on crafts (such as Japanese-style fishprinting), and performance (such as reader's theater of the 1,500-year-old Indian play *Shakuntala* and Child ballad sing-alongs).

And in terms of my deepening appreciation of the roots of my own culture in Southern Appalachia I never forgot Eliot Wigginton's phrase about that last generation of remarkably self-sufficient Southern Appalachian mountaineers: their "intricate tricks of self-sufficiency."

chapter nine

- -

Survival of the Great Shoal Fishtrap
and Other Old Practices

The Trap on the Mulberry

The first two photographs accompanying this chapter show a stationary fishtrap in some rapids on the Mulberry Fork of the Warrior River near Arkadelphia, Alabama. They were taken in August 1981, within months of the long-illegal trap's having been run for the very last time. State game and fish officers had apparently modified it somewhat in the interval, blowing small holes in each of the rocky wing dams and pushing over one side of the wooden trap. There was still enough left, though, to see how it worked.[1]

The trap was made to catch fish that were swimming downstream, usually after a heavy rain when the river colored and rose. The wing dams, in the shape of a V with the open end upstream, were designed to funnel most of the river flow into the mouth of the wooden part of the trap. The mouth of this particular fishtrap was six feet wide, and the whole downstream section of the trap maintained this same width. Inside the mouth, the river water poured through wooden slats called "fingers," which sieved out any sizable objects—preferably fish, although, as one photograph shows, leaves and limbs could also accumulate.

Sweet gum and oak were the predominant construction materials. The first set of fingers shown here were made of two-by-two lumber; the sections farther downstream were of one-by-three and one-by-four planking, less desirable because they are too wide to let water through easily and too thin for a fisherman to walk on them without danger of breaking. Each set of fingers was four feet long, with the downstream end of each set inclined upward at an angle of approximately twenty degrees. Solid six-inch-wide boards were nailed to the top of the downstream end of each section of fingers and the bottom end of the next section. This formed a succession of inclined steps, the drop after each solid board capable of holding any fish pushed over into it by the water. The plank walls on each side, some two and a half feet high, kept any fish on the trap from getting off the sides. The trap would catch fish from when the water first began pouring through the first (upstream) set of fingers, until it got higher than the end of the last set of fingers or higher than the sides. Wooden mudsills below the mouth of the trap were buried under the converging, downstream ends of the rocky wing dams, anchoring the trap during high water. This made for minimal rebuilding the next season.

The Mulberry Fork of the Black Warrior River, in the vicinity of Arkadelphia, is not a big river, and around the region these stationary fishtraps seem to have been more or less proportional to river size. Older fishermen near Cropwell with whom I spent time remembered fishtraps as large as fifteen feet across the mouth on the as-yet-undammed Coosa River. Sometimes rock formations in the river bottom itself

Figure 9.1.
Overview of
the Mulberry
River fishtrap

This side view shows the V-shaped rock walls made to funnel most of the river current into the trap, and the side wall of the wooden trap itself. (Photo courtesy of Bob Stiles.)

Figure 9.2.
Looking
downstream
over the trap

The trap has been partly wrecked, though you can still clearly see many of the four-foot-long fingers, or slats. (Photo courtesy of Bob Stiles.)

would naturally funnel the current into a shallow and swift chute; these may be the oldest of all the fishtrap sites, since they required the least construction. Most often wing dams were built in swift shallows that lacked ledges or other bottom structures. More sophisticated wing dams than the loose rock ones shown here in the Mulberry Fork, ones that worked better in deeper water, were made by framing. Two logs were pinned together a foot or two apart with wooden stakes, and the whole construction was weighted with rocks piled between the logs. Several such courses built up vertically and tied together made a wing dam that reputedly could survive floods until the logs rotted out.

The locations of fishtraps still in living memory probably correspond to Native American trap sites that considerably predate the sawn lumber technology of European pioneers. John Swanton's *The Indians of the Southeastern United States*, a Bureau of American Ethnology publication of 1946, includes a map illustrating "certain natural resources" of southeastern Native Americans. It shows an arc of fisheries running down the Eastern Seaboard and then turning up the east side of the Mississippi Valley, coinciding roughly with the fall line.[2] The best runs of spawning fish up the rivers could be intercepted here first. The runs down could be intercepted here or at any upstream shoals, with the potential gradually diminishing toward the headwaters.

Some rivers in the southeastern United States seem to have had fishtraps at every major shoal; George Washington reported prior to 1785, for example, that there were "many, probably 30 or more V-shaped 'fishpots' in the [Potomac] river."[3] The stacked-rock wing dams are still commonly to be seen in undammed rivers all over the Southeast, whether of Native American or pioneer construction or both. There's a much-photographed V-shaped fishtrap (also sometimes called a fishdam) on the Etowah River in Georgia within walking distance of the Etowah Mounds.[4] Geographic features named for fishtraps, in fact, show how common they were all over North America. There's a Fishtrap Branch and a Fishtrap State Park in Kentucky; a Fishtrap Shoals on Lake Oconee in Georgia; a Fishtrap Hollow on the Buffalo in Arkansas; a Fishtrap Bluff in Mississippi; and a Fishtrap Creek in Washington State. Lolokalka, to give an example closer to home, was a Creek Indian place name in Talladega County, Alabama, that is said to have meant "sequential fish traps."[5] And there's a Fishtrap Road near the Locust Fork of the Black Warrior, just downstream from the Millers Ferry power plant, running along the edge of a huge ash settling pond today where there are presumably fewer fish to trap than there used to be.

TERMINOLOGY: WEIRS VERSUS FISHTRAPS

At the time of the first European incursions, weirs and fishtraps were more widely used by the Native Americans of what is now the United States and Canada than were nets, spears, fish hooks, poisons, or any other fishing method, probably because they were more efficient in catching numbers of fish.[6] Sometimes the terms are used interchangeably, but they ought not to be; there are two distinctly different strategies and techniques here for catching fish!

Weirs, as the word is commonly used, predominated in coastal shallows and slow-moving freshwater bodies or lakes, and they consisted of lines of vertical poles driven partway into the bottom, connected by woven baffles, for channeling fish into narrower and narrower keeps or trapping them when the tide went out.[7] They relied more on the movement of fish than on the movement of current. The most interesting modern weir I ever read about was in the Bay of Fundy, where tides can change the water level sixty vertical feet or more. John McPhee wrote about it in his *Founding Fish* study of the American shad. He'd heard about a traditional weir still being run thereabouts and wanted to see it. He was initially worried about getting seasick, going fishing on this arm of the Atlantic Ocean. As it turned out, he needn't have been worried: when the friendly fisherman invited McPhee to join him aboard his "craft," it was a Honda three-wheeler with a cart attached, and they drove to the edge of the bay when the tide was ebbing. Before long a three-thousand-foot-long dark line broke the surface, slowly revealing itself as almost a thousand spruce posts driven into the bottom and interwoven with spruce, fir, and hardwood limbs and small trees. It was in the shape of a very shallow V, with the ends nearer the shore than the middle was. It stood about seven feet tall in the middle and tapered to five feet at the ends. "Fishing" the weir was child's play compared to the Herculean task of building it: every low tide you just drove down to the last little pool at the inner corner of the shallow V and scooped up the fish with a dip net. You just had to keep up with the timing of low tide.[8] Closer to home, perhaps the earliest record of fish weirs on the Gulf Coast came from the account of Álvar Núñez Cabeza de Vaca, one of only four survivors of the 1527–28 Narváez expedition, which explored the Gulf Coast of what's today the southeastern United States from Tampa Bay to Galveston. Somewhere between those two identifiable points in the narrative he said of the inhabitants: "they have weirs of cane, and take fish only in this season [winter]."[9]

By contrast, fishtraps or fishdams—the main subject of this chapter—were located in rivers where there was considerable current, especially after rains upstream. Native Americans mostly used V-shaped wing dams of piled rock exactly as shown in the photographs of the Mulberry River trap, but their usual means of capture was a loosely woven, cone-shaped basket with the mouth upstream. Fish that entered were kept there by simple pressure of the current. James Adair, writing in 1775, said that such loosely woven baskets in use by the Choctaw could be six feet in diameter at the mouth and fifteen feet in length.[10]

In 1974 the *Journal of American Folklore* published an article on the use of piscicides—fish poisons—used in the Blue Ridge Mountains of Virginia and North Carolina. The main argument of the article was that mullein (which most of us know as a roadside weed with a basal rosette of flannel-like leaves and a tall central spike with little yellow flowers) was brought to the Appalachians from Germany by forward-thinking immigrants who'd used it to stun fish back home in Europe. Apparently crushed mullein seeds (like the rotenone used by biologists and the pounded-up buckeye roots used by the Cherokee) temporarily paralyze the breathing apparatus of fish. In June 1967 a couple of local men took the author of the article to a fishtrap on Wildcat Creek in North Carolina, one built by their great-great-grandfathers and in operation for at least four generations. It had typical V-shaped walls funneling the current down to a narrow mouth, in this case about six feet wide (about the size of the Mulberry River trap we started with). They told him there used to be parallel log-and-stone walls running downstream from the mouth of the trap. In rising fast water they had used it (when it still had those parallel walls, presumably holding sets of fingers) as a conventional fishtrap, but more recently in slow, low-water times they'd plug the bottom end of the trap and spread crushed mullein seed upstream. A few people with hand nets would just wade down around the edges of the stream and scoop up the fish as they came floating up to the surface, with a few more down at the trap to get those that showed up there.[11]

Reading that reminded me of a passage in the 1972 *Heritage of Blount County* that had been particularly interesting to me, a fish drive ending in a communal fish fry. No fish poisons were used, and the end of the road for the fish so herded was the mill dam itself. Here's the description, attributed to Daisy Miller:

> The annual summer fish fry was the outstanding event of the year. Several hundred people from everywhere came. A group of men in the community started out early in the morning, upstream, and seined down to the swimming hole. It was great excitement for the children to stand on the side of the bluff to wait and watch for the seining crew "to turn the bend."

The fish fry was well organized. Different groups did different jobs. The huge pans of golden fried fish placed at intervals on the very long narrow table was a sight I shall never forget. In between these pans of fish the women had placed wonderful homemade breads, cakes, pies and cookies. That was the menu. Lemonade and coffee were in abundance.

After Alabama passed a law prohibiting seining in streams and rivers the dear old fish fries, country style, were gone forever. Fourth of July picnics tried to replace them, but they never did have the same atmosphere. Homebaked loaves of yeast breads turned into biscuits. The sweet water fish turned into chicken.[12]

Wow, a rural Fourth of July festival that was older—and in her eyes, richer—than the fried chicken (and barbecue) we think of as so traditional. I wonder how widespread the custom was, in the vicinity of water mills and rivers statewide.

Getting to Know Fisherfolk on the Coosa

In that first decade of teaching at Samford, in the mid-1970s, I had an older student in my classes who was a veteran of service in the US Army in Vietnam and Laos before such service in those places was even public knowledge. Dan was a part-time preacher in a church down south of Pell City in the little town of Cropwell. He introduced me to Claude Hayes (an older commercial fisherman on the Coosa, through whom I met Claude's sister Ellin Kelly, who taught me how to tie fishnets), and then to Claude's old friend Harold Daffron, at this point in time a successful industrialist. From them I first heard about "jump boxes" when laying trotlines, and about the old permanent fishtraps in the Coosa before it got dammed. They taught me the importance of nongame fish I knew little about: smallmouth buffalo, freshwater drum, and various species of catfish.

Ellin showed me how to tie netting using a net needle (a pointed shuttle that held a quantity of twine) and a mesh pin (a long rectangular spacer that was used to loop the twine around to establish the size of the mesh). The net needles were usually homemade from a thick strap of white oak, though you could order nylon ones from Memphis Net and Twine, whose mail-order catalog was commonly used by commercial fishermen all over the Southeast. Whether of brand-new nylon or decades-old white oak, the implements themselves, in design, were paleolithic and have been found worldwide wherever there were people and fish. I wondered whether the

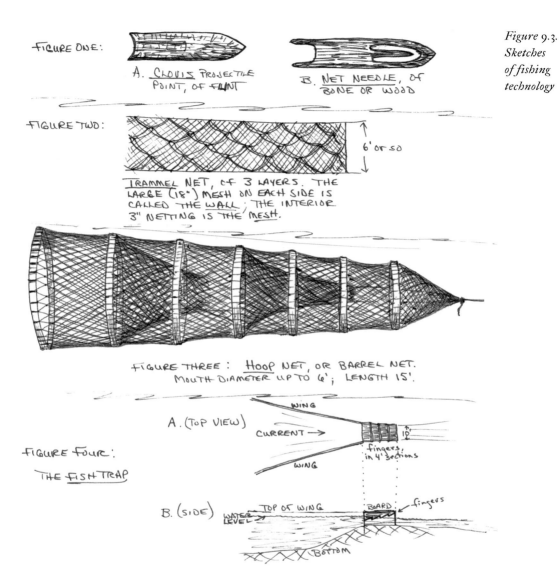

FIGURE ONE:

A. CLOVIS PROJECTILE POINT, OF FLINT

B. NET NEEDLE, OF BONE OR WOOD

FIGURE TWO:

6' or so

TRAMMEL NET, of 3 LAYERS. THE LARGE (18") MESH ON EACH SIDE IS CALLED THE WALL; THE INTERIOR 3" NETTING IS THE MESH.

FIGURE THREE: HOOP NET, OR BARREL NET. MOUTH DIAMETER UP TO 6'; LENGTH 15'.

FIGURE FOUR:

THE FISH TRAP

A. (TOP VIEW)

WING

CURRENT →

WING

fingers, in 4' sections

10'

B. (SIDE)

TOP OF WING

BOARD

fingers

WATER LEVEL →

BOTTOM

Figure 9.3. Sketches of fishing technology

Fishing technology the author was encountering back in the 1970s. The sketches were made for his folklore class.

shape had been invented by either one transcendent, ancient genius or a line of several such. In both outline and antiquity the net needle was much like a Clovis spearhead, I thought. And net needles are still found wherever fishnets are hand-tied or repaired: I later bought some old ones made of various sorts of hardwoods, polished by long use, on the upper Amazon in Peru, in a back harbor of Hong Kong Island, on the coast near Mombasa in Kenya.

In modern times, Ellin told me, the fisherfolk she knew who still made nets by hand had gone mostly to nylon twine for its durability and strength. But she thought the cotton twine they'd used back in the Great Depression would tie knots that weren't so liable to collapse as with the slippery nylon. She told about how, when she was being taught to tie nets, she was made to pick apart thirty-five knots to get back to a thirty-sixth that she had tied incorrectly. It was a good lesson, obviously so well learned that she remembered it forty years later: one collapsed knot and you suddenly had an opening in the net four times as large as the regular mesh opening, and there went your catch.

Trammel Nets and Hoop Nets

In the Memphis Net and Twine catalog, at least in those days, one of the common commercial fishing nets on offer was a trammel net. Ellin knew about such nets, though she didn't tie them herself. The name is as old as classical Rome, I learned later: trammel comes from *tre mail*, three-walled; and the structure of the net is probably much older than Rome, probably paleolithic as with the net needle. Imagine a long, linear net perhaps six feet tall, top to bottom. Not one but three webs of mesh connect at top and bottom: the two outer ones are of very large mesh, a foot or more square, and they are both about six feet high; between these two layers is a middle layer that is of much smaller mesh and is perhaps eight feet in height so that a fold or two of it lies loose between the two outer webs. It worked when a large fish came into it from either side, passing completely through the large mesh of the first net and then pushing a pocket of the smaller middle net through the large mesh of the third or outer net, and so "trammeling" itself up in a pocket of the smaller-meshed middle webbing. Later I heard of Alabama river fishermen who would set a trammel net across the deepest part of a stretch of river and then make a commotion first at one end of the stretch and then at the other, moving toward the net: banging on the boat with paddles, throwing big rocks from the boat into the water, even setting gasoline on fire on top of the water. It was all to get the big fish moving fast into the trammel net set across the bottom of the deep stretch.

The common nets Ellin Kelly tied were hoop nets. These were cylindrical nets that came to a point on the upstream end and were typically built around seven hoops: big hoops of five or six feet in diameter for the "bank nets," and smaller hoops of perhaps two feet in diameter for the "bait nets." They were made to be used in moving water. Imagine seven stout white oak hoops in gradually diminishing size, so one just fits inside the next. The largest was for the downstream end of the net. From hoops number 2 and 4, counting upstream, woven funnels (called "muzzles" or "fingers") were hung—easy for fish to go into, almost impossible for them to get out of again. Even in later years when the basic nets were purchased from Memphis Net and Twine, most commercial fishermen preferred to tie their own "fingers," the critical part of the hoop nets. The big hoop nets were fished against the bank especially in high water because fish going upstream hugged the bank as the path of least resistance. The bait nets could be fished anywhere there was a little current. They typically had tow sacks of spoiled cheese or cottonseed meal in their inmost, upstream parts, and catfish especially would follow the smell up into the hoop net. The pointy, upstream end was tied by a plow line to a tree or some sort of anchor.

In operation the nets took up a huge volume of space, but the beauty of their construction was that they were completely collapsible, and several would fit nicely in the bottom of a big skiff or across the gunnels of a small one. You wove three-inch mesh (tied on a one-and-a-half-inch mesh pin) from hoop 1 to hoop 2; two-inch mesh from hoops 2 to 4, including the first, downstream set of fingers; and one-and-a-half-inch mesh from hoops 4 to 7, including the second set of fingers, the inner keep of the hoop net. The three-inch mesh guided them in, the two-inch mesh constrained them a bit more, and the one-and-a-half-inch mesh of the inner keep kept every fish worth keeping.

Formulas for White Oak Fish Baskets and River Skiffs

Marvin Ogletree, a retired white oak basketmaker I encountered in Blount County in the course of the Folkcenter South field research talked about earlier, told me he had made white oak split fish baskets a foot and a half across the mouth, six feet long, and tapering to a five-inch round solid block. Those were "less tedious" to make than oak split cotton baskets, he said; his daddy had taught him to make them so that you only needed ten or twelve ribs.

He reminisced about fishing with such white oak catfish baskets as a youngster. He was picking cotton, which he hated doing, one hot summer day with his two older brothers, and to get out of it he said he believed he'd go check the three catfish baskets they had out in the river. They usually baited with "soured old cornbread" tied up in a tow sack and put inside the fish basket; a rope was tied to the tapered end, the current held the wide end downstream, and catfish would presumably follow the scent of soured cornbread up to and then into the basket. A heavy rain had raised the river about three feet and muddied it up. When he tugged on the plow rope tied to the first basket he had trouble lifting it off the bottom, and he figured it had silted in. But even after it broke loose from the bottom it was heavy. Lodged in the mouth of that first basket, dead, was a catfish he remembered as being longer than he was. Inside were two more live ones each three feet long. In a sack he brought back a hundred pounds of thrashing catfish from the three baskets, and he remembered bumping it across the fields, grinning, heading toward his brothers. That had been more than sixty years before the day I spoke with him, but he could still see it in living color. Later, when I was "driving and asking" somewhere in Cullman County, a man whose name and address I later misplaced gave me an old white oak fish basket that was collecting dust in the rafters of his garage. Today it is in the Center for Traditional Culture in Montgomery.

For every complex creation used by fisherfolk, as with the hoop nets, there seemed to be easily-remembered formulas for construction. I heard about Alabama formulas later for river skiffs to be made of five boards of cypress when you could get it, yellow (tulip) poplar when you couldn't: five boards, twelve feet long, twelve inches wide, and an inch or so thick. Two of the boards made the two long sides of the skiff. Most of the rest were used for the stern and the dozen partial boards nailed or screwed sideways across for the bottom, leaving just enough material left over for three seats or thwarts, and not forgetting the thin bracing strips where bottom and sides came together.

OTHER NEW (TO ME) WAYS OF FISHING THAT TURNED OUT TO HAVE NATIVE AMERICAN ROOTS

Claude Hayes, the old commercial fisherman on the Coosa south of Pell City, was the fisherman with whom I spent the most time. Once on a visit I had taken my

Figure 9.4.
Pump drill

This is a toy, much repaired, that Claude Hayes made for the author's children, modeled on a toy his grandfather had made for him. It is recognizably a Native American pump drill, minus the flint drill bit.

eldest (then only) daughter, who was second grade or so in age. The next time I went back, Mr. Hayes presented me with some hand-carved toys for my daughter and her younger brother. One was a set of thin wooden rectangles cleverly linked by straps so that when you tilted the top one, they flipped and flopped all the way to the bottom. The second was a little toy with a frame like a capital letter H, with a little wooden manikin suspended by strings from the tops of the H; when you squeezed the bottom ends of the H together, the mannikin danced and even somersaulted. I had seen newer plastic versions of both of those in the toy stores. But the third one was magical indeed, an old Native American–style pump drill that Mr. Hayes didn't recognize as an Indigenous tool, just a toy his grandfather, a pioneer who came in from

Georgia, used to make. It seemed to me to be just another proof that the European cultural wave didn't simply advance as an impermeable front, at once and totally replacing the Indigenous cultures on the land. There was apparently lots of interlacing across that slowly moving cultural border, including Native American women and their families who formed marital and trading alliances with Scottish men.

In fact, in that first decade I was in Alabama, the 1970s, I'd learned from either scholarly literature or local practitioners of several unusual (at least to me) ways of catching fish, and in almost every case had later learned they were essentially Native American in origin or at least paralleled in Native American experience. The main exceptions were "telephoning" (hand-cranking a generator to electroshock fish) and dynamiting, which were obviously newfangled inventions. Here are just a couple of those traditional ways.

A most friendly and personable physical education instructor at Samford, J. T. Haywood, introduced me to "jiggerpoling" the first year or two I was in Alabama. We'd go out at dusk or night, the steerer in the back of the boat working a trolling motor, trying to keep it close to the bank, and the fisherman in the front working a long cane pole with a noisy surface lure tied with strong line just a foot or two from the end of the pole. The fisherman's job was to run that noisy lure as close as possible to the bank, logs, and limbs, doing so back and forth a couple of times if the boat was going very slowly. A variation I was taught later was called "shaky pole," wherein the fisherman shakes the cane pole lightly up and down so the tip just pitter-patters on the water ahead of the lure, simulating a school of minnows being pursued by a small fish (the surface lure). Strikes came with explosive force, like dropping cement blocks into the quiet lake, and if you hooked the bass you'd hand walk the pole up to near the tip and net the fish. Later I found a great description by William Bartram of essentially that same technique as practiced by Native Americans in the Southeast around the time of the American Revolution. He wrote eyewitness accounts of the catching of "green trout" (largemouth bass) in Florida up to thirty pounds—way above the modern weight records of the species. About the only difference with the jiggerpoling as I was taught it, right down to the instruction to the sternman to paddle "softly," is that the lure was a treble hook covered with fur, cloth, and feathers that just dabbled on the surface. It's 1776, and in his travels Bartram is near Lake George, roughly the latitude of Daytona:

> They are taken with a hook and a line, but without any bait. Two people are in a
> little canoe, one sitting in the stern to steer, and the other near the bow, having a

rod ten or twelve feet in length, to one end of which is tied a strong line, about twenty inches in length, to which are fastened three large hooks, back to back. These are fixed very securely, and covered with the white hair of a deer's tail, shreds of a red garter, and some parti-coloured feathers, all of which form a tuft or tassel, nearly as large as one's fist, and entirely cover and conceal the hooks: this is called a bob. The steersman paddles softly, and proceeds slowly along shore, keeping the boat parallel to it, at a distance just sufficient to admit the fisherman to reach the edge of the floating weeds along shore; he now ingeniously swings the bob backwards and forwards, just above the surface, and sometimes tips the water with it; when the unfortunate cheated trout instantly springs from under the weeds, and seizes the supposed prey.[13]

Some of the fish caught, he said, "were so large and strong in their element, as to shake his [the fisherman's] arms stoutly, and to drag us with the canoe over the floods before we got them in."[14]

Then there is grabbling, with fishermen neck-deep in the water reaching—blind—up under rock ledges and inside sunken hollow logs to find huge catfish. The catfish actually swallows the exploring hand of the fisherman, who then grabs it by the inside of its mouth or gills and wrestles it out from under the ledge and up to the surface of the water. We're talking about the possibility of encountering snakes or beavers or catfish in the hundred-pound range, so you can understand nicknames of veteran grabblers such as "Seven-Finger Joe." James Adair wrote, poetically, about that very technique among the Chickasaw in West Tennessee almost 250 years ago:

> They have a surprising method of fishing under the edges of rocks, that stand over deep places of a river. There, they pull off their red breeches, or their long slip of Stroud cloth, and wrapping it round their arm, so as to reach to the lower part of the palm of their right hand, they dive under the rock where the large cat-fish lie to shelter themselves from the scorching beams of the sun, and to watch for prey: as soon as those fierce aquatic animals see that tempting bait, they immediately seize it with the greatest violence, in order to swallow it. Then is the time for the diver to improve the favourable opportunity: he accordingly opens his hand, seizes the voracious fish by his tender parts, hath a sharp struggle with it against the crevices of the rock, and at last brings it ashore.[15]

I wondered whether the cloth wrapped around the wrist and hand was not also partly to keep the skin from being abraded by the coarse, sandpaper-like teeth of the big catfish.

But of all the riverine culture and fishing techniques I was learning about, what still fascinated me most was the fishtrap. Harold Daffron had fished the Coosa River in central Alabama when he was a young man. He told me when I interviewed him in 1976 that he had watched an uncle run "a set of these traps" south of Pell City. This particular one was called the Old Harmon trap; there were three other traps in the general vicinity (today there's still a nearby unincorporated town over on the Talladega County side of the Coosa River, now Logan Martin Lake, called Fishtrap or, by the old-timers, Sims or Beavers Fishtrap). Mr. Daffron remembered standing on the wing dam near the Harmon trap's mouth during a fish run back in the 1930s. Sometimes a big fish would sense that something was wrong and turn and fight back upstream—"just like a salmon trying to jump these falls," he said—and occasionally one would make it. Most of the time, though, "they done waited too late." The fishermen would sit up all night at such times and run the traps every hour, picking up and throwing the fish off of the trap into the boat. These were mainly rough fish: drum, buffalo, some catfish, and "tons and tons of shad." When I asked whether he ate the shad, he replied with some disgust:

> No, you just threw them all right back in. My uncle tried raising some hogs on them, and when he killed the hogs you couldn't eat them. He threw the meat away [laughing]. He fed them on nothing but shad. You know, if he'd used his head a little bit and maybe a month before he got ready to kill them, put them on grain or something, it would have been all right. But he was throwing all that shad away, and he just put a pen full of hogs down there and said, "Okay, I'm just gonna raise me some free meat." And he did. The hogs got to where they would eat them. But they done nothing but eat shad. That was their whole diet. They didn't get a bite of nothing else their whole life, so they tasted like shad.

For most of the summer the water was too low for the traps, and for much of the winter they were covered by high water. The traps didn't work well if the water was too clear; the fish could spot them too easily and avoid them. Only when the water got dingy or muddy and picked up some speed did fish swim into the mouth, and "come shooting in there on the fingers." These Coosa River fishermen remembered that usually on a summer rise they would get drum and lots of shad, and on toward fall, buffalo, and then, at first frost, eel. When the eel ran, the fishermen would mesh their traps with one-inch-square wire mesh because the eels were so strong and so slick that without the wire mesh, even an eel that weighed as much as several pounds would get its tail down in the space between two fingers and spring them. The eels they caught survived in boxes in the water all winter without perceptible weight loss and could thus be sold off gradually to those locals with no dietary prejudice against them. Occasionally big catfish came in on the trap, but the biggest fish my informants ever saw caught on the trap was a sturgeon weighing upward of a hundred pounds.[16]

Lower down on the Coosa, some seventeen miles upstream from Childersburg, Alabama—before Lay Lake was raised—were two fishtraps known locally by the singular designation Willinghams' fishtrap, from Cecil and Albert Willingham, owners of the land. They consisted of V-shaped rock-and-log dams about four feet higher than low-water level, with the typical configuration of sets of wooden fingers followed by step-downs. In July and August 1949, Professor Donald Scott of the University of Georgia's biology department collected fish in the area by fish basket, hoop net, and the chemical rotenone, and he incidentally kept a record of what the fishermen were catching on the two fishtraps. In the thirty-nine-day period covered by his records, the traps produced 108 pounds of buffalo, ninety-seven of blue catfish, forty-six of drum, seven of channel catfish, seven of blue sucker, and four of blacktail redhorse.[17] That averages out to an anemic seven pounds a day, but it should be noted that this was late summer—after most of the spring spawning runs, during the period of least flow, and before the quickening pace of fish movement that comes to a southeastern river with fall rains and cooler temperatures.

Fishtraps in Alabama Law

Such traps are in evidence early in Alabama's history, judging by laws and legal records. An 1833 state law, echoing a provision in the Magna Carta more than six hundred years earlier, declares: "If any person or persons shall erect any fishdam on any such water courses, he or they shall open in the deepest channel . . . one-third of said water course."[18] That original law relating to fishtraps was probably aimed at keeping rivers open to small-craft navigation. Just after the Civil War, however, the first signs of a conservation ethic appear, reflecting an effort to preserve the rapidly declining fish resources. The first laws against poisoning streams came in 1865–66, for example.[19] In 1879 a state act called for fining anyone who prevented the passage of fish up the waters of any river or creek. With the continued decline of fish as well as game populations in the state, more drastic measures were called for, and in 1907 a state game and fish division was created along with a spate of new fishing regulations.[20] Meshing the traps with wire mesh was forbidden first. Then, as the older fishermen I talked to remembered it, the minimum space required between the fingers of the fishtrap was widened until finally fish of three and four pounds were slipping through, and a fishtrap was not worth the trouble it took to maintain.

Fishtraps and fish taken on them were clearly recognized as private property as early as 1876 by the Alabama code: "Any person who takes, in any manner, fish from a private artificial fish pond or lake, or fish trap, without the consent of the owner of such fish pond or lake, or fish trap, shall be guilty of a misdemeanor and shall on conviction, be fined no less than five, nor more than fifty dollars."[21]

Nearly a century and a half later, however, the fishtraps have all but disappeared. Most of the larger rivers in Alabama, as in the rest of the South, have been dammed for flood control, power generation, water storage, or recreation. Large impoundments drowned many a fishtrap site. Smith Lake, for example, flooded several fishtrap sites on the Sipsey known to older fishermen I spoke with back in the 1980s. Aerial surveying of the future Lake Harris on the Tallapoosa during a drought showed the remains of some sixty fishtrap wing dams in a ten-mile stretch of river.[22] The modern dams also cut off all the ocean runs of eel, great sturgeon, some species of shad, mullet, and perhaps even rockfish, the saltwater striped bass we usually associate with rivers of the Atlantic Coast.

In parts of the state, industrial pollution destroyed fish populations in those rivers still left undammed. In 1902, a part-time farmer and fisherman named Nichols launched a suit alleging this against Tutwiler Coal, Coke and Iron Company. Nichols's farm was situated on the Little Warrior River not far from Birmingham, and here he had a permanent fishtrap. Unfortunately for Nichols, fifteen coal washers with a daily capacity of 7,500 tons were built between 1893 and 1900 on two upstream tributaries, Village Creek and Five-Mile Creek. His suit claimed that fish had been killed and that "refuse and poisonous matter" had been deposited on his land. The lower courts all found in his favor, the siltation and fish kills being apparently beyond dispute and obviously traceable to the coal washers. But in 1905 the Alabama Supreme Court dismissed the suit against Tutwiler Coal on the rather technical grounds that the farmer should have sued all the coal companies that owned washers, not just the biggest one.[23] The end result seems to be that the farmer lost the fishtrap component of his livelihood, while the coal and iron companies, including Tutwiler, went merrily on their way. The progress of large-scale industrial corporations in this day and age, at least, was desirable enough to higher levels of government to make acceptable the loss of livelihood of mere individuals downstream.

A Game Warden's Lament

Despite the progress of game and fish laws, however, and the more troubling course of impoundment, channelization, and pollution, the rural culture over much of the state still preserves the memory of this classic means of catching fish. I first heard of the Mulberry River trap when some students (in the environmental history and folklore of Alabama class I was team-teaching with biology professor Bob Stiles, talked about in an earlier chapter) interviewed a Cullman County game warden in January 1977. This longtime warden lamented:

> Yeah, we'd blow the whole thing up, but they could put it back about as fast as we could blow up. Get a bunch of boys out there stacking rock, doesn't take long to put them back. [The stream is] I'd say, close to waist-deep down there where the trap is. They'll get any fish that comes on it, just about. Now a bass, they'll pretty well get off of it. But a catfish or a non-game fish, they'll stay up there. We have just about everything they've got anywhere in that river. Got drum, lots of drum; that's what they like to fish for, you know. They'd rather have the catfish, but they get more drum. And of course drum are real good eating, you know, when they're fresh. After they're out of the water awhile they're not so good; but if you cook them fresh they're just as good as anything. When you first get them out, just throw them in the pan. That's what they do mostly down there, just big picnics and all. Well, he does sell them. Customers out of Birmingham would line up there and get them whenever they was catching them real good. He denies it, but I know about it.[24]

According to a telephone conversation I had with that same warden some four years later, the fishtrap was still being blown up yearly. The owner had been ticketed by game wardens from three surrounding counties, but apparently the longtime judge who had just retired the year before had thought the practice was harmless: he merely fined the offender some token such as five dollars, and the latter was usually back at work on the fishtrap the next day. The Cullman County game warden thought that the new judge, however, might really "stick it to him" on any future conviction. He described the fishtrap owner as a likable farmer about seventy years old whose sons were grown and gone from home, and he gave me the man's name and phone number.[25]

Meeting Albert Cates, Fishtrap Owner/Operator

So a few days later I called the owner of the fishtrap, a Mr. Albert Cates, a bit concerned about how he would react to a stranger inquiring into this illegal operation. Even over the phone he was quite open and friendly, saying I should come up and see it: "Everybody else up here has, and most of them have taken home a sack of fish off it." With that encouragement I drove up to interview him, taking along my colleague Bob Stiles, professional ichthyologist and near-professional photographer. I took a

Figure 9.5. Albert Cates explaining the fishtrap

Another photograph of the Mulberry River fishtrap made that same afternoon in August 1981. Standing here are the author (forty years younger, *left*) and Albert Cates. (Photo courtesy of Bob Stiles.)

tape recorder; Bob took his camera. Mr. Cates was kind enough to spend most of an afternoon with us, walking us down to the river and showing us the trap.

Cates candidly admitted that "this fishtrap business is agin the law," but he said he could never stay away from it, from the time he first helped run one as a young man. "A fishtrap is the most fascinating thing I've ever fooled with," he said, and I think he may have bought this particular farm back in 1960 partly because it had this old trap site on it. According to oral history in the community, he said, that fishtrap site had been in continuous operation for at least a century, in successive ownership by three families: it was still called by the name of the first of those families, the old Stacks fishtrap, to distinguish it from the other fishtrap sites up- and downriver (there were at least three trap sites below this, two of them within a mile, and one or two on shoals upstream). "Old Man Stacks" used to take fish he had trapped and peddle them from a wagon in Empire and surrounding towns back when those currently old were young, according to Mr. Cates. Joe Boyd owned it for fifty years after that. Mr. Cates speculated that it was Native American in origin, though he had never heard or read anything specifically about that.

It became obvious during the interview with Mr. Cates that what really made a fishtrap worthwhile were the after-spawning downstream runs of various species of fish. He talked about two small species of sucker that ran first in later winter or early spring. One of these, which he called the redfin sucker, in a good run would come downstream onto the trap "at a thousand pounds an hour." He likened the sight to that of an industrial coal washer shaking coal out on the screen, and he said that if you didn't want your trap broken down by the weight of the fish you had better just take out the sets of fingers and let the water run straight through. Again he speculated about Native Americans, that they must have used this kind of small sucker to fertilize their corn hills: no other small fish were that numerous, or at least as easily available around corn planting time. Hard on the heels of the redfin sucker came the annual run of what he called the white sucker, averaging a pound apiece or less and also in impressive numbers. Then in late April came the big river redhorse, largest of the river suckers, averaging several pounds apiece.

The Drum Run

But what he waited for every year—the highlight of his whole year on the fishtrap and maybe of life in general—was the freshwater drum run in the last couple weeks of May or the first week of June. According to Mr. Cates, the drum in the river would have all worked their way upstream to "lay out," and with the first good rain after spawning they could come down the river in great numbers. I asked him what the signs were, and he said that you needed a change in the water and some good rains upstream. The best time was the first good rain after an extended dry period: "I'm going to tell you just like it is. I've sat there on that riverbank and watched that trap and it looked like the river was just perfect, like everything was ready and the time of the year was just right. And I'd get to thinking somebody had a net across the river and had them blocked coming down [laughter]. And they'd start a-running, and you'd wonder where they was all coming from."

These post-spawn late-spring drum runs on the Mulberry were as short as four hours or as long as twenty-four hours, but no longer than that. In one recent year, he had watched the trap on a likely day until ten at night, and nothing had happened, so he went to bed leaving one of his sons to watch. At half past one his son shook him awake, asking him whether he wanted to come see them run—"because he knew I did"—and in four hours they caught enough fish "to have filled a short wheel-base pickup truck level-bed full" of drum from one to five pounds, even after throwing back all the bigger fish, which are less tasty. They cleaned some of the fish while standing out on the trap and then brought them to the bank and rolled the fish in meal and salt to batter them. Two or three gallons of cooking oil in a wash pot over a wood fire were heated until a match would strike in the oil, and then the fish were thrown in to cook. Mr. Cates would eat his on a piece of bread to keep from burning his fingers.[26]

Everybody I spoke with about Albert Cates, including the game warden, said that except for "this fishtrap business" he was a model citizen. He was known locally, only half-jokingly, as "mayor of Arkadelphia" for his lobbying efforts in Montgomery on behalf of this unincorporated town. And his fascination with the fishtrap may not have been matched but was certainly widely shared over the years in the community. When the fish were running, word would spread rapidly along the grapevine, and often fifteen or twenty men would be on or near the trap on every promising night. The drum run and fish fry could attract fifty or one hundred. Said Mr. Cates: "People all over the country know when you're catching fish." It seems to have been a democratic gathering, with an occasional state legislator or businessperson coming to rub shoulders with the local farmers. Mr. Cates attributed his light sentencing at the hand of the former judge to the fact that the judge was raised farther up the Mulberry and had fished a trap as a boy; he knew that rough fish were being caught, not game fish, and he "would have liked to have fished with us."

In the last years of the fishtrap all Mr. Cates had to do was get on the phone and tell a few folks that he was going to rebuild the trap. They would build the four-foot-long, six-foot-wide sets of fingers up in the chicken house, where there was electricity to run the saws, and then load them on a truck and carry them to the river prefabricated. In this late mechanized phase a log skidder could apparently rake up rocks for the wing dams in short order. In Mr. Cates's words, "everybody wanted in on it," right up to volunteering to pay for the three hundred dollars' worth of lumber involved.

The fascination may be an atavistic one, stirred by one of the few migrations still intact in the region. The elk and woodland buffalo that used to migrate seasonally through Alabama are long gone. The passenger pigeons that stormed through in flocks of hundreds of thousands, breaking tree limbs by their weight like ice storms, fell to market gunners by the turn of the last century. The great runs of all the ocean-run fish were ended by dams during the past hundred years. On small, free-flowing rivers, however, seasonal migrations still go on under waters dingy and moving fast from recent rains, and their full scope was seen until recently only by the watchers on the fishtrap. Their feeling for it was obviously akin to the passion of bird-watchers and duck hunters spellbound by other surviving fragments of the great seasonal migrations of Native and early European colonial days.

End of an Era?

The new judge indeed ended the yearly running of the old Stacks trap. It was never rebuilt after these photographs were taken in 1981, and nothing much is left of the trap or even the wing dams now. For a time Mr. Cates toyed with the idea of trying to get it legalized for historical reasons: "I know it's older than any covered bridge in the state," he told me. He also said he'd thought about donating the trap site and a few acres around it to the state of Alabama for a park, if the state would operate it and let schoolchildren learn about the river and its fish by seeing it and studying it. What a nice idea. I personally know an ichthyologist and photographer who would like to see it rebuilt under special permit and run for scientific studies of populations of river fish and measurement of spawning runs. His interest is purely scientific, of course, but he wants to be there himself when the drum run is on.

chapter ten

River Redhorse and the Seasonal Snaring Thereof

It was in 1979 that I was first taken "redhorsing." I knew nothing much about the fish we were going after other than that it was a big river sucker with a red tail and that somehow people noosed or lassoed it. Looking back, I probably should have read up on it a little.[1]

Two Superb Books on the Fishes of Alabama

These days, if you would like to learn more of what science knows about this fish, you're in luck. Alabama now has not one but two great books on fishes of the state. Each has full-color illustrations, precise range maps, and descriptions of size, habits, and habitat of the river redhorse (and hundreds more species of fresh- and brackish-water fish), plus keys to identification and extensive bibliographies. "Fishes," incidentally, is not used here in this paragraph and in the titles of both these books just to sound King James English archaic, as in "loaves and fishes"; to ichthyologists "fish" means one or more individuals of the same species, and "fishes" means fish from two or more species.

In 1996 a team of scholars led by Scott Mettee of the Geological Survey of Alabama published *Fishes of Alabama and the Mobile Basin*.[2] Their coverage of the river redhorse, which is given a two-page spread, is typical of their treatment of each of the three hundred fish species covered by the book. On the left-hand page is a large color map of Alabama's river drainage system, with a small black dot placed where each of the 111 known scientific collections of this particular species was made, to date, and below that large map is a small black-and-white inset map of the entire United States, delineating the total range of the fish from its southernmost occurrence in the very south of the states of Alabama and Mississippi to its radiation way up the Missouri, Mississippi, and Ohio Rivers. Then at the top of the right-hand, facing page is a vivid full-color photograph of what appears to be either a live or a very recently preserved river redhorse, set against a shaded turquoise background. This full side view shows off the beautiful red dorsal (top), caudal (tail), and anal (bottom rear) fins of an adult male in breeding color. The silvery sheen off the scales makes the image appear almost three-dimensional. From the habitat and biology section of the text a reader learns that this fish prefers mid- to large-sized streams, with moderate to swift currents over sand, gravel, and cobble; and that it seems to thrive on the little imported Asian clam *Corbicula* that has colonized most Alabama waterways. The book also notes that adults in breeding condition were collected or seen spawning in April, a fact particularly important for the main subject under discussion here.

This *Fishes of Alabama and the Mobile Basin* entry also gives the etymology and origin of the Latin-based binomial nomenclature (a noun for the genus and an adjective for the species, a tradition established by the Swedish biologist Carl Linnaeus back in the eighteenth century) as follows: *Moxostoma*, "mouth to suck," and *carinatum*, "keeled." It was described and named by a nineteenth-century American biologist named Edward Drinker Cope, so a formal listing of the fish is *Moxostoma carinatum* (Cope). Interestingly enough, Cope himself is vividly remembered in the field of American biology for his epic feud with paleontologist Othniel Charles Marsh, a bitterly personal competition to unearth new dinosaur specimens that came to be called "the Bone Wars." Originally friends and fellow fossil collectors, they later let personal jealousies escalate to the point that they were poaching in each other's newly discovered fossil beds, bribing away the other's workers, and carrying on what you might call scientific character assassination of each other. And this was all by two independently wealthy Americans, each proficient in the German language, who became, respectively, professors at the University of Pennsylvania and Yale University—personalities you'd have thought secure enough in their own positions to be beyond such jealousies, but obviously not. Whatever the strain on each of them personally, the field of biology was arguably left the richer for their feud. In the end Marsh found the most new dinosaurs, but Cope published upward of a thousand scientific papers, and the chief American journal in the field of ichthyology and herpetology is still called *Copeia*.

The second great Alabama fish book came out in 2004, eight years after the first one, though it had been in preparation longer. Its authors were Professors Herb Boschung and Rick Mayden, both then of the University of Alabama, successive curators of its ichthyological collection for some forty years. Titled *Fishes of Alabama*, this book is even heavier than its predecessor.[3] It must weigh ten pounds, and each page is ten inches tall by a full eleven inches wide. It was published by the Smithsonian Institution (and beautifully printed in Italy), and the introduction is by the most famous living native Alabamian biologist, Harvard's E. O. Wilson. The space allotted to the river redhorse in this book is roughly the same space in square inches as in the earlier fish book, but instead of a single photograph, two small, hand-drawn and painted images of a juvenile and a female river redhorse head up the text and are repeated in larger size in the plates in the middle of the book. The artist's illustrations of the fish are magnificent, seeming to me to be equal or superior to anything done with birds by Roger Tory Peterson or David Allen Sibley in their standard field guides. There are state and national range maps similar to those in the earlier fish book. In the text more information is provided on how the species is endangered by siltation, which, among other things, kills the mollusks on which the river redhorse primarily feeds. There is also a much more detailed account of its spawning behavior—especially germane to the latter part of this chapter—including mention of a debate between university ichthyologists and fishery biologists on whether the male river redhorse purposefully builds a nest or courts females at spawning sites.

There are at least two reasons why Alabama has two full-color, sophisticated books on fish(es) of the state when other states are lucky to have just one as good as either of these. One is that Alabama has more species of fish than most any other state, making it a rich area to explore. The other reason is that these books emerged in the heat of an academic rivalry that is apparently well known to the state's ichthyological community, at least its older members—a sort of miniature Bone Wars. What I've heard about it is absolutely fascinating, but I'm not qualified to relate it; maybe somebody who is will write it up someday. I would add in the interest of full disclosure that academic rivalries and jealousies probably have played a more significant role in academic studies generally than most of us academics care to admit (and though it pains me to say it, in my academic life such motivation is not among the least). But long story short, what a fortunate state is Alabama, in which one can check out both fish books in a local library, open them side by side to the *Moxostoma carinatum* (Cope) sections, and enjoy a comparative literary and visual feast of scientific information.

Figure 10.1. Small, male river redhorse

This small male ("horse") was snared off a shoal at Bulldog Bend. Note the rough little spawning-season tubercles on its head and caudal and anal fins.

But even the best science has its limitations, of course, and can have no valid comment to make on the nearly spiritual belief that the river redhorse was created to be snared, in due season, by good old boys (and sometimes girls) on the Cahaba River.

THE REDHORSE SPAWNING SEASON

That due season, or peak spawning season for the river redhorse—the only time it is "tame" enough to snare—is about one week that usually falls between April 10 and May 10. If you had to pick one day to be on some proper fast-water gravel shoals of the Cahaba or the Little Cahaba (the lower one that heads up near Montevallo, not one of the other two Little Cahabas farther north), you should make it around April 20. But it changes somewhat year to year, probably because of variations in winter and spring temperature and rainfall. Scientists might be able to pinpoint the spawning week by water temperature, but the old tried-and-true folkloric guide is to use markers on the unfolding plant calendar of spring itself. Once I heard a Bibb County redhorse fisherman say that he looked for the flowers of the bush ivy, as what most of us call mountain laurel (*Kalmia latifolia*) is colloquially known there, to start to open along the river. But my chief instructor taught me some forty years ago to watch for the tulip poplar (*Liriodendron tulipifera*) in bloom: not freshly opened but fully, maturely open, as when a spring breeze can tilt the wide-opened blossoms enough to cause a light drizzle of nectar to fall on you from a hundred feet up.

That chief instructor was Mott Lovejoy, and it took me a while to find him. There's a catchy phrase attributed by some to the Buddha, by others to the Theosophists, that when the student is ready the teacher will appear. I don't think it's true. First, there are so many questions I've been ready to have answered for years and the teacher has never appeared; and second, I recognize just how lucky I have sometimes been to find a great teacher. Here was the process of finding Mott. I first heard about the snaring of redhorse sometime in 1978 from Joe Grammar, then proprietor of a popular canoe rental business at Bulldog Bend on the (lower) Little Cahaba. He told me about people using a twelve- or fourteen-foot cane pole tipped with a loop made of a guitar string, with a little piece of lead on the bottom of the wire loop, to catch the big river sucker by the tail. He said that he had never done it but had watched people doing it from his vantage point on the bridge where Bibb County Road 65 crosses the river there at Bulldog Bend. Mr. Grammar said there were just a few around who did it, not the whole community. Most of them were men who went by themselves, though occasionally one would take his wife. He had seen them come back with washtubs full from the Little Cahaba and the "Big River" (meaning the main Cahaba). He directed me to Mott Lovejoy and his uncle Morgan Lovejoy a few miles down the road in the community of Sixmile, known practitioners of the sport, warning me in particular about Morgan Lovejoy's sense of humor and predicting that he would "break one off" in us before the end of any conversation.

Stories from Morgan Lovejoy

So I showed up, unannounced, at Morgan Lovejoy's home in Sixmile the afternoon of December 22, 1978, with a folklore student in tow and a tape recorder in hand. Mr. Lovejoy, a bit unsure who we were and what we wanted, talked to us through the screen door for a while, then warmed up when he understood the topic under research. He took us around the house to show us the difference between Asian bamboo and the native cane, one of the latter stand being better than an inch in diameter. He told us he was born in 1895, which made him eighty-three or so at the time of the interview. He said he had last been to the river with his grandson Tommy Campbell, then in his twenties, that past spring. He had watched Tommy snare twelve big redhorse one after the other and not lose a fish. We walked back up to the house then, and with Mr. Lovejoy's approval we turned on the tape recorder.[4]

Part of what we got were jokes that started out as what we thought were serious stories and on which we were taking notes, to Mr. Lovejoy's great amusement when the joke broke on us. He talked about his brother Joe, who was once crappie fishing with a small hook and float down on the Big River, along with his wife and young daughter who had a Kodak camera. Joe had already caught a good many crappie when he hung some other sort of fish so big he knew the little crappie rig would never hold it. So Joe said to his daughter, according to Mr. Lovejoy: "C'mere, I got something large here and I'd like to get a picture of it if I could, if I could get it to the top. And says she walked up, and about the time she walked up that thing come up right lengthways, its back; and she snapped a picture, and he give a flounce and broke his line, and sent the negative to Birmingham, and when the picture come back *it* weighed fifteen pounds!"

But in a serious vein his memories about redhorsing went back for six decades and more. He had moved from the little community of Randolph, also in Bibb County, to the vicinity of Bulldog Bend in 1912, and one Charlie Edwards got him started gigging and snaring soon after he arrived. Trying to think back about others who in his earliest recollections fished redhorse, he named "old man Burns McGuire; he was a terrible fisherman" ("terrible" here meaning passionate, not inexpert!).

Morgan Lovejoy set us straight on a few other matters that Joe Grammar, an observer from afar, had not clearly understood. He described the spawning of river redhorse in a swift but smooth-water gravel run, from one to two feet deep, when a "mare" (female) would lean over on one side a little and begin vibrating against a "horse" (male) on that side to keep her steady, and often a third fish, another male, would come in then to press against her other side. As to the snaring of same, a twenty-foot cane pole was sometimes too short; you should cut a cane pole as long as you could find. The guitar wire noose described by Mr. Grammar was in reality a brass wire noose, softer and not so springy, with a one-ounce lead weight made to slip along the wire of the noose. The sliding lead weight was to drag along the bottom and so keep the plane of the wire loop at right angles to the current.

The overall aim was not to catch the redhorse by the tail with the noose, or snare, but to catch it just behind the gills and in front of the pectoral fins. Too big a loop and it would go completely over the fish without snaring it. When you got the noose positioned just right, you had hold of a strong fish on average between three and six pounds, with head and tail free, and no give in the wire or strong cord it was tied to. "They'll horse, too; they'll pull. They're a lot of fun," said Morgan Lovejoy, probably explaining the origin of the common name of the fish.

Mr. Lovejoy told one story about a time in the distant past when (I wish now we had asked exactly when) the sport became more popular, and whole families would go. He particularly remembered an "old man Turner" and his wife and son-in-law fishing on the shoals at Trot's Ford: "Well, old man Turner, he'd get out in front, and that'd run them off of the bed, see. And it was real swift there. And there was one extra redhorse there, and he hung it, and that water was swift. And his son-in-law was right there. And that redhorse jerked him down, with the help of that swift water, and his son-in-law grabbed the pole and he went down over them shoals. He was bony, they called him Bones. His son-in-law went down over there and you could see them skinny knees sticking up [laughter] and the redhorse got loose. See, if you give them slack they'd get loose."

He told another story from the more recent past:

Now this sounds unreasonable. A few years ago, I had a pickup truck here. And my son [and a nephew and one other person], we were down below Centreville, down on Big River. And we learned how . . . we used to put them on a string, you know, staging, trotline or something. And they'd slosh so 'til they'd tear their gills out and then they'd die quick. We learned to get tow sacks and put four or five in each sack and tie the sack to a sapling somewhere in the water. And we had so many when we come out of there . . . you know, fishermen can tell some big ones, but this is the truth. We got so many that we carried them out in those sacks and poured them in my pickup and that bed was, it was Chevrolet, that bed was half full, now, of redhorse. And those eggs was all over them, all slimy, you know, them eggs, slime and all. And I knew the fellow that had charge of the Waterworks at Centreville . . . and so I just connected up that big hose, and backed that truck down there over a drain, you know, and washed 'em out, just washed all that slime and eggs off.

As he remembered it, his son and nephew then peddled the still-living fish in an African American neighborhood where live fish were always in high demand, selling them for a dollar apiece no matter what the size of the fish.

Looking back at our questions on this tape from the point of view of someone who has since snared redhorse himself, I can see how vague on the actual technique of it we were. Morgan Lovejoy, of course, understood that at the time. Late in the interview he said, "Oh, I wish you could go one time. You see Mott and tell him you want to go with him." I didn't need any more encouragement.

Education at the Hands of Mott Lovejoy

A month later, on January 25, 1979, I caught up with J. Winfred ("Mott") Lovejoy at his home not far from Sixmile. He was about forty-eight or forty-nine years old to my thirty-four, a real outdoorsman who lived for the turkey and redhorse seasons but whose recent heart surgery had made his wife, Nellie Ree, nervous about him being out alone. He was tall and muscular and gruff talking, but with the friendly playfulness of a child, and he was one of the nicest people I ever met. Years later, I'd sometimes get a phone call at my home in Birmingham that would start out with a deep, gravelly, "Hey, boy," and then silence, no names or other introductions. I'd say, "Is that you, Mott? Where are you?" and it would usually be Brookwood Hospital, where he went when his blood pressure spiked uncontrollably.

Mott had his share of the family's sense of humor that we'd already seen in his uncle. In the shed where Mott kept his cane poles there were also some beaver traps hanging on the wall—jawed leg-hold traps each connected by a foot or two of chain to a steel ring, the ring for positioning around a notched sapling driven into the bottom of the creek. When I commented on the traps, Mott said that he'd only known real pain twice in his life, and that pain had been associated with this kind of trap. I was intrigued, and asked him how so. He said that one day he had waded out of the river in his overalls, answering a call of nature, to "drop trou" and squat on the bank. When he did it triggered a beaver trap hidden in the sand, which snapped shut on his nether parts. Then Mott was quiet, no more details forthcoming and the story seemingly over. I winced at the imagined pain inflicted and said something like, "Wow, what in the world was the second time?" And Mott, with a slow smile at how well things were going, looked at me and drawled, "That would have been when I took the slack out of the chain."

Mott had logged more hours of redhorse observation than all the scholars of fish behavior in all the universities in America put together, I suppose. He had the modesty of a true expert: "These things, we've watched them. 'Course we don't know that much about it, what goes on. All we know is what we see, you know, watching them bed. And those horses will go there and root this bed out. And maybe that'll go on three or four days before she [the mare] ever shows up."

I asked him whether you could snare the males at that time, or whether they would be too skittish or wild, and he said: "Yeah, you can catch them, but they're harder to catch. But whenever they start [spawning], when the mare gets there to lay the eggs, you can watch on both sides of her, just like that [holding his hands parallel, thumb side up] and she'll be right between 'em. And they'll get right on both sides of 'em like that and you'll see 'em just go to working, just like that [hands still parallel, trembling in unison]. And you can see the muddy water just a-flying. And then they'll squirt it [milt] out on those eggs, and that'll stick it to the rocks and fertilize them. And then they'll hatch in just a few days. And then they'll do that and then she'll drift off."

When I asked whether the spawning was discontinuous, Mott answered: "No, she'll come back afore long, you know, go to drifting back in there. And when she starts in there, you can catch 'em then. I don't care if he is wild, he won't run [laughter]." I asked whether they stayed to guard their eggs for a while, like bass or bream on the bed, and Mott said: "No, they're gone, and you can see small fish just eating them [eggs]—minnows and gars just ease up on the bed and you can see them little old suckers eating them, while you're fishing. But it's real interesting."

Later when we fished together—and I'd try to get down at least one day every April, while he was still living—he taught me to look for the bed horse, usually one of the smaller males that was a sort of watchman for the beds on the entire gravel bar: if you caught him off his spot, or in some way frightened him away, most of the others would follow his lead and vacate the spawning beds for a good while.

Later, while wade fishing for bass on Buck Creek, a tributary of the Cahaba that runs through Helena, I chanced on a redhorse fisherman. I also heard about redhorsing that had been done on the main Cahaba near Caldwell Mill Road just south of Birmingham, and even near Whites Chapel in the very upper stretch of the river, considerably east and a little north of Birmingham. When I asked Mott what he thought the limits on redhorse bedding in the river were, during that first interview, he replied: "They'll bed from one end of this river to the other. But most of the time there's just a bed, maybe, half as big as this room [speaking in a room maybe fourteen feet on a side]. And you can catch, oh man, no telling how many right there. And they just come for—it'll be the onlyest place for a mile they'll bed—and they'll come from all, from both ways there, see. And man, they'll just fill it up."

That first April, in 1979, when Mott called me and told me to come down because the redhorse were on the bed, the river had muddied up from a hard rain before I got there. We sat at Bulldog Bend on a child's metal A-frame swing set, minus the swings, that somebody had carried out onto an underwater gravel bar, and we dragged our three-and-a-half-inch-diameter wire snares in the fast muddy water, fishing blind and coming up empty. At the time I had no idea just how powerful a big fish—broadside to a swift current on a line and wire with no give—could be. I'd probably have been jerked off the swing set had I actually snared one.

The largest redhorse Mott had ever seen caught on the Little Cahaba, an estimated nine pounds, had been caught on or just after a night fishing trip: "I was about, I guess, fifteen years old. Daddy and me fished at that thing all night trying to catch him, and we couldn't. Every time we'd start to catch him, he'd back up under some bushes. There was a bunch of people there that night, and Dad and me just give out, and so we laid down to go to sleep, woke up the next morning, and this old boy was laying there about half sloughed [rhymed with "glued," and meant "drunk"], I call it. When I woke up, he'd been up there and caught him, and was letting the water drip off his tail in my face, you know. He'd slipped up there and caught him. Daddy 'n' me had fished at him all night, and couldn't catch him."

His favorite memory of night fishing, though, was this: "Oh, I caught—one night Uncle Morgan and Daddy and Uncle Morgan's youngest boy were there, down, well that was down close to the mouth of the Little River where it runs into the Cahaba. And it was cool that night. And I had an old green pole. You usually tried to fish with a dry pole, you know, on account of the thing, you have to hold it out on the end, and it just gets heavy. And they'd been wild that day and they'd just got right at the right stage, they fished. And a carbide lamp—did you ever see one?" I told him I had, that I knew how you could adjust it to cast a broad beam, and Mott went on:

> Well, it's broader, too, but they just blend in the water better, too. They're not as bright a light. And I caught, well I got out there and cut me a pole, you know, green. And them things got so tame that I was just holding the light with one hand and fishing with one hand, just had my pole choked up, you know, and had part of it sticking back behind me, and it wasn't so heavy then, you know, with it balanced in your hand. And they was on the bank asleep, now, I couldn't get them in there; but it was cool. I'd catch them things like that, and I just threw

them out there all night long. I caught one after a while, and instead of him going up and down the river, or out, he just come right back between my feet with it, you know. Well naturally he just broke my pole when he just doubled it up. Being a green pole, it just, you know, broke it down, but it didn't break it completely off. And when he broke it, I seen what happened, and I just turned and run with him, and just like a mule pulling a wagon or something, and run out on him. Then I had to quit, I just went out there then and went to bed. And then I had them in a, well, I caught thirty-two that night there [that] weighed a hundred and twenty pounds. That'd give you some idea about what they are. 'Course that was in the Little Cahaba, but now they get bigger than that in Big Cahaba.

The second spring I fished for redhorse with Mott on the Little Cahaba, in 1980, the water was clearer and we caught them in the classic manner. Even when the visibility was marginal, with shadows dappling the surface, most of the time the first thing you'd see of a fish would be that bright red tail fin, undulating in the water for all the world like a piece of red rag hung on a rock and waving in the current. Then the whole fish would gradually materialize. When you had one sitting still in a bed, the technique was to lower the wire snare quietly into the current a few feet upstream from the fish, which would be hugging the bottom in its shallow depression in the fast water, and bring your loop down with the current. You tried to keep the line and wire as vertical as possible while still letting the lead weight drag the bottom a little (so as to keep the wire loop square across the current) and so maneuver the snare over the fish's head. If you missed the fish and it was still tame enough to sit there, you'd gently raise your snare, swing it upstream over the fish, lower it in the water again, and make another pass at the fish. Two fishermen in tandem could stand side by side and do the same thing, as long as they dragged and then lifted and swung upstream in unison.

In clear water you could watch a fish shrug or twist when the noose went around it, and then you could pull the cane pole up to tighten the snare. More often, though, the fish would bolt at the touch and tighten the noose itself. If the fish ran upstream or downstream, the cane pole would absorb some of the tremendous pull, but if the fish darted straight away from you it was like being tied to a pickup truck. You, the fisherman, were often knee-deep or better in fast water, with the current trying to take gravel out from under your feet and you trying to keep tension on the snare as the big fish ran and flopped. As Mott said, on average you were lucky to get two of every ten you snared to the bank. Most often you missed the fish, and your wire snare collapsed. At that point you had to hand-walk your long cane pole up to the tip while letting the butt of the pole trail downstream in the current, reset the snare by opening it to the appropriate three-and-a-half-inch diameter and setting a bend in the wire to keep it there, and then hand-walk down to the butt of the pole again while trying not to jerk the snare shut. Mott prided himself on the smallness of his loop, which required more skill to maneuver around the fish but which resulted in more proper hookups. He kept a close eye on me in this regard as well, because after a period of catching no fish, I tended to widen my loop to make up for my lack of skill.

Whenever Mott kept fish at all, he only kept the males, or horses. The community conservation ethic, as long as he could remember, had always been to release all females to spawn and spawn again. Here are my field notes verbatim on that day (and night), May 2, 1980:

> Went down to Mott Lovejoy's in Sixmile, Bibb Co., AL, got there before 2 p.m., we headed down toward the Little Cahaba within a mile or two where it goes into the main Cahaba, or just little & big river, in local parlance. Drove pickup down by river at a shoal—a gravel bar cut the river in half & a whitewater rapid maybe 4 ft deep went around it. On the upper part of the gravel bar (upstream), the Redhorse were in prime breeding season. The other spot we checked they were gone, apparently finished. This population—you could see 20 at a time working across the river when we stopped the truck—may have been delayed by heavy fishing pressure—remains of last night's bonfire—& sure enough about dusk some other folks came in. Mott had fished on that same shoal as a kid, & his father & uncle fished it since 1913. We caught 23 fish, the smallest more than 2 pounds, the largest 6 and 7. Caught 6 mares, returned them to water; kept 17 horses. Kept them alive in a burlap sack tied in the current. Bag must have weighed 50 lbs. or more. You could see 3 or 4 in the same hole sometimes, & sometimes a frenzied burst of activity—"the mud'd just fly"—was the way Mott put it; he said that was the climax of the breeding, a horse coming up on either side of a mare. Mott says they press against her to help the eggs squirt out. All the fish we caught would squirt milt or eggs. Stayed till after midnight. Mott had electric headlamp, though he said carbide would have spooked the fish less.

My finest memory of fishing with Mott is when he, his younger cousin Tommy Campbell, and I went in Mott's pickup to a long shoal on the main Cahaba River some miles downstream from Centreville. We went through two locked gates, to which Mott had been given the keys by the landowners (he had a long familiarity with them), pulled the truck down to the river, and found no fish on the nearest shoal. Mott sent the two of us as scouts, one up and one down the river to the next gravel bars, and on the first gravel bar downstream there was a concentration of what must have been a couple of hundred redhorse, looking like small brown sharks holding in the current all across the yellow gravel bar, occasionally rippling the water with slashing runs at an encroaching rival. Mott said it was one of the biggest and ripest concentrations he'd ever seen. We—almost entirely Mott and Tommy, of course—landed forty-four horses and three mares, the latter returned to the water. That was May 7, 1983, and my field notes say that I'd seen my first tulip poplar bloom a week and a half earlier.

Mott always cut his own cane poles, from twenty to twenty-five feet long. While they were still green, he tied a bundle of three with cord every foot or so along their

Figure 10.2.
Wire and lead weight snare, with cord

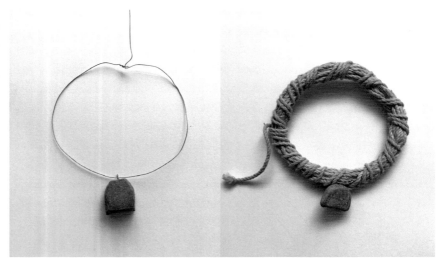

One of Tommy Campbell's snares, complete with homemade weight. When preparing to fish with it, "make it look like an apple." For storage, loop most of heavy cotton cord in the same circle as made by the snare; just save a little for spiraling around to lock it into place.

whole length as tightly as he could pull the cord, to begin the straightening process. Then he tied a rope to the gathered butt ends, threw the rope over a tall tree limb, hoisted the butts up until the tip ends cleared the ground, and finally tied a rock to the gathered tip ends as a weight so that all three poles would dry and cure straight from butt to tip. He made his wire snares from twenty-gauge brass wire from the hardware store, when he couldn't get twenty-four-gauge steel wire smuggled out to him from friends who worked at the old Hays Aircraft business in Birmingham: the steel wire would hardly ever break, while the brass wire, especially after it had been bent and rebent a few times, would sometimes pop under the strain of a big fish. Mott molded his own lead sinkers around little wire hangers, fairly flat sinkers to keep the wire snare close to the bottom, and with rounded edges so as not to catch on rocks. He tied stout nylon or cotton cord to his twenty inches or so of wire that made the actual snare, then fixed the cord to the tip of the cane pole with a knot, and finally spiraled the rest of the cord most of the way down the cane pole and tied it off. This last was to strengthen the cane pole and keep the tip from being broken off in the tremendous strain of trying to lift a thrashing five-pound fish completely clear of the water at the end of a twenty-foot-long lever.

Historical Musings on the Sport

Despite all the nylon, steel, brass, and lead used in this later phase of the sport, Mott was still convinced—as am I—that this noosing or snaring of fish had to be a surviving relic of a Native American fishing technique. John Swanton, for example, in his *Indians of the Southeastern United States*, quoted the English traveler Robert Beverley from 1705 on the Native American snaring of sturgeon: "The Indian way of Catching Sturgeon, when they came into the narrow part of the Rivers, was by a Man's clapping a Noose over their Tail, and by keeping fast his hold. Thus a Fish finding itself intangled, wou'd flounce, and often pull him under Water, and then that Man was counted a Cockarouse, or brave Fellow, that wou'd not let go; till with Swimming, Wading, and Diving, he had tired the Sturgeon, and brought it ashore."[5]

There is, however, an alternative view that such noosing might have been brought in as well by European settlers. A *Boat House and Net House* pamphlet from the Welsh Folk Museum, for example, talks about how "a wire loop mounted on a stick to slip over a salmon's tail was a common poacher's tool in Wales and probably many other parts of Europe."[6]

Figure 10.3.
Mott Lovejoy
with large
redhorse he'd
just snared

Mott had been given this picture around 1956,
he said, and gave it to the author to be copied
(on a copy stand, in those days).

Whatever the origins of this snaring, in modern times it seems to be limited to central Alabama; at least I've found no evidence of surviving counterparts anywhere else in the United States. Through the years, Mott Lovejoy and his dwindling band of fellow redhorse snarers were discovered, celebrated, and rediscovered by journalists and biologists as well as by historians and folklorists. Mott took sportswriters from the Tuscaloosa paper out redhorsing as early as 1956, and he was sent a copy of a black-and-white photo the paper had run of him with a six-pound redhorse; Mott gave it to me so I could make a copy of it on a camera copy stand back in those predigital days.

In 1966 a couple of district fishery biologists wrote an article called "'Redhorse Are Shoaling' Cry Calls Fishermen to Cahaba" in the journal *Alabama Conservation*. In it they talk about the beauty of the river redhorse and the way the Cahaba River is its last main stand in a state whose rivers were even at that time increasingly impounded and polluted. They very briefly discuss snaring, but the accompanying picture shows them with rods and reels, casting weighted treble hooks to foul-hook the redhorse and so snatch them off the beds.[7] Mott would have taken exception to such unsportsmanlike taking of his favorite fish; not only would it have required little in the way of skill, it would have permanently damaged the mares.

Clarke Stallworth, then associate editor for the *Birmingham News*, had an article in the paper on May 27, 1984, called "Romance with Red Horse Is One Family's Tradition." It's about Charlie and Frank Griffin and their traditional hunt for spawning redhorse on the Cahaba. The article is poorly informed on fish, calling the redhorse "vegetarian, nibbling on moss and grass on the bottom," but it is insightful on the people and their fascination with this seasonal migration.[8]

Mike Bolton, outdoors writer for that same *Birmingham News*, had a good article in the Sunday edition of May 3, 1987 (note that this too is a May publication date, obviously hard on the heels of the usual late April to early May redhorse bedding season on the Cahaba), on members of this same Griffin family. The article was called "Redhorse Roping: Griffin Brothers Keep Tradition Alive with Three-Day Vigil on the Cahaba River Shoals." Accompanying the article is the best action picture of snaring redhorse I've ever seen, captioned "Helena's Frank Griffin wrestles a hefty redhorse sucker from the Cahaba River." One interesting note from the article is on how the tasty but very bony fish was formerly pressure-cooked and canned, and thus became a year-round meal that would stick to the ribcage when times were hard.[9] These days almost no redhorse fishermen keep fish, either horses or mares; it's all for the sport, or the seasonal ritual.

As with all my enthusiasms, I inflicted this newest one on the members of my family who could tolerate it (not my wife or vegetarian-inclined younger daughter, Katy!). When my son, Josh, was around seven years old we were down wade fishing the rocky shoals just above where Sixmile Creek comes into the Little Cahaba, and I saw a big river redhorse, oddly enough, sitting still, leaning against a rock in a slow current. Looking back, I suppose it was resting after having spawned. I happened to have a snare in my little portable tackle box, so I fixed it up on Josh's rod, and after a few passes he maneuvered the loop around the head of the fish. The fish thereupon darted upstream, and I think if I hadn't grabbed the waistband of Josh's blue jeans he would have been pulled into the river. The fish got away, but both of us, I think, will always remember it. My older daughter and her current boyfriend caught river redhorse on a canoe run with me down the Little Cahaba. Later, when Josh was in high school, he and I took a Mexican exchange student who was staying with us down to Bulldog Bend. The exchange student snared a big redhorse before I ever even got down to the river from the car.

Flowering Trees and Documentary Films

By the early 1980s my folklore class had evolved from an occasional January mini-mester experimental class into a regular class every other spring semester. One requirement was to pick out a tulip poplar bud on some low tree limb on campus and submit a color pencil drawing of the same at a one-to-one scale every week from the first of February through a mature bloom in April. In February the end of the little twig mostly just changes color from week to week, going from brownish to greenish, but with March everything begins to happen in a rush: little leaves folded in half come out and unfold one by one; five, six, or seven of them each grow larger and change from light to dark green. Then the terminal bud swells and bursts open as a flower almost overnight.

This last event hopefully coincided with our scheduled class canoe trip down the Little Cahaba, courtesy of my friend Randy Haddock of the Cahaba River Society. We started such trips from Bulldog Bend—or, later, from the Glades a mile and a half downstream—and took out at the Highway 26 bridge on the main Cahaba. About half the prospective canoe trips had to be canceled or moved because of dangerously high water from the spring rains, and for another quarter we never saw a redhorse, much less caught one. But Randy would point out such sights as the red dogwood on the banks, the wild columbine in bloom, the hatched swarms of a rare aquatic moth, the rare mussels, and such, making the trip always a rewarding one just in terms of scenery and natural history.

In spring 2008, a student named Josh Crute took the folklore course and was on one of the April canoe trips on the Little Cahaba that didn't sight a redhorse. But the following spring he was one of six students in Samford's journalism department's documentary film class, and Josh's proposal of a documentary film on this strange-sounding snaring of redhorse was accepted as the major class project. The students interviewed me about it, and although Mott Lovejoy, my old guide, had been gone for about fifteen years, I drove down to Sixmile and looked up Tommy Campbell—Mott's younger cousin, whom Mott and I had fished with on that one memorable day over a quarter century before. Tommy was still as passionate in pursuit of redhorse every April as he had been as a young man. The highlight of the film, and the whole semester, was when Tommy found an unusually large number of red-horse spawning on a river bar on the main Cahaba, and four of the six students were able to get out of their Friday classes (or just cut them for this most worthy cause). It was a beautiful sunny day. Randy Haddock and I were there. We all caught fish, and we were all filmed catching fish with Tommy talking about it. The six students who made up the film class dedicated the film to the memory of Mott Lovejoy, although they'd only heard about him from Tommy and me.

They were proud of their documentary, and justifiably so, I thought. They had included an interview with Beth Stewart and Randy Haddock of the Cahaba River Society. These two explained among other things why the redhorse chose spawning sites with a particular size of gravel or cobble, because the only eggs that survived were those that were forced down into the gravel. There, sheltered but still washed with moving water flowing down through the cobble, they could develop in this most vulnerable phase of life. There was a special showing of the documentary on campus, and the students later entered it in some film competitions. The title of the final cut, about forty-four minutes long, was *Redhorse: A Cahaba River Tradition.*[10] I don't think it ever became publicly available, though there's a copy in Samford University Library's Special Collection for anyone really interested.

At the time the student documentary film was being made, I sent a copy of the first cut to my friend Joey Brackner, the Alabama state folklorist. He was, coincidentally, just beginning to work up a documentary series with Alabama Public Television called *Journey Proud* (an old country expression for the puffed-up and capable feeling you get when you start out on a major trip!). Joey, intrigued by the student documentary, put redhorsing on his list of nine topics for his first year's set of episodes on Alabama cultural history. In the resulting episode, Tommy Campbell is once again the star of the show, of course, along with his son William, his cousin Jimmy Lovejoy, and Jimmy's grandchildren Tristan and Morgan. The action part was shot on exactly the same river bar where Tommy had taken the Samford students for their film a couple of years earlier, though on this day there were fewer fish: it was late in the season, and a flood had covered up most of the spawning. But a few were caught, the first one by little Morgan, her ponytail bouncing as she hoisted the bucking cane pole up. Tommy Campbell, as natural a teacher as his cousin Mott, explained to Joey how to rig the pole and how to fish it.[11]

In terms of this topic, if a picture is worth a thousand words, either of these two videos is worth about ten thousand.

Last Words on Mott, Tommy, Redhorsing, and the *S-Town* Podcast

Mott Lovejoy himself died in late March 1995, just before the yearly redhorse season he loved so much. I didn't hear about it until I drove down to Bulldog Bend in mid-April, checking on the condition of the redhorse, and folks at the canoe rental business there told me about his passing. I remember the shock of the conversation: among other things, it was hard for me to imagine that the river redhorse could still shoal without Mott being there to appreciate it. He is buried beside his wife in the cemetery of the beautiful little Baptist Church in Sixmile, may he and Nellie Ree rest in peace. One of the lesser stars in their crowns has to be their kindness shown to a naive and nosy history professor forty years and more ago.

Not too long ago, in April 2017, I once again got a call from Tommy Campbell that the redhorse were on the bed. This was thirty-nine years after Mott had first taken me redhorsing, and I was just as excited about trying to snare them as I'd been back then. We were apparently either too early or too late for the expected big spawning on the main Cahaba down around Sprott, but we caught a few on the Little Cahaba at Bulldog Bend. Standing there in the shady run, trying to spot all the fish before we ever stepped in the river, we saw something I'd never seen and even Tommy had never seen. A five-pound or so spotted bass—a really big one for the Little Cahaba—was cruising around the redhorse beds as if it belonged there, mingling with the more stationary redhorse. Suddenly, a large horse, a redhorse male, came off his bed and charged the bass, harrying it off the beds and down the river. I suspect those rough little tubercles on a sizable horse's head in spawning season could remove scales from even the largest bass.

Tommy still revels in outdoors Alabama, the woods and the waters and their associated creatures, and it's contagious. And though he's had more than his share of personal tragedies of late, he still ornaments his life and those around him with his sense of humor. One of the more recent times I fished with him, I watched him making up a wire snare. The snare needs to have a little fixed loop in the wire at each end—one for tying the heavy line to, and the other for attaching the slip loop that holds the sinker and tightens around the fish. You can just twist the wire into loops by hand, making a rough teardrop-shaped loop, but Tommy made much neater and stronger wire loops by wrapping the wire around a small finishing nail to make the eye of the loop, and then cinching the wire around itself with a few wraps close to the

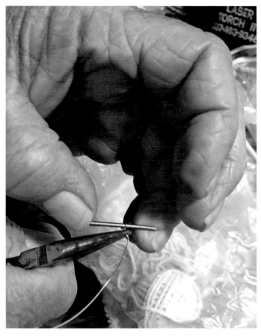

Figure 10.4.
*Completing
an eye on a
finishing nail*

Each end of the steel wire snare needs a circular, com-
pact eye; here Tommy Campbell works on one with
pliers and, presumably, his "favorite" finishing nail.

nail before sliding the finished loop off the nail. He let me try it out, and early in the
process I dropped the nail down into the tall grass, losing it. He said, "Don't worry,
I've got a handful," and handed me another one. But then he gave me a mournful
look and said, "but that was my favorite"—and then cracked up and me with him, at
the whole notion that one of a box of identical nails might be your favorite.

These days a seven-hour podcast called *S-Town*, by a New York interviewer about a
brilliant but tormented soul and some less brilliant, disoriented spirits around Green
Pond and Woodstock, is what the world in general knows about Bibb County, Alabama.[12] At last count tens of millions of people have downloaded and presumably
listened to it, and for most of them I would guess that "Bibb County" is the only
county of Alabama's sixty-seven they could name. My view of Bibb County, Alabama,
has been colored more by getting to know the Campbells and the Lovejoys over the
years. Mott and Tommy and kin were and are kind to strangers, and quick to make

them feel at home. Their work ethic makes me feel lazy. They've honored their word better than I've tended to do. They've done right by their older kin: Tommy physically saw about his ailing father, daily, for the last two years of his life; Tommy's wife, Bonnie, spent every Saturday through Tuesday for eight years with her mother so that her last years could be spent at home. And for Tommy and Mott, at least, Bibb County is where a big and a little river always beckoned, rich enough in aquatic life and varied enough in water level and mood to be endlessly fascinating.

Figure 10.5.
Tommy
Campbell
snaring a
redhorse

The setting is one of those typical yellow gravel shoals favored by bedding river redhorse. Note the twenty-foot-long cane pole bent like a horseshoe and ending in a watery explosion on the other end. The photograph is from spring 2007. (Photo courtesy of Tommy Campbell.)

chapter eleven

The Mountain Workshop of the
Alabama Audubon Society

It was in either 1979 or 1980 that I first attended the Mountain Workshop, just a couple or three years after its inception. It was put on by what was then the Birmingham Audubon Society, today the Alabama Audubon Society.

Lookout Mountain and Alpine Camp

The Mountain Workshop is so named because it's held up on Lookout Mountain, at a spot about a two-hour drive northeast from Birmingham. Although Lookout is most often associated with Tennessee because of the Civil War battles for Chattanooga in which that extreme north face of it figured, there's less than three miles of Lookout Mountain itself in Tennessee, from its foot at Moccasin Bend of the Tennessee River to the Georgia state line. As the long linear mountain—a plateau, really, averaging five or six miles wide—runs on down southwest, Georgia has about twenty-five miles of it, and then Alabama has the remaining fifty miles or so. It ends where Wills Creek and Interstate 759 run around its southern end at Attalla, the first going on east to join the Coosa River and the second heading northeast for the city of Gadsden. The long narrow plateau, unusually, has a river running down much of it—the Little River. There's a West Fork (with its scenic DeSoto Falls) and an East Fork that come together, and then lower down—starting with Little River Falls just downstream from the Highway 35 crossing—the unified river cuts a most spectacular canyon before slicing its way east out of the plateau to join the Coosa in what's today Weiss Lake. The heart of the canyon might strike a viewer more like something from the mountains of West Virginia than from Alabama; and even much of the west and east branch courses of the Little River above it are deeply incised into the surface of the plateau.

From the first the workshop has been held one long weekend in May at Alpine Camp for Boys, located on the West Fork. The main part of the camp is in a wooded bay of land maybe a hundred vertical feet above the river and a couple hundred feet below the open farmland on the plateau behind it. It's in DeKalb County, four or five miles south of the little summer resort town of Mentone and four or five miles west of the state line with Georgia. The weekend workshop runs before the summer camp for boys officially opens, but the camp staff is already there for training, and the cafeteria is up and running. For over forty years now Dick and Alice O'Ferrall (and more recently their daughter and son-in-law Carter and Glenn Breazeale, the current managers) have rented the place to the Alabama Audubon Society, from registration Thursday afternoon through departure after lunch on Sunday. I think it's been the best gathering of nature-minded folks in seven states, with a core of professional biologists and a wider circle of good amateur naturalists and craftspeople. They've even found room for the occasional cultural historian and sometime folklorist.

Thoreau Quotations and a Funeral

I was involved, tangentially, from close to its beginning, mainly because of my friendship with Bob Stiles of Samford's biology department. Sometime in the mid to late 1970s I met Dan Holliman, chair of the biology department at Birmingham-Southern College, at a social at the Stiles' house. Bob and Dan were already good friends. They had taught regularly the past few years in Alabama's marine biology summer programs at the Dauphin Island Sea Lab, and, as I heard it from Bob, they had socialized regularly after hours down there: it was, after all, a fairly tight-knit teaching staff in a fairly isolated place. But at this particular social at the Stiles', somehow Dan and I wound up in a quiet corner swapping quotes from Thoreau. Dan, who'd made a pilgrimage to Walden Pond, pronounced the name in New England fashion as "thorough," with stress on the first syllable. A pillar of the local Audubon Society chapter in Birmingham and one of the best all-round naturalists Alabama ever produced, he was at just that time one of a small group creating a yearly "mountain ecology workshop" at Alpine Camp. On the strength of my interest in Thoreau (and probably my friendship with Bob Stiles), Dan later asked me to come teach natural history and folklore-related classes there.

My earliest memories of all this were stirred up, like coals from the ashes of last night's fire, in May 2016. Bob's wife, Linda, had died that month after a long illness, and Bob asked me to say a few words at the memorial service. Linda had slipped away on Wednesday before Mother's Day, and the memorial service was the following Monday; the long weekend in between had been that year's Mountain Workshop—which our families years before had traditionally spent together, sometimes sharing the same cabin. So at the memorial service I recalled those early years, when our kids were all growing up and running around the camp as loose as free-range chickens, only corralled at mealtimes and bedtimes; when the adults would sit out on the screened porch until late at night in what Dan Holliman, an invariable participant, called "philosophizing sessions." Here matters both trivial and profound, mostly but not always about natural history, were debated to the soft clink of glasses and bottles. It would always be for us a time "when all the world was young," to use G. K. Chesterton's lovely phrase from *Lepanto*.

Still in the grip of those memories months after the funeral, I asked Michelle Little of the Samford Traditions & Oral History Recording Initiative (STORI) whether she would have the staff, equipment, and interest needed to interview those still around who were actively involved in the Mountain Workshop over the years. Michelle took on the project with enthusiasm, in effect lending me two honors students who had each worked with STORI for over a year, already veteran interviewers and technicians. The Audubon Society offered them free room and board for the May 2017 Mountain Workshop. A lot of the material to come in this chapter is from those interviews with a dozen of the principals of the workshop over the years.[1]

The Place

Alpine Camp adjoins DeSoto State Park, a Civilian Conservation Corps/Works Progress Administration (CCC/WPA) creation of 1934–39 (part of Roosevelt's Depression-era "stimulus package," we'd say today, as are most state parks in the United States). It was just Camp no. 5 while it was being built, and was only named "DeSoto" about the time it was finished. But the nucleus of Alpine Camp was from a decade earlier than the construction of the state park, and was the product of an even more surprising process than the New Deal, which is saying a lot.

Colonel Milford Howard (his was the honorary title awarded to most anyone admitted to practice law in the South in the nineteenth century) was born in 1862 as a tenant farmer's son in North Georgia. He grew up handsome, adventurous, and charismatic—a natural orator and politician—but he was apparently incapable of sticking with any idea or plan more than three or four years running. When he was eighteen and traveled through Fort Payne with his family, he discovered that the little village had three lawyers. Howard got one of them to tutor him, was admitted to the bar at age nineteen, and hung out his shingle. He married a local girl named Sallie just after he turned twenty-one. Some three years later, in 1886, he was elected county solicitor, and so he was very nicely positioned to capitalize on the short-lived but spectacular "Fort Payne boom" that was about to happen. He helped a Massachusetts entrepreneur get options on land for a railroad and was cut in on the Fort Payne Coal and Iron Company, which was organized in 1887 and was supposed to make of Fort Payne a new Birmingham. The company was capitalized by the sale of $4 million—1887 dollars!—worth of stock, which sold out in New England in less than five weeks, and Colonel Milford Howard, age twenty-five or twenty-six, was suddenly quite wealthy.

Apparently, though, it had all come so easily that now Howard speculated wildly, investing in other potential boomtowns in Alabama and as far afield as Kentucky. He lost virtually all his fortune in the 1893 financial panic, bolted the Democratic Party, and ran with the Populists. He was elected to Congress in 1895 and spent four years there. But the Populist Party faded, and his own financial situation became increasingly dire.

You really wouldn't believe a novel based on his life. In 1919 he was inspired to go to California to write books for the rising new Hollywood to be turned into movie scripts, and he indeed starred in a silent movie based on one of his books. But he'd tried to support himself in the meantime by opening a grocery business there. It went bust and—financially, at least—seems to have negated any success he'd had in the film business. The subject matter of his novels was mostly Appalachian, which of course is what he knew best and which had an exotic appeal in Southern California. In one of his novels of this time, *Peggy Ware*, the protagonist had dreamed of and then established a free school for all nearby mountain children—and in a case of real life imitating art, this became Howard's newest passion. He came back to Lookout Mountain, and with his vision and marvelous persuasive abilities he raised enough money to buy 750 acres. On it in mid-1923 he established his "Master Schools" at

Alpine. Community volunteers finished the main building, a two-story lodge with approximately the same foundations as the Alpine Camp lodge today (the original burned down in 1971 and was rebuilt), and the Alabama governor actually came to preside over the opening ceremonies. Back Howard went to California to raise money for his struggling new school, though it was a tough time because his wife, Sallie, died there.

Then he was back to champion a scenic highway running the length of Lookout Mountain. Sale of lands he just happened to own there let him and his second wife go to Italy on vacation. Howard was already a big supporter of the Ku Klux Klan revival of 1924, attributing his own original rise from poverty to what he believed to be his superior white racial heritage (and not just his exceptionally lucky timing)—and now he enthusiastically interviewed Mussolini and came back home endorsing fascism without reservation.

By 1928 the Master Schools had financially collapsed. Howard tried to give the property new life by re-creating it as "River Park," a summer retreat for wealthy refugees from smoky Birmingham. He flirted with the idea of making it an artists' colony, and then a summer school of psychology, but the Great Depression put an end to all such fantasies. His new wife drifted away, apparently unable to cope with the even more spartan living arrangements now necessary. In 1934 he finally sold Alpine Lodge and some of the associated acreage to a woman from Miami who wanted to open a girls' camp there.

The colonel's last eccentricity is probably the most visible reminder of his life that is left thereabouts. Anyone who has driven north through DeSoto State Park on Highway 89, and then turned right (east) on Highway 165, will surely remember the sight: at the crest of the first hill on the right is a small church built into an enormous rock formation. Colonel Howard's first wife, Sallie, had fallen in love with a California reproduction of the Annie Laurie church in Scotland. So build another reproduction of it he would, in her memory and eventually for his own ashes. In six weeks in the winter of 1936–37, sickly and as usual strapped for funds, he presided over the building of the basic structure. Sympathetic CCC boys helped him finish it, finally, by summer. He died that December.[2]

In addition to the Sallie Howard Memorial Chapel, the dam with Lake Howard behind it, and Alpine Lodge and a few smaller buildings up on the bluff close to it, all that was left was the surrounding "million-dollar scenery" that the colonel had always emphasized in his money-raising ventures.

Figure 11.1.
*Sallie
Howard
Memorial
Chapel*

The chapel built by Colonel Howard in memory of his first wife, Sallie Howard. The photograph was made in May, the month the Audubon Mountain Workshop was always held.

The girls' camp (which was known as Camp DeSoto) had a successful quarter-century run, but in 1959 the owner, aging and in declining health, sold the property to a partnership of an older man from Dallas, Texas, and twenty-three-year-old Dick O'Ferrall of Jackson, Mississippi, who intended to make a boys' camp of it. The older man retired from camp operations just a few years later; Dick is still with it as of this writing, sixty years later. In the bicentennial volume of the *DeKalb Legend* is a picture of Howard's original Alpine Lodge, a substantial two-story structure made of small logs, and above it a picture of the current lodge as rebuilt by Dick O'Ferrall essentially on the old foundations after the original burned in June 1971.[3]

Figure 11.2.
*Lodge at
Alpine Camp
for Boys*

The half-century-old "new" lodge, rebuilt on the foundations of the original Master Schools building, which burned in 1971.

The Environmental Inspiration of Blanche Evans Dean

Everything is so interconnected over time, I suppose, that it's next to impossible to say that any single movement started, bang, just here or there—born full grown, like Athena, straight from the mind of Zeus. But if there was such an intellectual birth of a process that came to fruition with the Audubon Mountain Workshop, those who remember unanimously agree, it was with Blanche Evans Dean. Born in rural Clay County in 1892, she was the youngest of twelve children and the only one really interested in education beyond grammar school. She boarded in Lineville, thirty miles from home, so as to be able to attend the closest high school; then she came back to Hatchet Creek to teach school in a two-teacher public school held in the local Presbyterian church building. Family members helped her afford a year at Jacksonville State Normal School (now Jacksonville State University) and then go finish a college degree in domestic science in Valparaiso, Indiana. After teaching a few years at Shades Cahaba, south of Birmingham (today a City of Homewood elementary school at one of the busiest of Homewood intersections, but back in those pre-Homewood days a rural Jefferson County high school), she tired of "domestic science," went back to college, to the University of Alabama, and got a chemistry degree. In 1924—about the same time that Colonel Howard was setting up his Master Schools in Alpine—Blanche was hired to teach biology at Woodlawn High School in Birmingham.

She was soon frustrated by the ongoing destruction of beautiful natural places nearby. Some were lost forever, including Clear Creek falls and canyon near Jasper, which were flooded by the raising of what's today Smith Lake (reading of this was the first time I ever had the thought that, much as I've enjoyed it, Smith Lake was built at a steep environmental cost). Some she saved, or at least set in motion the machinery for saving, including Sipsey Wilderness, the heart of the Bankhead Forest. She recruited younger friends to campaign for it, and she got some unexpected help from those with legal and lobbying expertise, as you'll see directly. It was an uphill battle: "wilderness" was presumed to exist only out west. But in 1975, the year after her death, the Sipsey received federal wilderness status ("eastern wilderness"!).

Blanche Dean found few decent field guides to Alabama's remarkably diverse flora and fauna, so she made her own: on birds of Alabama (she started the Alabama Ornithological Society in 1952), on ferns, and on shrubs and trees, for example. Late in life she produced, with biologist Joab Thomas of the University of Alabama, a guide to Alabama wildflowers; it came out in 1973, the year before she died.

Most relevant for this story, though, is that Blanche Dean was a teacher to the core, and it didn't stop with her high school students. She had attended a National Audubon Camp at Hog Island, Maine, in 1937, and been inspired by it as a model hands-on introduction to the interconnectedness of the natural world. She said that she'd never worked so hard, learned so much, or enjoyed anything so completely—and thereafter she usually went to one such camp every summer. In 1951 she started a series of "Outdoor Nature Camps" for adult education in the natural history of Alabama. These ranged from Dauphin Island to North Alabama, sometimes with cooks borrowed from the high school kitchen, and with specialists such as Samford biologist Herb McCullough or Alabama birder Tom Imhof cajoled into serving as faculty. The camps went on, several times a year, from 1951 until 1964. The very first of these was held at DeSoto State Park.

Dan Holliman was involved with these camps from the time he was just a graduate student at Alabama and was later brought in as an instructor. He was amazed by Blanche Dean's breadth of knowledge in field biology, and said that she taught him "the three musts of being a good field naturalist: to make your own observations; to never refuse a source of information; and to create a sense of place, that is, to really know where things are."[4]

The Reids, the Hancocks, and the O'Ferralls: Critical Personnel

Although I came to town in 1971 and got a copy of Blanche Dean's 1973 wildflower book as soon as I discovered it, I never met her. But I came to know the next two links in this connecting chain very well. They are, to use their married names, Elberta Reid and Jeanette Hancock. They were both from Birmingham, about the same age, and although they went to different high schools they debuted together (how old-fashioned *that* sounds, said Elberta when I showed a draft of this chapter to her recently) and frequented the same social circles. And they both married lawyers who came to Birmingham to practice. Elberta spent her first two college years in Randolph-Macon Woman's College (today Randolph College) in Lynchburg, Virginia, then took a summer term at the University of Colorado, and finally finished college at Alabama in political science. She says of herself that she was always very outdoorsy, but she was not particularly interested in birds until she met and fell in love with Bob Reid, a young lawyer with an ecological bent who was already a keen birder. So she got involved in the Birmingham Audubon Society, as did her friend Jeanette Hancock. As Blanche Dean got to know them in Audubon and other environment-friendly circles, she encouraged them to revive her educational nature camps, and the two talked about it.

Sometime in this era—Elberta Reid thinks it was 1959 or 1960—four young couples went up to DeSoto State Park for a nature outing on their own, mainly led by Bob Reid. I only got to know Bob later in his life (he died in 2006), mainly at Audubon events and occasionally at a meeting of the Friends of Shades Creek, and until I started inquiring about the origins of the workshop, I had no idea what a critical link in the environmental movement hereabouts he had been. A Kentuckian who'd graduated Harvard Law, he'd come to Birmingham almost accidentally while exploring job options in larger southern cities, and he really liked the place and took a job here. Bob brought a sharp legal mind to the budding conservation movement hereabouts. He was quite a character. Never remarkable for being on time, he arranged it so that his funeral service was announced to start five minutes late "at the request of the deceased." The announcement put a sweet and knowing smile on the face of everyone present.

In the mid-1960s, when Bob became president of what was then named the Birmingham Audubon Society, he set up a conservation committee that included, among others, Mary Burks as chair, Blanche Dean, Weesie Smith, Margarette Persons, Gussie Arnett, and Mary's husband, Bob Burks. They met and involved members of the Cherokee community in the area of the Bankhead National Forest, including Tom and Ruth Manasco and Lamar Marshall. A sympathetic University of Alabama professor who taught public policy and was also a former lobbyist for a Fortune 500 company taught them how to talk to congressional representatives, congressional staff members, and executive branch staffers. The Nature Conservancy was incorporated, and after a number of years of concerted effort by all involved, the Sipsey Wilderness became a reality in 1975.[5]

But to get back to the story of those four young couples visiting DeSoto State Park in or about 1959: besides Elberta and Bob, those on the trip included Jeanette and Jimmy Hancock and two other couples, friends in the same circle. Elberta wasn't married to Bob just yet, and in fact the only married ones were Jeanette and Jimmy. The couples took two rental units, one for the women and one for the men, and considered the newlywed Hancocks to be proper chaperones. One day as they were working upstream from DeSoto State Park on the west side of the west branch of the Little River, still a pretty rugged hike even today, who should Elberta see, waving to her from across the river, but an old college friend from Randolph-Macon who had also been her roommate in that summer term in Colorado. So the hikers all walked across the dam that backs up Lake Howard and climbed up the bank to talk to her, and she showed them around. Jimmy and Jeanette, over time, became great friends with her and her husband, and the Hancocks first rented and then bought a house of their own within easy walking distance of Alpine Lodge. Soon, naturally enough, the Hancocks got to know their neighbors Alice and Dick O'Ferrall, the owners and managers of the just-founded Alpine Camp for Boys.

Dick and Alice O'Ferrall were born within a block of each other in Jackson, Mississippi. He was six years older, but his father was the obstetrician who delivered Alice, and their sisters played together, so as they will tell you today they knew each other forever. Dick's father was, because of his specialty, one of the few local doctors not drafted for World War II. Most of Dick's associations in those war years were with girls, and he apparently longed for male companionship. When he was eleven, as he remembers it, he begged his parents to send him to a summer camp for boys on Lookout Mountain way over in northeast Alabama. Says Dick today: "So I would spend my summers up here, and loved it; and it was the happiest time of my life, and I've just been so blessed to spend my time here on Lookout Mountain." Alice's father insisted that his children experience the outdoors. He took the family to places such as the Smoky Mountains, where they'd spend their time hiking instead of wandering the amusement palaces in Gatlinburg and Pigeon Forge. Alice in her turn went to Girl Scout camp, then to a girls' camp on Lookout Mountain—though in the first years homesickness got the best of her. But then she went back as a camp counselor beginning as a college student, spending eight years on the staff at Camp DeSoto: "And that's where I just fell in love with the mountains—and I just grew to love camp; I just loved it." In the video interview she turns to her husband and says, "I think it became just more of a passion for me than with you, do you?"

When Dick O'Ferrall was asked about the circumstances of buying the camp in 1959 (just before Elberta and Bob and friends had been waved up from the river to see it), he reminisced: "Well, I had spent eight summers at another boys' camp, and loved it; it was just wonderful memories for me. And I saw the value of what camp could mean to a child in teaching them independence, and being in the out of doors, and building relationships, and experiencing God's creation." He and an older friend who had been a program director at the camp heard it was going up for sale, and bought it.

It took years to get the camp going in the black, switching from a girls' to a boys' camp. The original 135 acres were not all contiguous and didn't included the flatter land where the athletic fields are today. But by 1967 additional purchases made it some four hundred contiguous acres, beautifully sheltered (from other development) by DeSoto State Park on the west and a big block of Alabama Power lands on the south (and since 1992, when those Alabama Power lands were purchased by the federal government, the Little River National Preserve, an even better shelter!).

Understanding all this about Alice and Dick O'Ferrall, then, you won't find it surprising that in the mid-1970s, when Jeanette Hancock and Elberta Reid pitched their idea of a Blanche Dean–style adult education workshop on the grounds of Alpine Camp, the O'Ferralls were immediately on board. Jeanette and Elberta talk even today about how encouraging and supportive the O'Ferralls have been over the years. On their side the O'Ferralls will tell you it has deepened and enriched their appreciation for the natural world around them, and inspired them to protect it and to awaken in the summer campers a sense of wonder about it (as late as 2018 Alice still taught a session to the Alpine Camp counselors based on Rachel Carson's 1965 book *A Sense of Wonder*).

IGNITION AND LIFTOFF

The idea, the place, and the supporting institutions all came together when Elberta Rein, then president of Birmingham Audubon Society, introduced Dan Holliman and Jeanette Hancock to each other. The last piece of the puzzle, the proper time for the workshop, fell into place when the O'Ferralls agreed to rent space to the group the week before their regular summer camp opened. As Elberta recalls, "I finally said to Jeanette, 'If you will do the administrative part, I will see if Dan Holliman won't be the academic head.'" And he said yes. It started out slowly, Elberta remembers— just fifteen to twenty people all taking the same class, such as birding in the mornings and botanizing in the afternoons. But from the very beginning the Mountain Ecology Workshop, as it was originally called, was scheduled from Thursday late afternoon until after lunch on Sunday. Elberta churned out all the paperwork needed for the whole workshop—advertisement, program, registration, and such—on Bob's office mimeograph machine after regular office hours.

Elberta remembers the birth of the children's program with some humor. Some of the adults began bringing children, and as long as they were well-behaved, they were not much problem (Jeanette for her part remembers there were some who were indeed problems!). But on one course evaluation, one bright little boy wrote, "stop treating children like dirt." So the immediate response was to start a children's program, and over the years it's grown until today the Young Naturalists program is one of the best-loved features of the whole workshop experience. My grandchildren, as of this writing all in their teens, still have vivid preteen memories of sorting through a truckload of river gravel for shark teeth; of attending classes on edible plants; of making solar prints of leaves on special papers; of participating in daylight canoe trips and nighttime "owl prowls" and "ghost firefly" walks; and especially of attending herpetology showings that included lots of personal handling of the nonvenomous kinds.

Recently several of us who were around from near the workshop's beginnings were trying to pinpoint the year it started, a difficult task since the workshop grew gradually those first few years. For Elberta, who should know better than anyone, it was 1976. For Jack Johnson, who may be the only person who has been there every single year since then, it was May 1977. Jack had been a biology major at Birmingham-Southern and had worked as a student assistant for Dr. Holliman, devoting two hours every weekday to this work for much of his undergraduate career. He'd driven regularly on bird surveys, driving the university van all over the state on class field trips with Professor Holliman navigating from the shotgun seat. As Jack remembers it: "The way I came to the workshop is, I graduated from Birmingham-Southern in 1976. I believe the first workshop was the following year. I had been out of school for at least a year and received a call from him saying, 'Hey, why don't you come out to Mentone and participate in this workshop. I think you will enjoy it, and I can use some help.' So even though I was no longer his student or his employee, it was as if the relationship had not changed [laughter]."

Jack, who over the years has taught workshop courses on areas of his particular expertise such as beekeeping, magnolia species, and plant propagation, led day-long and half-day canyon hikes, and latterly even taught meditation techniques, didn't teach in his first year, 1977. As he remembers it, Dan Holliman was still doing most if not all of the teaching. And when, in what Jack counts as the second year of the workshop, Dan "assigned" him a class to teach—orienteering—it was not something Jack knew much about or was particularly interested in, and he remembers having to hustle to learn enough to teach it.

For others, the beginning year was 1978, judging by the fact that a special Tenth Anniversary award was handed out to instructors in 1987. Certainly by 1978 it had pretty well taken on its modern form.

The Intent, in Dan Holliman's Words

In 1984 Dan Holliman had an article in the *Journal of the Alabama Academy of Science* titled "Alabama's Mountain Ecology Workshop: A Model for Conservation Education." He boiled the intent of the workshop down to four things:

1. To create a conservation ethic by using a humanistic approach. An attempt is made to show man's place in nature and how human values relate to a sound conservation ethic;

2. To teach environmental education by using a multidisciplinary approach. The areas of botany, zoology, geology, history and other humanities are integrated into the subject matter;

3. To teach Alabama natural history by using knowledgeable instructors who are aware of environmental and cultural changes in the state; and

4. To teach that life on this planet depends upon diversity of many different forms of animals and plants. Every effort should be made to preserve living things and to appreciate their position in the ecosystem.

The bulk of the article is an alphabetical listing of some twenty-five classes offered, perhaps not every year, but at least ones that had been regularly offered in those first six or seven years of the workshop to date. There are ones in subjects you'd expect from a camp so named: birds, butterflies, carnivorous plants, edible plants, entomology, ferns, herpetology, limnology, mushrooms, trees and shrubs and wildflowers, and benthic ("river bottom") and riparian ("bankside") biology. But there's also geology, caving, canoeing, fly-fishing, astronomy, mountain crafts, and oral history. Dan's definition of "mountain ecology" had a real breadth to it, kin to those "telescoping time" techniques of Ian McHarg and Carl Sauer I'd come to appreciate earlier.[6]

The Maturing of the Institution

For twenty years Dan, Jeanette, and Elberta met for at least one long session every winter at Dan's office at Birmingham-Southern to plan and define the coming spring's workshop program. They tried as best they could to sort out what had worked well, what had worked somewhat and needed fine-tuning, and what hadn't worked at all and needed replacing. From early on a traveling library was assembled by Elizabeth Cooper of the Birmingham Public Library—the books set out on tables, to be freely borrowed by workshop participants on the honor system. And for decades one proud claim to fame was that not a single book was ever lost.

In those first two or three years Dan, Jeanette, and Elberta gradually shaped a routine of having two three-hour workshops per day, one in the morning (8:30–11:30) and one in the afternoon (2:30–5:30). Bird walks every morning at six o'clock would get you back to the cafeteria at half past seven for breakfast; and time after lunch for a long siesta, or tennis, or a swim, or social visits would leave you refreshed for the afternoon class. Keynote addresses Thursday and Friday evenings usually came from visiting experts. Saturday night started out with astronomical viewings, but since the skies were often overcast it morphed into a square dance in the gym/auditorium; most years the acoustic instrument band was the current band of Jim and Joyce Cauthen of Birmingham, with Jim on lead fiddle and Joyce as the caller. The name of the band was changeable; my favorite was from one year when they called themselves "Aldo Leopold and the Riparian Rounders." Dancers have always ranged from octogenarians to three-year-olds, and from the graceful to the two-left-footed; it's a measure of Joyce's skill as a caller that the dance always works! And outside the gym, if you want to take a break or stop by after the dancing ends, entomologists will have hung up white sheets and brightly illuminated them, attracting insects by the hundreds, most spectacularly the big luna and cecropia moths.

Early faculty members and administrators of the workshop widely agree that one key to recruiting faculty who would enthusiastically come back year after year was the financial arrangement. Payment for faculty was minimal: at first twenty-five dollars per course, later a little more, about enough to pay for the gas to get there and back from Birmingham, for instance. But the faculty member and immediate family also got free room and board, and could sign up for workshop classes if there was space. And everybody agrees that the other great draw over the years was in being able to hang out for a long weekend with lots of other folks concerned with the value of the natural environment and the dangers facing it.

A Local Lesson in Folk Architecture

One folklore class I taught there from early on was in the evolution of "vernacular" housing, meaning cultural traditions passed down in the community instead of from outside architectural influences. In my postgraduate semester in Intercultural and Folk Studies at Western Kentucky University, I'd been reintroduced to the humble log cabin as a cultural tradition originating in northern and western Europe. I'd always assumed that available building materials pretty well determined the shape of folk architecture, but no, most anthropologists said that cultural tradition was probably more important: for example, straight tree trunks can be used to make an eight-sided, almost-round Navajo hogan or a rectangular Appalachian-style cabin. The basic log cabin in the northern European tradition was a "single-pen" cabin usually favoring proportions of two by three, that is, something like twelve feet on the gable ends by eighteen feet on the eave sides, with a fireplace and chimney on one gable end and a doorway in one of the eave sides.

When the family grew in numbers or became more prosperous and a second room was needed, there arose the problem of how to attach the second "pen" to the original one: the dovetailed log corners didn't admit easy attachment of another structure. The solution was to build a complete *second* pen near the first. If it was built on the chimney side of the first pen, doubling the fireplace so it opened into both pens, you got a "saddlebag" house. It was so named because the chimney came up in the middle of the ridgeline, looking a little like the pommel of a saddle as seen from the south end of a northbound horse. The extra space between the pens, on front and back sides of the chimney, was often closed off with light walls to make little storage rooms. The other basic solution was to locate the second pen opposite the existing chimney and then build a new chimney on what was now the other end. Roofing over the gap between the two pens made for a "dogtrot," a shady breezeway much favored by the hounds in summertime, and the old and new doorways often faced each other on either side of the breezeway. The saddlebag construction predominated in the northern Appalachians; the dogtrot was more common farther south.

Then if more space was needed, it was added vertically. The loft of the dogtrot house was floored and the roof raised a little to make a story-and-a-half dogtrot, with a stairway usually coming up from the dogtrot itself to the second floor. And then a full second story was added to make an "I-house." When I first heard the term, I assumed that the I was what you saw when looking at the structure from one of the chimney sides: a structure one room deep but two rooms (plus a taller chimney) high. But instead, it was named by a folklorist from Michigan who taught in Louisiana; as he traversed the states in between, the names of several of which began with I, he found this style to be the standard farmhouse. The facades were symmetrical, with a central doorway and either one or two windows on either side, echoed on the second story but with a central window instead of a doorway, and matching chimneys on each end. Often the dogtrots were closed in later; giveaways were little panels of glass or wood above and on either side of the central door, often a double door. In many cases an L or T extension was built off the back of the house—in this case the shape of the letter describing the view from above.

When the folk architecture class gathered in one of the chair circles before setting off on our road trip, I'd talk a little about vernacular architecture versus outside influences. I remember one year I brought my kids' Lincoln Logs, divided the class into two groups, and had them build a single-pen cabin (proportions of two by three) with a door in one eave side and a chimney on one gable end. Then I asked them to double the size of their house, and when they were generally stumped by how to do it, I suggested the two groups put their pens near each other for saddlebag and dogtrot double-pen solutions. After such a short orientation session we'd reassemble in a car caravan and drive back toward Fort Payne until we hit Highway 35. We'd turn left (east) on it, drive across the width of Lookout Mountain, crossing from DeKalb to Cherokee County when we crossed the Little River just above the waterfall. Then we'd curve down the other side of the mountain, losing six hundred feet of altitude in less than two miles. At the little crossroads of Blanche, we'd turn right on Highway 273 (known locally as Blue Pond Road), which heads southeast toward Leesburg about fifteen miles away. Paralleling Lookout Mountain on the other side of Blanche is a low, intermittent ridge called Shinbone, so the valley Blue Pond Road runs in is naturally enough called Shinbone Valley. This had been our destination all along, the first eight miles of it southwest of Blanche.

Immediately after the turn were (and are) two classic I-houses, one close to the road on the left and the other way off on the right, originally matching houses built by brothers soon after the Civil War. I'd made arrangements with the owner of the near one for us to park and walk around so we could also see the house from the chimney side. A little farther down the road on the left was a Georgian structure, two stories high but two rooms deep and with a hip roof—built by a doctor from someplace else, an intrusion into the countryside of an outside (nonvernacular) tradition! On down south a couple of miles on the right was a single-pen cabin.

And there, right on the corner where a road turns into the Canyon Mouth Park of the Little River, was the first of the two concluding architectural pièces de résistance of the tour: a story-and-a-half dogtrot built in 1835 on land acquired from the local Cherokee, who hadn't yet been forcibly evicted. One Chisolm Daniels, born in Virginia in 1790 (says his tombstone in the nearby church cemetery) and a veteran of the War of 1812, built it. It had tiny little windows in the low second-floor walls. Dixie, the older woman who lived there back when I took touring groups in the 1980s and 1990s (and whose last name I can't find in my notes), was always sweet as she could be about us roaming all around the house, and even walking up on the porch to open the door and look down the length of the dogtrot. She told me she remembered when the dogtrot was open, before a doorway was constructed to make a room of the former breezeway. Knowledgeable botanists in some of my tour groups saw heirloom varieties of flowers in her flower garden they'd never seen before, I remember.

And lastly we'd go not quite half a mile farther south down Highway 273, the road rising, and find on a knoll on the right the local Tara, a beautifully kept, classic I-house with a Greek portico on the front on four tall pillars and with an L extension on the back, looking out over the flat fields of the floodplain of the Little River as it

Figure 11.3.
Chisolm
Daniels house

This 1835 story-and-a-half dogtrot has a shed-roof porch running the entire front of the house. Note small windows in low wall above porch.

Figure 11.4.
Len Daniels
house

In this 1840 I-house, a classical portico has been added to the front, and you can see a bit of the L extension off the back of the house.

approaches the Coosa proper. It's still worth the ninety-minute drive from Birmingham just to see this house. It was built in 1840 by Len Daniels, son of the builder of the 1835 house half a mile down the road, but now on land emptied in the five-year interval of Native Americans—the Cherokee having been dragged from their homes and driven off on the Trail of Tears, leaving only their burial ground on the ridge down from the house, their cleared agricultural fields, and, adding insult to injury, the county name.

SAVED BY THE FEMALE LINE

The owner and occupant of the Len Daniels house when I knew about it was Mary Wood, an elegant older woman with a passion for the house and local history. She told us stories of the house going back to Civil War days. General Hood's army, having retreated from the Battle of Atlanta in late July 1864, camped down around the 1835 story-and-a-half dogtrot Chisolm Daniels house to recuperate—and in fact Hood used the house as his headquarters for a few months, before heading off to the even more disastrous (for the Confederates) Battle of Franklin. As I remember the story Ms. Wood told, two daughters of Len Daniels, ages thirteen and fifteen, once accompanied farm workers taking wagonloads of supplies down to the battered army. On their return to the house, the thirteen-year-old informed their mother that her fifteen-year-old sister had been "making eyes" at a Confederate captain, whereupon the fifteen-year-old was forbidden to go back down to the camp. But after the war the former captain came back and won the young woman as his bride, and they went back to his home in Tennessee to live. When he died in 1877, his still fairly young widow came back down to the old home just in time to find her brothers about to sell the whole estate. She claimed the manor house and surrounding acreage as her share.

Mary Wood was obviously proud that it was mostly women who had saved the old home place and kept it in the family. She herself, even in her early eighties, was raising a copse of tightly planted (for close-grain lumber) pine trees to repair the house; they'd be ready in twenty years, she said, and she intended to be there. As it turned out, she wasn't, but it wasn't from lack of pluck. On occasion I'd be invited into the house, usually to be shown some architectural feature. On the wall hung a giant portrait of General Robert E. Lee. Ms. Woods and I were about as far apart on the political spectrum as you could get, I'd guess, from this "Marse Robert" icon to her die-hard opposition to the attempts to make a national park out of the canyon, the canyon mouth, and those farmlands along the little river that contained the Chisolm and Len Daniels houses. That last would probably have necessitated condemning some lands for forced sale, and she led a spirited resistance to it and may indeed have been the sharpest rock on which the project foundered. But she cut her way through life like a diamond saw, and I was an awestruck younger admirer.

Much as I enjoyed taking workshop participants around on my folk architecture tour every couple of years, I knew there was somebody better to do it—Joey Brackner, the state folklorist. While I was just a historian with folkloric tendencies, Joey had degrees in anthropology and folklore, and as a bonus was distantly related to Mary Wood. The workshop administrators were, of course, amenable to getting somebody better to teach the class. Once Joey took it over, he'd start in with Henry Glassie. I knew of Glassie, one of the academic stars of my generation in the field of folklore, having really liked his first major book, the 1968 *Pattern in the Material Folk Culture of the Eastern United States*.[7] From his detailed studies of such features as shapes of roofs and styles of tools, he came up with persuasive maps of culture regions. But Joey knew Henry Glassie personally, and Henry had actually given Joey a copy of his notes on his two 1964 folk architecture tours of Shinbone Valley, complete with photographs both modern and old—tours made when Glassie was about twenty-three years old. These materials included a copy of a 1915 photo with the Faulkner family all standing on the porch of that first (distant on the right) I-house in Blanche, as well as Glassie's own photographs of the Chisolm and Len Daniels houses. As of this writing twenty years after the change of instructors, Joey is still with it, teaching one of the workshop's real classics.

CONTINUITY AND CHANGE

In 1997, at the concluding Sunday lunch session of the nineteenth year of the Mountain Workshop, Jeanette Hancock announced—on behalf of the whole volunteer team that had run it—that twenty years was enough, and they were stepping down after the next year. Greg Harber, a medical researcher who had just recently come to Birmingham to work with Southern Research, and who had immediately gotten involved with Birmingham Audubon, remembers the shock: "And I just thought, 'Oh no. [laughter] You can't stop now, I just found out about this place.'" He went up afterward to Jeanette and said, "You know, this is great; I've thoroughly enjoyed it. Would you mind if somehow we can keep this going?" He recruited Hans Paul (to be academic director), Mary Waldrop, Mary Porterham, Betty Susina (to be librarian), and Lee Brewer—several people who were willing to just kind of step right in. Jeanette, years later, remembers thinking how the old guard stood ready that twentieth year to step in should the new leaders need help, but the transition went so smoothly they really weren't needed. I suppose it was about half the result of a solid, already fine-tuned Mountain Workshop structure and half the talents and energy of the new guard that made it happen.

And then again, roughly twenty years after that first transition, when Greg Harber's day job responsibilities changed and made it impossible for him to continue, there was another leadership change: the growing professional staff of the Birmingham Audubon Society itself took over the leadership. Ansel Payne, the new head of what is now the Alabama Audubon Society, is shouldering the load as of this writing.

Even with all that's been said above, it's still hard to describe the range of subjects at the workshop. The sessions I've been closest to have been, of course, those taught by close friends and kin—Bob Stiles's classes on fishes of the Little River; the classes of my son-in-law Reed Brozen, an emergency medical doctor, on wilderness medicine, especially high-altitude problems encountered on his treks to Everest base camp; the session my older daughter, Andrea, a veterinarian with a degree in One Health (human-animal-environmental health), once taught on permaculture. For years Tena Payne, proprietor of Earthborn Pottery in Leeds, taught wonderful ceramics classes, which included taking all the greenware back to Leeds with her, glazing and firing them, and bringing them back the next year to be claimed by their creators. In 2019 Malia Fincher of Samford's biology department taught a most interesting class on vegetable fermentation, wherein we all prepared our own sauerkraut and other fermented delicacies.

Faculty Kids

Ken Marion, herpetology professor and later chair of the biology department at the University of Alabama at Birmingham (UAB), was involved from early on with the workshop, both as a faculty member and then as the unofficial assistant director to help Dan Holliman. He tells a story that I expect has improved a bit over the years, but it's still a good story. In his field herpetology classes in those early years, he was hampered because Jimmy Stiles (Bob's son) and my son, Josh, would have turned over every rock and log in and around camp within hours of their arrival, in search of salamanders, frogs, and snakes. The boys usually saved their best finds for him in little jars and aquariums, but, as Ken says, his nature walks were abysmal because there was nothing much left to find.

But the good Dr. Marion had a pedagogical inspiration one year, and he approached the boys with a deal: a couple of hours before Ken's herp walk, they were to take their critters back and put them under whatever log or rock they'd originally found them under, and then show Ken. So on the walk, as Ken said, he'd point to a log as a good habitat for the northern red salamander, and lo and behold, there'd be one there, and so on. The class members "thought I was a god," he said, the best field biologist ever—although with Jimmy snickering in the background the truth apparently eventually came out. But for Jimmy, it was the beginning of a career as a professional herpetologist himself. He and his wife, Sierra, in between more formal educational studies and classroom teaching, today bring their traveling menagerie of herps including some venomous snakes, and their programs at the workshop generate the same enthusiasm among those now the age Jimmy was then. Jeanette Hancock uses Jimmy Stiles as an illustration of the cultural continuity of the camp—that little boy whose birthday was in May, so small we'd have to put him up on the table to sing Happy Birthday to him, and now he's a professional herpetologist who hasn't missed an Audubon Mountain Workshop since his first one thirty-seven years ago.

Even the current generation of "faculty kids" at the camp is interesting in this regard. Two or three years ago, Ellie, oldest of the two little blond-haired daughters of Birmingham-Southern College biology professor parents Megan Gibbons, herpetologist, and Pete Van Zandt, entomologist, was trying to get her mother to explain what orienteering was all about. When Megan told her it was about using compass bearings to get from point A to B and so on in the fastest time, usually through the woods, Ellie was still puzzled: "But momma, how can you turn over logs that way?" How indeed, so why would anybody want to just run on by them, all of us amateur herpetologists would agree. And the most passionate naturalist in the whole camp may be eleven-year-old Rowan, older son of Samford biology professor parents Malia Fincher and Grant Gentry; you can already see where he's heading in life. Since he was five or six years old, he and I and his family and some other friends have gone up on the plateau to seine ponds for frog and salamander larvae, particularly looking for tiger salamanders. We usually do this in one of the siesta times after Friday or Saturday lunch, and for years that was about the only place he ever saw me. His mother laughed later that he had told her that when he grew up he wanted to have "Dr. Brown's job," thinking I spent all my days seining ponds for amphibian larvae. I told her that may have been my academic dean's view of me, too . . .

Bird Walks and Camaraderie

I vowed when I retired from full-time teaching in 2016 that I was finally going to get serious about learning my birds. So far my progress is right up there with learning Latin and becoming a great cook, which I also vowed to do, and which I haven't done much with yet. But for three morning bird walks every year at the Mountain Workshop I get reminded of how rich a field it is. One of my favorite memories is of a bird walk up to the farmland plateau above Alpine Camp one frosty morning. There at the crest of the hill several hundred cedar waxwings were perched in the top of a row of trees, all facing the rising sun, their breast feathers puffed up and soaking up the morning sun. If you've ever seen a peach tree with such a great crop that it threatened to break the limbs down, that was the vision. And they were taking turns raiding a grove of mulberry trees below, which was defended by a single male scarlet tanager—brilliant red body, black wings, valiant but hopelessly outnumbered.

For close on forty-five years without a break, then, as of this writing in 2021 (though called off on account of COVID-19 for 2020 and again for 2021), for one long weekend every May the Alabama Audubon Society has hosted a Mountain Workshop at Alpine Camp. For longtime faculty and many repeat participants, it's been a really important part of our lives. We all start from that common ground of being fascinated by the natural world and our relationship to it. It's a brother- and sisterhood beautiful to behold, a real sense of family. Judge Jimmy Hancock told his wife, Jeanette, that what she did at the workshop for twenty years—getting folks housed compatibly, getting newcomers grounded and connected, fine-tuning the program year to year, handling all the responsibilities of emcee at every meal's announcement time—had touched more lives than any ministry she'd been involved with in her church.

The Walter Coxe Blessing

Walter Coxe was a Birmingham advertising executive and very much an environmentalist. He was most public spirited, and among other things he ran a Boy Scout troop that drew mainly from public housing in downtown Birmingham. He published Blanche Dean's 1973 *Wildflowers of Alabama* book. He sponsored lawsuits back in the late 1960s and early 1970s, on environmental grounds, against the building of the Tombigbee Canal, and against the Birmingham Waterworks' sale of the old Camp Horner property on the Cahaba—though neither of these were successful. He toured a nature film on the Bankhead Forest around the country during the push to get eastern wilderness status for the Sipsey, picking up considerable non-Alabama congressional support. Most active in the Birmingham Audubon Society, he went to the president, Elberta Reid, with an idea for Audubon-sponsored spring field trips around the Southeast. They started up just after the Mountain Workshop was born (the first spring field trip was in 1978), long weekends that sometimes stretched even longer: to Four Holes Swamp near Charleston, to the Okefenokee, to the vicinity of Apalachicola, to Reelfoot Lake, just for starters. Walter and Elberta either singly or jointly reconnoitered the lay of the land in each place—visiting twenty-six separate springs in Central Florida to ascertain which single one was best for a group visit, for example! In a way, they just extended the Blanche Dean field trip model from Alabama to the broader Southeast region, the way the Mountain Workshop just made one of her workshops a regular yearly event.

Not being very active in Birmingham Audubon itself, other than going to an occasional nature film, I never really knew about these trips, or about all of Walter's other conservation-minded activities. But the "Walter Coxe Blessing" he's left us with at the workshop is both short and sweet and—for me, at least—never seems to get old or trite with use. It's compounded of a quotation from President Theodore Roosevelt, something from the Episcopal Book of Common Prayer, a phrase of legalese that Elberta Reid swears had to come from her lawyer husband, Bob ("because Walter didn't talk like that: 'assets . . . enhanced and not impaired'"), and some words of Coxe himself. Before each and every meal, somebody with a microphone gets everybody's attention and asks for this singular blessing from a genderless and most ecumenical God:

> O God of all Outdoors and of every living thing
>> Help us make Thy Way our way,
> And keep us mindful always of the needs of others.
>> Give us a reverence for all Your Creation
> That we may be good stewards of Your many blessings
>> And will treat them as assets to be passed on to future generations
> Enhanced and not impaired,
>> And that we may use Your resources wisely in the service of others
> To Your honor and glory forever.
> Amen

We diners echo "Amen," and the immediate tintinnabulation of silverware on platters and ice in glasses is gradually submerged in a buzz of conversation, mostly but not always about matters of natural history.[8]

chapter twelve

For the Amusement of the Boys

John Mealing, Railroad Caller

Looking for Music Associated with Labor

In 1981, when I'd been in Alabama for a decade and had begun to recognize the social and historical lay of the land, I was asked to do some field research into work-related music.[1] The askers were from Birmingfind, a short-lived, grant-supported venture based at Birmingham-Southern College, mainly funded by the National Endowment for the Humanities (NEH). Birmingfind's project was to study several neighborhoods in Birmingham, and to focus particularly on five ethnic groups in the city: African Americans, Greeks, Italians, Jews, and Lebanese.[2] The audio collected in such research was intended to accompany community history presentations of the written and visual variety. I found some great union music (management is disadvantaged by having no music!) from the 1930s and 1940s in and around Birmingham. Among other things, I interviewed well-known union organizer Eula McGill and got her to tell me stories about the Amalgamated Clothing and Textile Workers Union strikes in Birmingham from the middle of the Great Depression, around 1934. She was born in 1911 and so would have been about seventy when I met her in 1981—a tall woman with a strong voice. She sang for me old Woody Guthrie songs including "Union Maid" and Joe Glazer's haunting classic about a mill worker who dreamed of heavenly work after this life. I can still hear her on the chorus after all these years:

Oh, the mill was made of marble
The machines were made out of gold
And nobody ever got tired
And nobody ever grew old

I was particularly interested in her critique of Communists who tried to find a home in her favorite unions: they weren't really working for improvement in worker conditions, she said, because they were single-mindedly focused on an upcoming world revolution.[3]

Railroad music, however, which I was sure was my guaranteed ace in the hole, didn't pan out quite as I thought it would. I'd signed up to work on the project, in part, because one of my history students—quite a musician, and I still have a guitar I bought from him—worked part-time on the railroad. When I'd asked him whether the workers out there knew lots of railroad songs, he told me yes, lots and lots. But once I signed on to work with Birmingfind, I could never quite get back in touch with the student. In desperation I finally spoke with his ex-wife, another former student. She told me that since he liked me and hadn't wanted to disappoint me, he had probably invented all that singing of railroad songs on the conversational spot and was now carefully avoiding me. So I found out, to my disappointment, that modern-day railroad workers seemed to know no more of the old railroad ballads—"Casey Jones," "The Wreck of the Old 97," and such—than the general public. But if you're reading this, Mack, it all worked out even better than finding railroad ballads. Come on by for a visit and I'm buying whatever you're drinking—partly because of the guitar, and partly because I'd never have signed on to Birmingfind without your assurances.

SECTION GANGS AND THEIR "CALLERS"

Because what I found out, to my great delight, was that some of the old-time section gang callers were only recently retired, and their work chants and songs were still in their memories if not in current practice. On the bigger railroad lines the callers began to be outmoded and replaced by track maintenance machines as early as the 1950s. This happened on the medium-sized lines a decade or so later, and a few callers lingered on even after that on the smallest and most isolated lines. To find them in and around the big cities of the South, judging by my experiences in Birmingham and to a much lesser extent in Atlanta and Greenville, you didn't hang around railroad company retirement offices and expect to learn much. You didn't go to the railroad employees' reunion banquets. You didn't visit the union halls. You learned not to spend a lot of time on the phone with administrative assistants and higher management. I tried about two months' worth of things that didn't work. What worked best, simply enough, was to find the oldest active or most recently retired roadmaster, as he is called on most lines, the man in charge of track maintenance and thus in direct contact with every section gang. He knew who all the call men were, and if anybody did, which of them were still alive and where they were last heard to be living.

Before mechanization of track upkeep, a section gang on a line like the Frisco (after 1980 the Burlington Northern, and after 1995 the Burlington Northern Santa Fe, BNSF) would typically take care of ten to fifteen miles of track. These workers had to "grass" it with shovels, slicing the weeds out by the roots. They had to keep the ballast straight-edged and full between the ties, using scoops to move the coarse gravel, or "chat," that was the commonly used ballast. They swapped out rotted crossties for new ones. They either turned or swapped out worn rails (they wear out on the inside top edge, especially along the outside rails on curves). But a good half of a typical workday, in blazing and breathless summer or cold and windy winter, was keeping the track level and in line. Especially for the old steam locomotives with their rigid undercarriages, the track needed to be straight. With modern, more flexible undercarriages, it's not supposed to be so critical, though the frequency of wrecks on ill-maintained track might argue otherwise. Railroads have made a comeback in the forty years since I first interviewed these railroad workers and call men, but I remember standing back then with an old section gang hand who just clucked and shook his head as a slow train passed us, car tops rocking back and forth from the unevenness of the track.

The enormous weight of passing trains, then and now, gradually works the track (the two rails and the crossties they're spiked down to) up and down and especially sideways through the ballast. The section gangs raised the low spots with a jack and crammed the coarse gravel ballast under the raised ties with square-ended picks. Mostly, though, they worked on side-to-side alignment, using five-foot-long, heavy "lining bars"—giant, straight crowbars weighing almost twenty pounds. The bars had a chisel end (for digging down into the gravel below the rail), above that a

Figure 12.1.
*Lining bar
and sixteen-
inch spike
maul*

The lining bar is the longer of the tools in this photograph. This one weighs in at nineteen pounds. The
sixteen-inch spike maul is so named because it is sixteen
inches across the asymmetrical head; it weighs thirteen
pounds, almost all of the weight in the head. The yard-
stick is included for scale.

square-shafted section of a foot or so (the part coming in contact with the rail itself
when you were levering it over), then the rest of the shaft round, and finally a point
at the top (for standing the tool up in the gravel when you weren't using it; laying it
down in the summer sun would make the lining bar too hot to handle).

Depending on the weight of the track and the urgency of the job, a gang might
be as small as four or five men or it might number thirty or forty or even more. Each

man had his own lining bar. Facing the rail their lining bar was under, usually with right foot forward and lining bar on their left side, left hand well back on the end of the lining bar and right hand close beside it with their right arm across their bodies, they would all pull up and forward on their bars together to lever the track, crossties and all, over through the ballast. They were popularly called "Gandy Dancers," supposedly because the railroad tools came from a Gandy Tool Company in Chicago—though no researcher has ever found a Gandy company that produced railroad tools. An alternative theory for the name is that the flat-footed repetitive "dance" the section gang did when lining looked like a gander strutting.[4]

It was long, boring work, and the timing or coordination of the pull was much more important than the brute force each man put into it. This is where the caller came in. He motivated, entertained, and set the timing all at the same time. This was a position of some prestige. In the South, on typical lines such as the Frisco and the Louisville and Nashville (L&N, later Seaboard and today CSX), management from the foreman of the section gang on up was all white until the later 1950s. The section gangs themselves were almost altogether of African American workers, and the highest an African American employee could move was assistant to the roadmaster; a close second was lead worker on the gangs, almost always a caller.

In pursuit of the work chants of these callers, I eventually ran down three in the greater Birmingham area who were reputed by fellow workers and roadmasters to have been the best around. Two of them refused to ever let me turn on a tape recorder (and this despite my openness, winsome character, and, when those failed, my devious manipulation of their friends and former bosses). There was a generation gap or two between us, not to mention the old problems of African American informants and white interviewers, and those of white-collar professors trying to query blue-collar labor. All that was missing was the gender gap to doom any interview, questioner and subject passing each other on the horizon as distant ships not knowing what life was like on the other. So the third, who not only let me tape from the first five minutes on but actually seemed to welcome it, was surely atypical. His lining songs were also a good deal cleaner than the verses I had heard repeated from the other callers' repertoires. He was a good Baptist Sunday School teacher who didn't drink—both traits that were unusual in the section gangs, according to one of his old friends and fellow workers. Too, in other areas of his life, including church and quartet singing, he was not just a regular performer but once a semiprofessional entertainer.

JOHN MEALING, A BIOGRAPHICAL SKETCH

He was John Mealing, born in or around 1908 in a little hamlet in Lowndes County named White Hall. Lowndes County, classic Alabama Black Belt, is famous for some of the finest surviving antebellum homes in the state, and as such is a popular tourist drive. John Mealing described society there from the bottom looking up; from his early childhood he remembered "gallowses, and they wasn't for no white people." He went through elementary school there through the fifth grade, lived with his father for a few years in Selma, and then came back to White Hall to stay with his mother again. He told me that his mother had been cooking for the foreman of a work gang on the Western Railroad, which ran through White Hall, the halfway point on the seventy-mile run between Selma and Montgomery. She couldn't get free railroad housing without a man in the family working on the railroad, so in 1926 the foreman slipped John, underage but the biggest of eight children, onto the section gang as water boy. The railroad forms required a middle name, and John, born and raised within sight of the tracks, signed them "John Henry Mealing."[5]

"Totin' the bucket" wasn't all that easy, he remembered. He had to walk to the closest spring or well, sometimes a matter of miles, and by the time he got back the water in the bucket might be lukewarm. Workmen would each get a dipperful and after a couple of sips throw the warm water on the ground, so that all too soon it was walking time again. John, anxious to be a real worker anyway, got off the bucket by an interesting stratagem. In exchange for putting an engineer in touch with a moonshine source, he got the engineer to stop the train around a curve out of sight of the work gang, where John, using a pair of tie tongs in place of ice tongs, wrestled a three-hundred-pound block of ice out of a refrigerator car. He buried it in the cinders beside the track so it would last all day, and all afternoon he brought iced-down creek water to the workmen. Either from the ice or the creek water the workers all got stomach cramps and fell out, and the foreman thereupon fired John from the bucket and set him to following the jack—working on the small crew that carried the tool that jacked up low spots in the track. Soon he was a regular hand on the gang, taking his turn at the lining of the track.

In summer 1928 the Alabama River rose up in a major flood and washed out a section of the Western's track embankment about thirty yards from a short trestle. I went down there once with Mr. Mealing and a film crew from Birmingfind, and you could tell by his emotion it had been a bit of a traumatic and exciting time for him, the sort that usually makes for more vivid memories and better oral history. As he remembered it, the rails and crossties hung like a string over the gap with water rushing under it at what looked to the workmen like "seventy-five miles an hour." One workman tried to go across on a railroad handcart, but it tipped and dropped into the rapids. He couldn't swim, and they only found his body four days later when the flood went down. The white foreman couldn't understand why all the African American section gang workers took the rest of that first day off.

Hearing That First Caller Lining Track

But most important for the subject at hand, a special gang was brought in from Atlanta to help with track repair. It included "a boy named Eddie, about forty years old," the first real caller John Mealing ever heard. John was fascinated and kept right at his heels. They were lining track before the water even fully uncovered the tracks, and were working from before dawn until after sunset—long, long days in a humid lowland in a hot Alabama summer. As Mr. Mealing remembered it:

> Well, it done me so much good I was laughing at him, you know, keeping up with him, laughing, because I liked it. But now, everybody had been working all night, and they was done got exhausted, done give down. They was tired. But you see, by him went to singing, that made it better. And everybody got uplifted and they all went to work and forgot they was tired. That was in 1928; oh, it was in the summertime long about this time of year [this was June 30, 1982], because the corn was up high as I got out there, and the water was all over it. And you know it must have been somewhere along right now, 'cause them peoples in the country had them laid by [the last plowing done, just waiting on crops to finish ripening]. But I never would have thought that I'd ever be a man to catch that off of that boy—and went all up and down the Frisco, all on the mainline here.[6]

Some of the verses of the Atlanta caller—a "heap of them old bad ones"—John Mealing never did as a call man; but a few he kept up all his working career. The lining verse he especially associated with that first caller goes:

Way down yonder in Durant Bend[7]
Heard my hammer come a-whistlin' through the wind

Visualizing the Scene

To know exactly what the caller was doing, it helps to visualize the whole scene. The white foreman would be hunkered down a hundred feet or more from the work gang, sighting along one of the rails. If close enough, he could have called out what needed doing, but distance and long practice made hand signals easier. The section gang would usually line the tracks in a leapfrog method—at the joint of the thirty-nine-foot long rails and then the halfway point, then back to the quarter point and on ahead to three-quarters, then back to midrail and then ahead to the next joint. This apparently resulted in a straighter track than if you simply did joint, quarter, half, three-quarters, and next joint, as the track just behind where you had lined in that manner got marginally out of line again. If the foreman wanted to change the routine, he would point either to his elbow ("joint") or the middle of his forearm ("midpoint") and then to his rear ("behind") or his head ("ahead").

The caller would be watching the foreman, and the rest of the gang would gather in close to the caller, on either side of him on his rail and in a matching file on the opposite rail, all facing the way the rail needed to go. The caller gave them time to jab their lining bars in under the rail and get a purchase on the gravel, and then he commenced singing a couplet of two four-beat lines, or on rare occasions a double couplet of four lines, like so (the downbeat of the four-four time shown by underlined syllables):

Oh my <u>wife</u> needs a <u>hat</u> and my <u>baby</u> needs <u>shoes</u>
<u>Come</u> on, <u>dice</u>, and <u>gimme</u> two <u>twos</u>

As he sang, the workers clicked their lining bars against the rail, keeping ragged time in the first line of the couplet as they fell into rhythm and got their feet set, making good time in the second line, and sounding like a single lining bar hitting the rails by the end of the couplet. Then came the refrain, which went on indefinitely, until the foreman signaled that the point had come in line:

Come on, <u>move</u> it! <u>Huhn</u>! [pause]
<u>Boys</u>, can you <u>move</u> it! <u>Uhmm</u>! [pause]

The lining bars tapped the rails on the first two beats of each line of the refrain, and the heavy hauling took place on the third beat as everybody put their backs into it, torsos moving forward toward the rail they were working, arms straight back and down on their left-hand sides, hands on the very end of the lining bar for maximum leverage. The fourth beat, the silent one, was for repositioning themselves. Sometimes the verse and refrain called for an especially good pull, or an especially light one:

<u>Shake</u> it to the <u>east</u>, <u>shake</u> it to the <u>west</u>
<u>Shake</u> it to the <u>one</u> that I <u>love</u> the <u>best</u>
Shake it <u>lightly</u>! [silent next three beats]
Just <u>lightly</u>! [silent next three beats]

The first time John Mealing patiently explained it to me went like this, with special emphasis on each of his four uses of the word *time*: "But see, here's what that is. It's a *time*. You carry the *time* with it. You don't just jump and go on; you carry a *time*. 'Cause see, when the man's calling, he started the *time*: 'Hey, hey,' then everybody else answer him when he calls, 'Hey, hey, [caller]; 'yeah' [gang]. Then I start":

Oh <u>come</u> on <u>boys</u>, let's <u>go</u> round the <u>wall</u>
<u>Don't</u> want to <u>stumble</u> and I <u>don't</u> want to <u>fall</u>
<u>That</u> <u>suits</u> me . . .

"And then all of them's lining, see? It'd go on over, when I'd say that—'Hey, hey,' and it'd go on over, when they'd say it."

Print is a poor substitute for the original audio, but the following six verses are from the first tape recording I did with Mr. Mealing. It was June 17, 1982, and after having spent fifteen minutes trying to record and talk over the window air-conditioning unit and the sounds of his wife washing dishes (clashing them with what I thought was the energy of suspicion of this stranger in their parlor), I'd gotten him to move out to the porch of his house at Pratt City, right behind the old East Thomas yard of the Frisco. On the tape you can hear songbirds and kids way in the background, and some occasional wind noise in the mic, but it is still far and away the most interesting taped interview I ever did:

> Woke up this morning' 'bout half past four
> Somebody knockin' on my door
> Boys, move it [silent two beats]
> Hey, move it [silent two beats]
> Hey, move it . . .
>
> Me and my wife had a fallin' out
> Now stop, let me tell you what it was about
> She jumped at me, and I give her a load
> She wanted me to work on the Southern Railroad
> Can you move it?
>
> I got my learnin' on Number Four,
> Boy, I'm tellin' you, and I'm ready to go
>
> I got a gal, her name is Kate
> She movin' in her hip like a Cadillac Eight
>
> Oh, a handful of nickels and a pocketful of dimes
> A house full of chillen, ain't nary of 'em mine

The audio recording from this June 17, 1982, interview is available through YouTube as of January 2021, and is well worth a listen.[8]

John Mealing said he had worked on the Western until he was laid off in the Great Depression in July 1932. Most of the 1930s he did construction work in Montgomery. In 1939 he moved to Birmingham, and in 1940 he got a job on the Frisco, where he stayed until he retired in 1976. It was on the Western, making a dollar a day, that he first did any calling of his own. "Oh, well, I called some down in the country, but it was after '28, long about '30." On a lunch break near Benton (Lowndes County), he said, he carved this verse on a crosstie with his pocketknife:

> Bury me between the railroad ties
> Where I can see the train pass by

When I'm <u>gone</u>, <u>hey</u> <u>boys</u>, <u>when</u>
I'm <u>gone</u>...

The way he gradually learned to sing—practicing to himself, then trying it out with a small critical audience on the Western, and later on calling three or four hours of lining at a time on the Frisco—reminds me somewhat of Albert Lord's 1960 *The Singer of Tales*, a study of the stages in which mainly illiterate Yugoslav epic singers of the early twentieth century learned their epic songs. Even the formulaic composition Lord identifies as the key to how a singer put a song together fits: they performed not by rote memory of the whole epic, but by the memorization over time of a collection of thousands of phrases that fit the meter of the traditional performance, which lets the performer put them together on the fly, to fit the mood and attention span of the audience.[9] In this kind of calling on the railroad, of course, the meter is four-by-four-beat couplets. Some of the more successful verses even became the base for a series of four-line songs:

> Oh, ain't no need in me workin' so hard
> I got a gal in the white folks yard

And then:

> She kills the chicken, saves me his head
> Thinks I'm a-workin', I'm at home in the bed

Or:

> She kills the chicken, saves me his wing
> Thinks I'm a-workin', I'm not doing a thing

Or:

> She kills the chicken, saves me his feet
> Thinks I'm a-workin', I'm just loafin' the street

According to Clyde Terrell, a good friend of Mr. Mealing's and a fellow worker for some thirty-five years, he wouldn't sing the same verse twice in a whole day of lining track. A few verses he would make up on the spot topically; most of them were in his head. As Mr. Mealing put it very seriously to me in our first interview, "I had to satisfy sixty to seventy men on the job. Now *you* worried me when you called . . . ," because he hadn't done any calling since he'd retired in 1972, ten years before, and now he was going to have to "satisfy" me with it.

The verses do different sorts of things. One set expressed work gang feeling about the white foreman, just out of earshot:

> Well, look at the foreman, how he stands
> Standin' more like a farmer than he do a railroad man
> Can you move him? . . .

A lot of verses call the foreman the "captain," from a tradition earlier than railroad work:

> Well, my cap'n can't read, my cap'n can't write
> My cap'n can't tell when the track is right

One of these is a broad hint that it's time to quit, and the foreman's watch must not be a real jeweled railroad watch at all, but a cheap imitation called a Waterbury:

> Well, the cap'n got a Waterbury just like mine
> Wind it up, it won't keep no time

And even more direct was:

> Oh, you can work me soon and work me late
> But when dinnertime [the midday meal] comes, don't hesitate

And:

> Oh, I sang this song, gonna sing no more
> Get your hat and let's us go

One way the section gang could strike back at a foreman they disliked—and the likes and dislikes of years ago were still passionately remembered by John Mealing and his friends—was to "hump" the track. The foreman could judge side-to-side alignment better from his vantage point than he could up and down, so the gang could raise the track in a spot or two and the foreman be none the wiser until an inspector ran a vehicle over the tracks and then made him redo it.

In other verses the caller would call maverick members of the work gang to account. Sometimes they'd go out to work on a wreck and take perhaps a week to build temporary track around it, tear out the mess, and then re-lay the original track. Camped out, some of the men wouldn't wash or shave, and Mr. Mealing would work such morality as this into the day's calling:

> Oh, eat him up, crab lice, he won't bathe
> Eat him up, hair dogs, he won't shave

There were verses about hard times and visions of good times:

> Oh, holes in my pockets and patches on my pants
> Behind in the house rent and they want it in advance

> Oh, when I die, bury me deep
> Jug of molasses at my feet
> Thousand biscuits in my hand
> Gonna sop my way to the promised land

Some were from gambling, especially crap shooting:

> Shoot my dice, the point was nine
> Six come a-runnin' and the trey come to flyin'

Many had to do, logically enough, with the lining process and trains:

> Joint ahead and quarter back
> That's the way we line this track

> Hey, the hotter the sunshine, the better I feel
> Workin' on the railroad and getting' no meal

Well, the freight train is a-runnin' and the passengers a-flyin'
The old people's a-fussin' and the babies are a-cryin'

Some had to do with wives in particular and women who weren't:

I love my wife, I love my baby
Like my flapjacks swimmin' in gravy

Well, a nickel is a nickel and a dime is a dime
A woman gets tired of one man all the time

And as close to risqué as Mr. Mealing ever got:

My Uncle Jack is the jelly roll king
Got a hump in his back from shakin' that thing

Local Fame

Apparently by the time John Mealing had spent a year or so on the Frisco, he had already achieved some local repute as a caller. This occasioned an event he was as proud of as anything that he ever did on the railroad. It was 1941, and a section gang was lining some track between Fifteenth and Seventeenth Streets North in Birmingham, and got stuck. They didn't have a real caller, said John Mealing and Clyde Terrell, who was also there, just a workman who sang out rather ineffectively, "Joe! Joe!" "Well," said John Mealing, "'Joe' had done give out." So the foreman took John Mealing off another gang, took his lining bar away, and gave him a pick handle to drag along the rail for the foreman to sight on. John remembered the foreman saying:

"That's all you need; just touch the rail where I want you to get down." And that's what I done. And I started to singing—'cause he told me, "Talk your Latin!" just like that. Then I started. *He* was there [pointing to Clyde Terrell, who nodded] and that track just moved, just went on over there. The fellows got uplifted. That's what that song was for, to make a man feel good. 'Cause if he gives out, you just as well to sit down and let him rest. But if he's down and out and somebody can really talk it, he'll get uplifted. And I have did that a-many a time. I've went on a wreck, and folks were so close to the track we couldn't move—following us, every which way we'd go. Every time us'd move down, they'd move down, women and men, children, white and black, just keeping right up with us, just right jammed up, and they'd make them get back. They'd listen at me, and everybody would answer.

A second kind of calling done regularly by John Mealing was the dogging call. These were the instructions by the caller for carrying or "jumping" rails. A heavier set of tongs than tie tongs, called "rail dogs," worked on the same general principle—two pieces of metal pivoted on a bolt so that the raising of the handles caused the wide-flange clamp to close on the ball, or bole, of the rail. The handles are solid steel about an inch in diameter, and it's a heavy tool just by itself (it was a standing joke with section gang hands that all the tools on the railroad were too heavy to begin with, and then they would want you to *do* something with them!).

Before the days of continuously welded track, rail came in standard thirty-nine-foot lengths. When John Mealing began working, it was mostly with ninety-pound rail—ninety pounds to the yard, that is—and by the end of his career most track was laid with 132-pound rail. At a hundred pounds to the yard, to strike a low average, a rail weighed in at some thirteen hundred pounds. A gang of twelve men picking it up would be heaving upward of a hundred pounds each if they all were carrying exactly their share. No man alone could hope to hold it up if it was dropping or stop it if it was moving. If you thought the rail was going from you and stepped toward it, and the rest of the gang thought it was coming toward your side, you were going to get thirteen hundred pounds of steel dropped on your leg, guaranteed to break it.

CALLERS IN THE RULE BOOKS

Here a lead worker as caller was a must; in fact, it got written into the rule books of at least one major railroad. Even though old-time section gang hands will tell you the rule book was "not to work you by, but only to fire you by," this inclusion reveals the view management took of calling. The following rules of the predecessor of the CSX system come from a 1984 pamphlet titled *Seaboard System Railroad: Safety Rules*:

Section 210. When two or more employees are handling a heavy or cumbersome object, have a definite understanding as to the way it is to be handled and observe the following precautions:

a. Remove slipping and tripping hazards if practical. If not practical exercise care to prevent slipping or tripping.

b. Designate one employee to act as "call man" to give commands for all movements (lifting, walking, lowering or throwing). When practical, the "call man" should be at one end of the object being handled.

c. Employees other than the "call man" must not give commands or do any unnecessary talking.

d. Move only on command.[10]

One other interesting rule in the book, under Section 216, says that employees must not "jump" rail (that is, jerk it suddenly about a yard at a time and let it drop, dangerous to feet). As you'll see, however, that was the ordinary way of moving rail when John Mealing was an active caller.

Another point of pride Mr. Mealing felt about his time on the railroad is that no one ever got hurt while he was a caller. The key, in his mind, was in making sure everyone knew what was going to happen: "But the first thing you got to do is get people to know what you want done. Where you get a man hurt is when he don't know. Because you got a greenhorn in the bunch. There's somebody in there that's hard to catch on to what you're gonna do. Yeah, and you got to watch out for him."

Dogging Calls

Here is some transcription of Mr. Mealing demonstrating dogging calls. First, he goes through the process for a loose (spikes pulled), worn-out rail in its bed on the ties. It has to be shifted first to the center of the crossties, then over the other rail to the end of the ties (called the "head" of the ties), then down into the ditch. Then he demonstrates the reverse process, setting a new rail from the ditch up onto the end of the ties, then jumping it into the bed (where it is to run), and finally sliding it up to butt against the end of the last rail so the two can be bolted together:

> Hey, listen at me, now, boys [caller]
> Yeah [response]
> Dog your rail, son [caller]

Well, if I'm over this way [on the side toward which the rail is to be moved], go:

Set't on me

And all of 'em gonna come to me; and I want to go further:

Set't on me

And all of 'em come to me:

That's all right, move on down the line

Get down there:

Hey, boys—what you gonna do down there, man?
Yeah [gang response]
I want you to set't on me
Oh, set't on me
Alright
So, man

Got it in here [loose rail still in its place on the crossties]:

Look a-here, now, boys
I want you to set it in the center—whoomp!
Alright, I want you to set it over the rail—whoomp!
Then I want to set it in the ditch, yeah

You put it in there:

Come on, boys, and go with me

Everybody come and go with me, get the other one:

Alright now, dog him, now, now, boys
Yeah [response]
Alright, set't over the rails

Set it in the ditch one time
Alright, now come on, follow me
Oh, boys, dog him now, man
Yeah [response]
Oh, look a-here, can you do what I want you to do now, boys?
Look a-here
Set it on the head, man
Yeah [response]
Set it in the bed, man
Join iron on me, son—whoomp!
Alright, move on down the line

Just tell 'em which a-way to go. See that was the way when you was laying it.

TAMPING CALLS

A lot of other work on the railroad didn't lend itself to music or chanting; two-man teams driving spikes when the heads of their sixteen-inch spike mauls would be just a blur, for example. But there was a third and last kind of calling Mr. Mealing did, a tamping song. It is completely unnecessary for safety or even timing; it seems to have been done out of sheer exuberance, or again, just "for the amusement of the boys." Men in pairs with square-ended tamping picks leaned shoulder to shoulder, so much so that they wore holes in their shirts where they leaned against one another, and swung their square-ended picks together between two crossties to cram the ballast up under them. Here is some transcription of John Mealing's tamping songs. This too is four-four time, with a "chunk" put in where the tamping picks hit the gravel on the third beat:

I got a
Mu-ule (chunk) on the
Moun-tain (chunk), bring him
Down boys (chunk), bring him
Dow-own (chunk) . . .

I got a mule on the mountain
Bring him down, boys, bring him down

Who in the world gonna ride him
But bring him down, boys, bring him down

. . . and on and on through many peregrinations of said mule.

Mechanization of track upkeep ended John Mealing's daily calling just as it did for callers all over the South and indeed the whole industrial world. By the early 1960s the Frisco in and around Birmingham had "bump tamp" machines, a vehicle that clamped to the rails and with an internal side-to-side hydraulic bumper knocked the machine, track and all, to either side. About the same time "ballast regulators" appeared, which, in the hands of a single skilled operator, mechanically pulled the ballast in full under the crossties. In the mid-1970s, the Frisco got "torsion-beam tampers," which lined and surfaced at the same time. After that only an occasional odd job needed the call man's old art.

Like folk art everywhere, I suppose, it began to be appreciated only when it was dying out. I've seen a videotape done by ethnomusicologist Alan Lomax of a section gang lining track in Mississippi; it was shown at an Alabama Folklife Association meeting, though I'm not sure it ever became publicly available, having not been able to run down a citation. There are also very similar "ax" chants and other work song chants in an audio collection Lomax put together, "Afro-American Spirituals, Work Songs, and Ballads," which originally came out on LP records from the Library of Congress in 1960.[11] That same year, Lomax published *Folk Songs of North America*, including lining calls such as "Can't You Line It?"[12] A decade later, in 1970, historian William Ferris released an article with transcript on the caller for a railroad bridge gang in Mississippi.[13] Both scholars agreed that these railroad work chants are an aspect of African American folklore. This they obviously are, at least in the South, though other norms apparently held up north and out west. In 1982, the year after I first met John Mealing, I had a former roadmaster on the Southern—in the process of explaining the westward growth of many Georgia lines in the nineteenth and early twentieth centuries across Alabama and on west—describe this sort of calling. He said that it was used "east and south of Kansas." Ferris in his article further noted that despite the accessibility of the last of these African American callers, they had received little study by folklorists and others interested in African American music.

I find this curious as well, especially in light of all the scholarship devoted to African American spirituals and rural and urban blues.

Spirituals, Blues, and Railroad Calling

There is a clear connection between the words of John Mealing's lining chants and the traditional blues on the one hand and African American church music on the other. He grew up hearing cotton chopped to work chants in the fields of Lowndes County. He sang in church from age four, and he did so in choirs and as a soloist right down to when I met him years into his retirement. He was in his first quartet as a teenager, and he sang in gospel quartets in Birmingham for thirty-seven years, mainly with Willie McKinstry and the Evangelist Singers, and later with the Gospel Southern Aires. This included weekly television appearances on Birmingham's Channel 6 in 1950 and 1951, which, unfortunately for the folklorist, were before things were regularly videotaped; it was all evanescent live performance. John Mealing was never much into singing the blues himself, but he could sing lots of the spirituals both the way he grew up with them and the jazzed-up way the quartets did them. He had a clear idea which folk songs on the railroad were based on some historical happening ("Casey Jones, he was an engineerman on the Frisco") and which weren't ("There never was but one John Henry on the railroad, and that was *me*"). He spoke of the strong influence of traditional African American church music on the blues, and even thought that was some of the inspiration for his own railroad calling: "Well now, all of that *tune* comes from the same song. Now, you can believe it or not, but in what I was saying on the railroad, the same *tune* come from the other song, and that came right out of the Bible. You take, well, you don't know nothing about it, and I don't know nothing about it, but in the time of slaves—I got a Baptist hymnbook in there, a Baptist songbook—every song in there was sung by slaves, folks was enslaved. But they was depressed; and a person get depressed, the Lord'll give him something to say."

The Effects of Being "Discovered"

When Ed Bradley of *60 Minutes* reporting fame died back in 2006, CBS and even the other networks ran all sorts of old footage of him. One was of an interviewer asking him which of his news stories he was most proud of, of all the things he had ever done. He replied that if Saint Peter ever inquired of him what he thought he had done that entitled him to admission to heaven, he would say to Saint Peter, "Did you see my interview with Lena Horne?" On a smaller scale I suppose one of the things I'm proudest of is having "discovered" John Mealing, though I wonder if it wasn't something of a mixed blessing for him.

His life in retirement had fallen into a fairly established and comfortable pattern: Sunday church activity; two days a week light yard work for a family in the Mountain Brook area of Birmingham who, children and grown-ups all, thought the world of him; and the rest of the time spent around home or with relatives and friends. Then in 1982 I popped up for a tape-recorded interview and came back for several more. And I brought friends and photographers, and then I got Mr. Mealing to give a half-hour performance to a luncheon audience in the gleaming new Harbert Center of downtown Birmingham.[14] Joyce Cauthen, who for years was the real dynamo that made the Alabama Folklife Association run, featured Mr. Mealing in an Elderhostel program at the University of Alabama at Birmingham (UAB); other college appearances followed. Joyce was also the driving force behind the "Talking Tent," the folklife narrative tent, put on for years at Birmingham's annual City Stages festival, and several times she got John Mealing and friends to perform there—going so far as to have a short section of track built for the purpose. A segment of audio tape of his calling made it onto National Public Radio. A local newspaper columnist gave John a half page of the Sunday paper, anchored by a color photo of him standing on the tracks somewhere. *Guideposts*, the national Methodist magazine, sent an interviewer down to feature him in an article on work, and when that article appeared Mr. Mealing's phone began to ring as people from all over the area called wanting him to come to their civic club or church group, or to sing at some folk music get-together including at the new stage at Sloss Furnaces. In 1991 he performed at the Smithsonian Festival of American Folklife. In 1994 he was one of a half dozen area call men featured in the documentary *Gandy Dancers*, mostly filmed at the Heart of Dixie railroad club yard in Calera.[15]

In March 1995 he and other "gandy dancers" performed at Wolf Trap.[16] In 1996, he and Cornelius Wright Jr., a former call man from the US Steel network of tracks—consisting of over 1,100 miles of track, I was astonished to learn—received National Heritage Fellowships (the highest honor of the National Endowment for the Arts, including an award of $10,000 to each individual) in a ceremony in Washington, DC, and a year later Mr. Mealing rehearsed his railroad calling as one of a group of folk artists who performed at Carnegie Hall.

Figure 12.2.
*Reenactment
of a work gang
lining track*

This photo was made at the Heart of Dixie Railroad Museum in Calera, Alabama, on December 10, 1988. The occasion was a reunion of railroad callers and friends. (Photo by Joey Brackner, courtesy of the Alabama Department of Archives and History.)

In 2017, in the process of updating all this for the book in hand, I said something to Marjorie White of the Birmingham Historical Society about having always regretted missing John's funeral in 2007, and not even knowing where he was buried. She had John's daughter Linda Mealing-Nelson's phone number, and Linda agreed to guide us to Mount Zion Cemetery between Roebuck and Tarrant and show us the site. It was mid-August and had threatened rain, but it turned into a beautiful day. I've got a lovely photo of Linda and Marjorie side by side just behind Mr. Mealing's grave marker, new silk flowers on top from Linda and rose petals from Marjorie's garden scattered all around. Linda had so much of her father's personality and understanding of human nature that it brought him back to me more vividly.

Over lunch for the three of us at the Chick-fil-A in Roebuck she allayed some of my fears of having totally disrupted her father's retirement life. Earlier Linda had said: "I had no idea at all that Daddy had done this; he'd never talked about it around me."[17] As she remembered it, the rediscovery of his call art had been a blessing to him, and had made lots of other people aware of history not many knew existed. Although she had two young sons in the 1990s, she (and the whole family) had gone with him to the folklife celebration at the Smithsonian Institution in Washington and to the gandy dancer performance at Carnegie Hall. She remembered how proud she personally had been, his daughter, going into the sold-out performance in Carnegie Hall in the heart of Manhattan, passing people without tickets who were making substantial offers for hers.

But Mr. Mealing's performance gradually changed, too, in these new venues. The cadence of the lining chants lost its strict timing, and there was a lot more flowery hand motions and ad-libbing on the refrains. Going back through my tapes it seems to me that the second half of our first recording session and some of the second

Figure 12.3.
John Mealing
in retirement in
the 1980s

John Mealing in retirement. This is more or less how I remember him from visiting with him in the early 1980s. (Photo courtesy of Linda Mealing-Nelson, daughter of John Mealing.)

session a week or so later were the best in terms of that elusive goal, authentic recording of folk art. John was sitting on his porch with me and sometimes Clyde Terrell too, slapping his hands and tapping his heel, trying to think back into the old lining verses. The only way to have done a good audio or videotape with him later on, as much as his delivery had changed, was (as you can see in the *Gandy Dancers* film) to get him out on some track with his old buddies from the Frisco, lining bars in hand, and actually try to move some track. Doing the real job with his natural audience listening straightened things out in a hurry.

Honey in the Rock

I'd like to close with John Mealing's use of the "honey in the rock" image for the (oh so slowly!) changing South. The metaphor is from the Bible, Deuteronomy 32:13. The whole book of Deuteronomy up to that chapter seems to be about rules—short chapters on how to dress, eat, punish criminals, and such, spliced with historical occurrences such as the episode of the Golden Calf that help explain the rules. And then comes this long chapter 32, the "canticle" of Moses, the words of a song that some scholars conjecture was already old when Deuteronomy was composed and it was included therein. The "honey in the rock" phrase comes toward the end of a passage describing the ways God promises to provide for a loyal Israel (here in the King James Version):

> [10]He found him in a desert land, and in the waste howling wilderness; He led him about, He instructed him, He kept him as the apple of his eye. [11]As an eagle stirreth up her nest, fluttereth over her young, spreadeth abroad her wings, taketh them, beareth them on her wings: [12]So the Lord alone did lead him, and there was no strange god with him. [13]He made him ride on the high places of the earth, that he might eat of the increase of the fields; and He made him to suck honey out of the rock, and oil out of the flinty rock.

Perhaps because getting honey from stone so succinctly and magically summed up what African American Christians especially in the South hoped could happen to them, the "honey in the rock" phrase became a staple of folk song and folk preaching. John Mealing obviously felt it to be such a common metaphor as to need no explaining to me:

It's honey in the rock in the South. This is one of the best places in the world for a man to want to live, in the South. And my granddaddy lived to get ninety years of age pecking in this rock trying to find honey. But he died, he didn't get it. My daddy lived to get up in age, but not as old as my granddaddy, pecking in the rock trying to find honey. But he couldn't get any. All of the old peoples on my momma's side died pecking in that rock hunting honey. But they couldn't find it. But I knowed it was honey in this rock in the South.

My brother was living in Detroit and he tried to get me to come to Detroit in '50 to live. But I told him this, I said, "Boy," I said, "I don't want to stay up here"; I said, "But there's honey in the rock in the South." I say, "But somebody gonna find it," I say, "and I want to be there when they find it. I may not be able to sop none of it, but I can see somebody else soppin' it."

Now there's the mayor of great big old Birmingham [Richard Arrington, at the time of the recording], and he's a black mayor in the South. And that's some of that honey. Now I can't do that, but he's soppin' it. And if you go to the City Hall to pay off a traffic ticket, you're gonna have to pass the black. Now that's true, because I done been *down* there! And if you go the county courthouse to buy a driving license you got to go past the black. You go on around there to get your tag, you got to pass the black. Everywhere you go, you're passing the black. Now that's some of that honey.

My daughter works for the telephone company, and she's got a [good] job. That's some of that honey. Now I ain't got sense enough; I'm too old now to sop that honey, but she's soppin' it. But I'm here seeing it, and it's a blessing to me to be here seeing it. And I told them, I'd rather be here hungry in the South than to be in the North with a pocket of money. And I will. I don't want no part of nothing but the South. It's honey in the rock in the South; you've just got to live to get it.

Epilogue

Life is what happens while you're making other plans, they say. In this case I like what "they" say; among other things it seems to excuse me for not having had the personal discipline to focus single-mindedly on Russian history.

On the surface of it, there's huge diversity in the twelve major topics that have been dealt with in the chapters of this book. They've followed the courses, geographic and historical, of some of Alabama's medium-sized rivers, the life cycles of some local plants and animals (mainly herptiles and fishes), the use of local botanical materials in traditional medicine and basketry, the history of a culvert built by enslaved laborers from way back in the Civil War, the practice of African American railroad work gang calling that survives in recent memory, and the evolution and survival of archaic, backwoods hymns and ballads. Lots of time has been spent remembering the personalities that either introduced these to me or explained them for me, on the educational movements that let many of them be a part of my teaching career, and on the environmentally or historically inclined institutions that championed their conservation.

It may be, when looking back from retirement age, that you tend to see more unity to your life than was really there. But I do feel there's an underlying commonality in all the variety of topics discussed herein: my interest in them was a response to my being swept along too rapidly in modern technological and societal currents I didn't understand very well. It was like dropping a sea anchor overboard, a sort of underwater sail that drags and slows a boat's drift. There was just something about older, slower cultures, and about the natural world in which they existed in such a direct and intimate way, that filled some empty space in me.

Similar interests might have developed had I moved to any other state in pursuit of a college teaching job, but Alabama was where I found myself those first formative ten or eleven years after graduate school. It wasn't nirvana, and it wasn't love at first sight. Back in the 1970s there were many days every year that the air was so polluted you couldn't see from Red Mountain to the hills north of downtown Birmingham just a mile or so away. Racism hereabouts was more flagrant and hateful than where I'd come from, and we surely had our share. But there was a driving force about greater Birmingham that I think was left over from the city's founders, some of whose still-impressive descendants I got to know. There was a vibrancy that may also have come from the unexpectedly rich ethnic mix in the greater city that included not just white and African American but distinct Jewish, Italian, Greek, Lebanese, and Palestinian communities, scattered Cuban and Syrian and Iranian and Russian and Kenyan and Chinese families, and more, all of which I got to know here in part because some of their college-age young people attended Samford.

And from that very first week in town in mid-June 1971 the natural world that began not far out of the city offered me endless entertainment. Some years ago Samford's geography department helped host a national meeting of geographers here in town. Being on the university payroll I qualified as an insured van driver for one of their excursions, down to Perry Lakes near Marion, hard by the Cahaba River. I drew a vanload of academics mostly from New Hampshire. Without much effort the local guides turned up rare mussels and fishes, and on the trail between the parking lot and the Cahaba we found sheep frogs and other uncommon amphibians. One of the New Hampshirites bent down a stalk of rivercane to examine a leaf more closely, and there on the cane right next to his hand was a sleeping green treefrog. Since neither rivercane nor green treefrogs get much north of the Ohio River, he was understandably really excited about his finds. It dawned on me later that in terms of profusion of life-forms, if you're from New Hampshire, Alabama is about halfway to the Amazon rain forest.

In half a century here I have explored corners of Alabama from Estill Fork of the Paint Rock and the Walls of Jericho up near the Tennessee line to Wolf Bay on the Intracoastal and Bayou La Batre on the Gulf, and I must confess I still love exploring the state. It seems that for all of my plans for self-education and world travel in retirement, I'm still being distracted by Alabama. The general direction of it was set back in that first decade I was in the state. It was a period in my life, to borrow geographer Carl Sauer's words as he reflected back on his early fascination with Hispanic culture after moving to California, "when field work was unrestricted by endurance or time."[1]

Notes

Chapter 1

1. See W. M. Howell, R. A. Stiles, and J. S. Brown, "Status Survey of the Cahaba Shiner (*Notropis* sp.) and Goldline Darter (*Percina aurolineata*) in the Cahaba River from Trussville to Booth Ford, Alabama," US Fish and Wildlife Service, Contract no. 14-16-004-81-055, unpublished report, 1982.

2. Harvey H. Jackson III, *Rivers of History: Life on the Coosa, Tallapoosa, Cahaba, and Alabama* (Tuscaloosa: University of Alabama Press, 1995), 237–38.

3. Todd Keith, *Cahaba: A Gift for Generations; A Series of Historical Essays Revealing the Cahaba River Past, Present and Future*, designed and illustrated by Guy Arello, with photography by Beth Maynor Young (Birmingham, AL: Birmingham Printing, 1997).

4. The most readable summary I have found of this event is "Jefferson County Sewer Construction Scandal," Bhamwiki, edited January 9, 2020, https://www.bhamwiki.com (the Birmingham-focused Bhamwiki was launched in 2006 on the Wikipedia model by John Morse).

5. Jim Allison's website includes photos of most of the rare and unique plants. See "A Botanical Lost World in Bibb County, Alabama," Jim Allison (website), last updated January 12, 2010, http://www.jimbotany.com/lostworld.htm.

6. See the Nature Conservancy website on the Glades: "Kathy Stiles Freeland Bibb County Glades," Nature Conservancy, accessed March 15, 2021, https://www.nature.org.

Chapter 2

1. For an earlier version of this chapter, see Jim Brown, "The City of Homewood's Great Suburban Spotted Salamander Migration," *Wild South*, no. 27 (Winter 2004): 26–32.

2. For the full text of Gibran's "On Marriage" passage in his *The Prophet*, see Kahlil Gibran, *The Prophet* (New York: Alfred A. Knopf, 1923), 19, Project Gutenberg, last updated February 1, 2019, http://www.gutenberg.org.

3. Henry D. Thoreau, *Walden*, ed. J. Lyndon Shanley, introduction by Joyce Carol Oates (Princeton, NJ: Princeton University Press, 1989), 159.

4. Recently Marjorie White of the Birmingham Historical Society showed me a *Birmingham News* article dated March 20, 1960, describing how that nature trail would be dedicated on April 8 of that year with a speech by the executive director of the national Nature Conservancy.

5. See Patrick Hickerson, "Caution! Salamanders Crossing: Homewood Salutes Its Biodiversity," *Birmingham News*, April 12, 2003.

6. Joe Mitchell and Whit Gibbons, *Salamanders of the Southeast* (Athens: University of Georgia Press, 2010).

Chapter 3

1. Michelle Blackwood still has the planners' maps handed out at that 2002 Hoover City Council meeting. Recently I borrowed the one with the topographic lines and overlaid the photo into Google Maps (an aerial photograph dating from 2019). Ross Bridge Parkway appears to have been curved a bit east in the immediate vicinity of the causeway when built (in comparison with its original plans), probably so as to miss the eastern end of the (newly identified) causeway and small park.

2. Most of this discussion comes from a conversation with Michelle Blackwood on January 7, 2017.

3. "The History of Ross Bridge," Ross Bridge: A Classic American Resort Town (website), accessed February 12, 2019, http://www.rossbridge.com/history-ross-bridge/.

4. Birmingham Historical Society, "'Ross Bridge' Goes On the Record," *Newsletter*, June 2017, https://birminghamhistoricalsociety.com/news-and-newsletters/.

5. See Marjorie L. White, *Shades Creek: Flowing through Time* (Birmingham, AL: Birmingham Historical Society, 2019).

6. Marjorie L. White, interviewed by Jim Brown, March 8, 2019, transcript and audio recording of interview are available in Samford Traditions & Oral History Recording Initiative (STORI), Samford University Library, Special Collection 6297.

7. Marjorie L. White, Richard W. Sprague, and G. Gray Plosser Jr., eds., *Downtown Birmingham: Architectural and Historical Walking Tour Guide* (Birmingham AL: Birmingham Historical Society, 1977).

8. Marjorie L. White, *The Birmingham District: An Industrial History and Guide* (Birmingham, AL: Birmingham Historical Society, 1981).

9. The Library of Congress's photography collection can be searched at its website through the Prints and Photographs Online Catalog, https://www.loc.gov/pictures/. A search for "Alabama Sixteenth Street Baptist Church," for example, brings up thirty-six items as of 2020, all but three of them digitally available, as shown by thumbnails of the photos. To obtain a copy of as-yet-undigitized photos (all the Library of Congress photos of Ross Creek culvert, discussed later, for example), visit the Library of Congress's Duplication Services, https://www.loc.gov/duplicationservices/.

10. See Historic American Engineering Record, *Ross Creek Culvert*, HAER AL-214 (Washington, DC: National Park Service, n.d.), Library of Congress, accessed April 2, 2021, https://loc.gov/item/al1362.

11. James Gage, quoted in Birmingham Historical Society, "'Ross Bridge' Goes On the Record," 8; and Historic American Engineering Record, *Ross Creek Culvert*, 15.

12. Marilyn Davis Barefield, *A History of Hoover, Alabama and Its People* (Hoover, AL: Hoover Historical Society, 1992).

Chapter 4

1. Eliot Wigginton and His Students, eds., *The Foxfire Book: Hog Dressing, Log Cabin Building,*

Mountain Crafts and Foods, Planting by the Signs, Snake Lore, Hunting Tales, Faith Healing, Moonshining, and Other Affairs of Plain Living (Garden City, NY: Doubleday, 1972).

2. Eliot Wigginton launched the whole enterprise, obviously, but Margie Bennett may have been as important in the whole *Foxfire* experience as he was. She was co-editing the compendium *Foxfire* volumes as early as 1979, and was listed as sole editor of *Foxfire* 9 (1984). For years she and Bob actually lived at the Foxfire Museum and Heritage Center, where she was full-time host to visiting teachers and students, and also guided the summer work program. Most of this information comes from Joyce Green, Casi Best, and Foxfire Students, eds., *The Foxfire 45th Anniversary Book: Singin', Praisin', Raisin'* (New York: Anchor Books, 2011), 505.

3. Blount County Historical Society, *Heritage of Blount County* (Blountsville, AL: Blount County Historical Society, 1972), n.p., see the "Old Mill" passage in section 8, Folklore.

4. An earlier version of this section appeared as Jim Brown, "The Brief, Mostly Happy, Life of Folkcenter South," *Tributaries*, no. 6 (2003): 9–16.

5. Jim (James R. Bennett) eventually authored a half dozen works of local history. Especially pertinent for this topic is his highly regarded *Tannehill and the Growth of the Alabama Iron Industry: Including the Civil War in West Alabama* (McCalla: Alabama Historic Ironworks Commission, 1999).

Chapter 5

1. Carl Carmer, *Stars Fell on Alabama* (New York: Literary Guild, 1934; Tuscaloosa: University of Alabama Press, 1985), 53.

2. Carmer, 57.

3. George Pullen Jackson, *White Spirituals from the Southern Uplands: The Story of the Fasola Folk, Their Songs, Singings, and "Buckwheat Notes"* (Chapel Hill: University of North Carolina Press, 1933; New York: Dover, 1965).

4. See N. S. MacDonald, "A Singing School," Washington copy, November 30, 1938, Works Progress Administration Files, 1936–43, Government Records Collections, Alabama Department of Archives and History, Montgomery.

5. H. L. Jackson, *The Colored Sacred Harp* (Ozark, AL: n.p., 1992). Recordings of "Florida Storm" are available through YouTube; see, for example, "Florida Storm," uploaded October 7, 2016, by Andy Alexis, YouTube video, 4:59, https://www.youtube.com/watch?v=n1MGgKjUTIw. Even better is a 1979 short film project directed by Landon McCrary. See "Dewey Williams, 81st Birthday Singing, Wiregrass Sacred Harp Singers, Film," uploaded December 11, 2015, by Steve Grauberger, YouTube video, 16:58, https://www.youtube.com/watch?v=4aCHWxc3pT8. Dewey Williams himself leads "Florida Storm" in this recording, beginning near 12:50.

6. See Milton Oliver, interviewed by Jim Brown, May 20, 1994, Samford University Oral History Collection, SUHist/Folklore/003, audio recording, 54:11, https://www.samford.edu/departments/oral-history/projects/folklore/Milton-Oliver.

7. See D. W. Steel, "Sacred Harp Singings," University of Mississippi (website), last modified April 9, 2021, http://home.olemiss.edu/~mudws/singings.html.

8. Buell E. Cobb, *The Sacred Harp: A Tradition and Its Music* (Athens: University of Georgia Press, 1978).

9. Cobb, 116.

10. Cobb, 117.

11. Buell says the book came out in late 2013, despite its publication date. See Buell E. Cobb, *Like Cords around My Heart: A Sacred Harp Memoir* (Denver, CO: Outskirts Press, 2014).

12. See *Journey Proud*, "Camp Fasola," November 17, 2013, online episode, 27:34, Alabama Public Television (website), https://aptv.org.

CHAPTER 6

1. E. F. Schumacher, *Small Is Beautiful: Economics As If People Mattered* (New York: Harper and Row, 1973; New York: Perennial Library, 1975), 53–62.

2. This was a series of four articles on land use planning that came out in a week's time in the *Birmingham News*. As the historian of the group, I wrote the first two: "Awe for Natural Beauty Begins with Thoreau," May 4, 1977; and "Wasteland of 'Concrete Cemented by Grime,'" May 5, 1977. Economist Fred Hendon wrote the third, "Affluent Citizens Escaping to Suburbs," May 6, 1977; and political scientist David Gillespie wrote the fourth, "Open Countryside in Center of the City," May 9, 1977.

3. See Ian McHarg, *Design with Nature* (Garden City, NY: Natural History Press, 1969; with expanded illustrations, New York: John Wiley, 1992). All the quotations from McHarg in the first pages of this chapter are from pages 1–4 of the first chapter, "City and Countryside," from this twenty-fifth-anniversary edition, which I assume is dated in reference to the 1967 grant that supported the work.

4. Fernand Braudel, *The Mediterranean and the Mediterranean World in the Age of Philip II*, first published in French in 1949, trans. Sian Reynolds, 2 vols. (New York: Harper and Row, 1976).

5. See Carl O. Sauer, *The Early Spanish Main* (Berkeley: University of California Press, 1966).

6. The BRPC has been since renamed as the Regional Planning Commission of Greater Birmingham. The BRPC published a separate McHarg-based study for each county; see, for example, BRPC, *Chilton County: Land Suitability Plan* (Birmingham, AL: Commission, 1976).

7. For a complete list, go to "Project List," Jane Reed Ross: Land for Living (website), accessed April 1, 2021, http://www.janereedrossla.com/project-list. There, she lists her major projects by category: parks and trails, campus work, site design, and urban spaces and planning. Each category, on average, includes a dozen major projects.

8. In 2015, the TIGER grant program was renamed BUILD, for Better Utilizing Investment to Leverage Development.

9. See William Lynwood Montell, *The Saga of Coe Ridge: A Study in Oral History* (Knoxville: University of Tennessee Press, 1970).

10. See Rec Childress and Mrs. Childress, interview by Jim Brown and Judith Schottenfeld, Cub Run, Hart County, KY, September 14, 1977, recording (Folklore class project, Western Kentucky University, Bowling Green), transcript in William Lynwood Montell Papers, Kentucky Museum Library Special Collections, Western Kentucky University.

11. See Avencio Villarejo, *Así es la Selva* (Iquitos, Peru: Centro de Estudios Teológios de la Amazonia, 1979).

CHAPTER 7

1. Allen's thesis on Tommie Bass was completed two years later: Allen Tullos, "Tommie Bass:

A Life in the Ridge and Valley Country" (MA thesis, University of North Carolina at Chapel Hill, 1976).

2. Joseph E. Meyer, *The Herbalist*, revised and enlarged by Clarence Meyer (Glenwood, IL: Meyerbooks, 1960), 5.

3. See Dixie Miller and Tommy Hill, "Tommy [*sic*] Bass of Mackey Is Known Far and Wide . . . as the 'Herb Man,'" *Birmingham News*, September 30, 1978.

4. For the *Wall Street Journal* profile, see Linda Williams, "Doctors May Frown, But Hill People Say Herbalist 'Gives Ease'; Tommie Bass, 77, Even Lures Folklorists and Academics to a Leesburg, Ala., Shack," *Wall Street Journal*, July 8, 1985. The film can be viewed online: Allen Tullos and Tom Rankin, producers, *Tommie Bass: A Life in the Ridge and Valley Country*, 1993 film, 49 min., Folkstreams (website), accessed April 2, 2021, http://www.folkstreams.net /film-detail.php?id=83.

5. Eliot Wigginton, Margie Bennett, and Their Students, eds., *Foxfire 9: General Stores, the Jud Nelson Wagon, a Praying Rock, a Catawba Indian Potter—and Haint Tales, Quilting, Home Cures, and Log Cabins Revisited* (New York: Anchor Books, 1986), 12–82.

6. Steven Foster and James A. Duke, *A Field Guide to Medicinal Plants and Herbs of Eastern and Central North America* (New York: Houghton Mifflin, 1990).

7. Foster and Duke, vii–viii. The discussion of bloodroot is on p. 48.

8. James A. Duke, *The Green Pharmacy: New Discoveries in Herbal Remedies for Common Diseases and Conditions from the World's Foremost Authority on Healing Herbs*, illustrated by Peggy Kessler Duke (Emmaus, PA: Rodale Press, 1997), 465.

9. John Crellin and Jane Philpott, *Herbal Medicine Past and Present*, vol. 1, *Trying to Give Ease* (Durham, NC: Duke University Press, 1990).

10. Crellin and Philpott, 1:215.

11. Crellin and Philpott, 1:127.

12. Crellin and Philpott, 1:30–31.

13. See John Crellin, Jane Philpott, and Allen Tullos, *Wintertime for a Backwoodsman: Reminiscences of A. L. Tommie Bass of Leesburg, Alabama, "Same Address since 1925."* (Chapel Hill, NC: n.p., 1983).

14. See *Journey Proud*, "Herbal Medicine," August 11, 2017, online episode, 27:36, Alabama Public Television (website), https://aptv.org.

15. See Darryl Patton, *Mountain Medicine: The Herbal Remedies of Tommie Bass* (Birmingham, AL: Natural Reader Press, 2004).

16. John Crellin and Jane Philpott, *Herbal Medicine Past and Present*, vol. 2, *A Reference Guide to Medicinal Plants* (Durham, NC: Duke University Press, 1990), 233. Crellin cites D. B. Mowrey, *The Scientific Validation of Herbal Medicine* (Toronto: Cormorant Books, 1986), 158–59.

17. Crellin and Philpott, *Herbal Medicine Past and Present*, 2:466. Here, Crellin cites T. Hussein et al., "An Investigation of the Quaternary Alkaloids of Rhizomes and Roots of *Xanthorhiza simplississima*," *Lloydia* 26 (1963): 254–57.

18. Crellin and Philpott, *Herbal Medicine Past and Present*, 2:193–94.

19. Duke, *The Green Pharmacy*, 438.

20. See Michael J. Barry et al., "Effect of Increasing Doses of Saw Palmetto Extract on Lower

Urinary Tract Symptoms: A Randomized Trial," *Journal of the American Medical Association* 306, no. 12 (2011): 1344–51.

21. Just a few years ago, as an addendum to this herbs and herbal medicine topic, I had a conversation with old friend and former student Jane Reed Ross, the local landscape architect talked about at length in the last chapter. At the time she was working with Francesca Gross of the Nature Conservancy on various kinds of gardens (woodland, prairie, etc.) that they were helping students at Birmingham's Woodlawn High School build on nearby empty lots. Jim Duke, who had grown up just down the road from Woodlawn early in the Great Depression some eighty years earlier, was still active at his six-acre herb garden he called "Green Farmacy" in Fulton, Maryland, not far from Washington, DC. How neat it would be, I thought, to be able to bring him down to connect with students just down the street from where his interest in botany had first begun.

Jane was on board with the project, and I loaned her both Meyer's 1918 *Herbalist* and Jim Duke's book on medicinal plants of the eastern United States. My older daughter and grand-daughter, coincidentally, were driving from Birmingham back up to their New Hampshire home, so I asked whether they would swing by Jim's place in Maryland on their way north. They thoroughly enjoyed their visit to the Green Farmacy herb garden and their chat with Jim and his wife, but they told me they thought the state of Jim's health would probably rule out any more long trips for him. Meanwhile, other progressive plans around Woodlawn were resulting in buildings replacing the newly constructed gardens, so the gardens only had a one-year life span. Sure enough, Jim passed away not long afterward, in 2017. So once again, as with my plans for a joint appearance of Tommie Bass and Jim Duke at the Birmingham Botanical Gardens a quarter century before this, I was a day late and a dollar short.

Maybe, in light of my newfound skepticism about herbal remedies, the failure of these projects was for the best.

CHAPTER 8

1. John Dewey, *Experience and Education* (New York: Macmillan, 1938), 15.

2. Dewey, 45.

3. Dewey, 50.

4. Dewey, 85.

5. Eliot Wigginton, ed., *Foxfire 2: Ghost Stories, Spring Wild Plant Foods, Spinning and Weaving, Midwifing, Burial Customs, Corn Shuckin's, Wagon Making and More Affairs of Plain Living* (Garden City, NY: Anchor Books, 1973), 9, 13–14.

6. Laurence Ivan Seidman, *Once in the Saddle: The Cowboy's Frontier, 1866–1896* (New York: New American Library, 1973).

7. John Jacob Niles, *The Ballad Book* (New York: Bramhall House, 1961).

8. Evelyn Kendrick Wells, *The Ballad Tree: A Study of British and American Ballads, Their Folklore, Verse and Music, Together with Sixty Traditional Ballads and Their Tunes* (New York: Ronald Press, 1950).

9. Thomas Percy, *Reliques of Ancient English Poetry*, ed. Henry B. Wheatley, 3 vols. (London: Swan Sonnenschein, 1886).

10. Francis James Child, *The English and Scottish Popular Ballads*, 5 vols. (Boston: Houghton Mifflin, 1882–98).

11. See Elizabeth McCutchen Williams, ed., *Appalachian Travels: The Diary of Olive Dame Campbell* (Lexington: University Press of Kentucky, 2012), 85–86. The actual quotation comes from the six-hundred-page-long unpublished manuscript Olive wrote, "The Life and Work of John Charles Campbell," integrated into the diary entries by the editor.

12. Cecil J. Sharp, *English Folk Songs from the Southern Appalachians*, ed. Maud Karpeles, 2 vols. (1917; London: Oxford University Press, 1932).

13. See Byron Arnold, *Folksongs of Alabama* (University City: University of Alabama Press, 1950).

14. See Olive Dame Campbell, *The Danish Folk School: Its Influence in the Life of Denmark and the North* (New York: Macmillan, 1928).

15. Eliot Wigginton and His Students, eds., *Foxfire: 25 Years; A Celebration of Our First Quarter Century* (New York: Anchor Books, 1991), 216. In the same chapter as the quotation here, "On the Road," former *Foxfire* student participant Lynn Butler remembers speaking at "Samford College in Alabama" (p. 223). This retrospective was, unfortunately, the high point of Wigginton's career; the next year he pleaded guilty to child molestation of a ten-year-old boy, and his educational career ended. All those of us who had ever been the subject of his sharply critical remarks about our shortcomings as educators, I suppose, found this development thought provoking.

16. Bob England, pers. comm., 2020. "The Flight of Sparrow Hawk" is a five-page typescript manuscript, circa 1995, that England loaned to the author years ago.

17. I have a copy of the *Birmingham News* article here quoted and so can vouch for its accuracy, though the top of the pages (with the dates) is cut off, unfortunately.

18. Tracey Leiweke, "Experiential Learning: The 'Foxfire' Approach," *Center for Southern Folklore Newsletter* 1, no. 1 (Spring 1978): 6–7. The same general story is told from Eliot Wigginton and his students' points of view in *Foxfire: 25 Years*, the chapter titled "Transplanting Foxfire," 242–50.

19. See *Half-Modelling*, introduction by Lance Lee, text by David King (Bath, ME: Apprenticeshop, 1976), 24.

20. Eliot Wigginton, ed., *Foxfire 5: Ironmaking, Blacksmithing, Flintlock Rifles, Bear Hunting, and Other Affairs of Plain Living* (New York: Anchor Books, 1979). See especially the first few pages of the "Ironmaking and Blacksmithing" section, including p. 78 with its cutaway drawing of old Tannehill Furnace #1, which was refired on September 19, 1976, and p. 80 with the photo of Professor Farabee pointing to the charging point of the old furnace.

21. James Brown, Adolph Crew, and Joyce Lackie, "Experiencing History," *Journal of Experiential Education* 1, no. 1 (May 1978): 29–37, reprinted in *Experiential Learning in Schools and Higher Education*, ed. Richard J. Kraft and James Kielsmeier (Dubuque, IA: Kendall/Hunt, 1995), 230–43.

CHAPTER 9

1. The nucleus of this chapter was first presented as a keynote address to the Birmingham Audubon Society's Mountain Ecology Workshop, sometime in the early 1980s, at the invitation of Dr. Dan Holliman, then also chair of the biology department at Birmingham-Southern College. It was published in more formal form in 1994 as an article titled "Survival of the Great

Shoal Fishtrap" in *Tributaries*, Summer 1994, 11–22, the initial issue of the occasional journal of the Alabama Folklife Association. And although I don't know this for a fact, I always hoped the article influenced the choice of the journal's name!

2. John R. Swanton, *The Indians of the Southeastern United States*, Smithsonian Institution, Bureau of American Ethnology, Bulletin 137 (Washington, DC: US Government Printing Office, 1946), xiii, 943. The title of map 13 is "Map to Illustrate the Distribution of Certain Natural Resources in the Southeast Drawn on by Indians."

3. See Carl H. Strandbery and Ray Tomlinson, "Photoarchaeological Analysis of Potomac River Fish Traps," *American Antiquity* 34, no. 3 (1969): 312.

4. One such photograph of the fishtrap on the Etowah River is available for viewing through Wikimedia: Jflo23, "Fish Trap on Etowah River," photograph uploaded December 16, 2009, https://commons.wikimedia.org/wiki/File:FishTrap.JPG.

5. See Albert S. Gatschet, "Towns and Villages of the Creek Confederacy in the XVIII and XIX Centuries," ed. Thomas M. Owen, in *Report of the Alabama History Commission to the Governor of Alabama* (Tuscaloosa: Alabama Historical Society, 1901), section titled "Lolokalka."

6. Erhard Rostlund, *Freshwater Fish and Fishing in Native North America* (Berkeley: University of California Press, 1952), 102.

7. See good visual illustrations in Emma Lila Fundaburk and Mary Douglass Fundaburk Foreman, *Sun Circles and Human Hands: The Southeastern Indians—Art and Industry* (Luverne, AL: Emma Lila Funderburk, 1957; Tuscaloosa: University of Alabama Press, 2001), 188; and in Fred Breummer, "Fishing Weirs of the St. Lawrence," *Canadian Geographic Journal*, no. 71 (July 1965): 14–19.

8. John McPhee, *The Founding Fish* (New York: Farrar, Straus and Giroux, 2002), 116–20.

9. See Frederick W. Hodge, ed., "The Narrative of Alvar Nuñez Cabeza de Vaca," in *Spanish Explorers in the Southern United States, 1528–1543* (1907; New York: Barnes and Noble, 1971), 50.

10. See James Adair, *History of the American Indians* (London: Edward and Charles Dilly, 1775; New York: Promontory Press, 1973), 432–33.

11. Gene Wilhelm Jr., "The Mullein: Plant Piscicide of the Mountain Folk Culture," *Journal of American Folklore* 64, no. 2 (April 1974): 235–52.

12. Blount County Historical Society, *Heritage of Blount County* (Blountsville, AL: Blount County Historical Society, 1972), n.p., see "Old Mill" passage in section 8, Folklore.

13. William Bartram, *The Travels of William Bartam* (Philadelphia: James and Johnson, 1791; New York: Dover, 1955), 108.

14. Bartram, 194.

15. Adair, *History of the American Indians*, 433–34.

16. Claude Hayes and Harold Daffron, interview by author, November 18, 1976, transcript in Samford University's Oral History Collection. Hayes was a commercial fisherman on the Coosa south of Pell City, and his old friend Daffron fished with him when they were young men. My first publication of any of this fishtrap lore came in 1978, in a series of short newspaper articles as part of Alabama Folkways, arranged by the Alabama State Council on the Arts; one of the old clippings I still have in my file is an article in the *Marion Times Standard*, June 1, 1978, titled "Alabama Folkways: The Great Fish Trap, by Jim Brown."

17. Donald Scott, "Sampling Fish Populations in the Coosa River, Alabama," *Transactions of the American Fisheries Society* 80 (1950): 28, 38.

18. See John G. Aikin, compiler, *A Digest of the Laws of the State of Alabama Containing All the Statutes of a Public and General Nature in Force at the Close of the Session of the General Assembly, in January 1833* (Philadelphia: Alexander Towar, 1833), 442.

19. In A. J. Walker, preparer, *The Revised Code of Alabama* (Montgomery, AL: Reid and Screws, 1867), 712, sec. 3753, "Poisoning Stream for Fish," the fine is set "at not less than ten nor more than one hundred dollars."

20. See James J. Mayfield, preparer, *The Code of Alabama*, vol. 3, *Criminal* (Nashville, TN: Marshall and Bruce, 1907), 544, sec. 6901, "Seines, Nets, Traps or Other Devices for Catching Fish Prohibited."

21. Wade Keyes and Fern M. Wood, prepapers, *The Code of Alabama, 1876* (Montgomery, AL: Barrett and Brown, 1877).

22. These details are from notes on a 1982 conversation between the author and personnel from the Geological Survey of Alabama. Most of the rock dams were thought to be Native American in origin, and of some antiquity: a paleolithic projectile point was found at one site. An article on the subject was being planned but may never have been published.

23. Tutwiler Coal, Coke & Iron Co. v. Nichols, 146 Ala. 364, 39 So. 762 (1905).

24. Mansell Goodwin, game warden, interviewed by Joel Alvis and Gary Uhrig, January 11, 1977, tape and transcript in possession of author.

25. Mansell Goodwin, phone interview by author, August 1, 1981. Albert Cates remembered the fine usually being eleven dollars; see Clarke Stallworth, "Trick Trap Yields Kettles of Fish," *Birmingham News*, March 23, 1983 (I had told Clarke about Mr. Cates a few weeks before he wrote this article). Clarke asked Mr. Cates, as I had done, "Isn't the fish trap illegal?" Mr. Cates replied: "Oh, there's a little old chimbly-corner law that says it's illegal, but Representative Drake is working on a local bill that would make it legal." I don't remember "chimbly-corner" being one of the legal categories I looked into when researching this article!

26. Albert Cates, interviewed by Jim Brown and Bob Stiles, near Arkadelphia in Cullman County, August 1981, tape and transcript in Samford University's Oral History Collection. See also shorter interview with Mr. Cates by Bill Gullett, August 15, 1984, transcript in author's collection.

Chapter 10

1. An earlier version of this chapter appeared as Jim Brown, "River Redhorse and the Seasonal Snaring Thereof in Alabama," *Tributaries*, no. 9 (2006): 9–26.

2. Maurice F. "Scott" Mettee, Patrick E. O'Neil, and J. Malcolm Pierson, *Fishes of Alabama and the Mobile Basin*, illustrated by Karl J. Scheidegger (Birmingham, AL: Oxmoor House, 1996), xii, 820. The river redhorse appears on pp. 358–59.

3. Herbert T. Boschung Jr. and Richard L. Mayden, *Fishes of Alabama*, illustrated by Joseph R. Tomelleri, with foreword by Edward O. Wilson (Washington, DC: Smithsonian Books, 2004), xiii, 736.

4. Morgan Lovejoy, interviewed by Jim Brown and Bill Finch, Sixmile, Bibb County, AL, December 22, 1978, tape and transcript in possession of author.

5. John R. Swanton, *Indians of the Southeastern United States*, Smithsonian Institution, Bureau of American Ethnology, Bulletin 137 (Washington, DC: US Government Printing Office, 1946), 333–34.

6. J. Geraint Jenkins, *Boat House and Net House* (Cardiff, Wales: Welsh Folk Museum, n.d.).

7. Peter A. Hackney and Walter M. Tatum, "'Redhorse Are Shoaling' Cry Calls Fishermen to Cahaba," *Alabama Conservation* 36, no. 6 (1966). These same two authors, with the addition of S. L. Spencer, also wrote "Life History Study of the River Redhorse, *Moxostoma carinatum* (Cope), in the Cahaba River, Alabama, with Notes on the Management of the Species as a Sport Fish," *Proceedings of the Southeastern Association of Game and Fish Commissions* 21 (1968): 232–49; a map in the article shows the Cahaba River from Centreville downstream.

8. Clarke Stallworth, "Romance with Red Horse Is One Family's Tradition," *Birmingham News*, May 27, 1984.

9. Mike Bolton, "Redhorse Roping: Griffin Brothers Keep Tradition Alive with Three-Day Vigil on the Cahaba River Shoals," *Birmingham News*, May 3, 1987.

10. *Redhorse: A Cahaba River Tradition*, Bravefellows Production, 2010, 43:52, available in Samford University Library, Special Collection.

11. See *Journey Proud*, "Redhorse Fish Snaring," January 19, 2014, online episode, 26:45, Alabama Public Television (website), https://aptv.org.

12. The *S-Town* podcast can be listened to online at the *S-Town* website, https://stownpodcast .org. All episodes of the podcast were posted online on March 28, 2017. It was said to have had ten million listeners in its first four days of posting.

Chapter 11

1. Some of this material can be accessed through the Samford website; see "Birmingham Audubon Mountain Workshop," published May 8, 2018, Samford University Oral History Collection, SUHist/Folklore/004, video clip, 24:34, https://www.samford.edu/departments /oral-history/projects/folklore/Birmingham-Audubon-Mountain-Workshop. The same video clip can also be viewed through YouTube; see "Celebrating the History of the Birmingham Audubon Mountain Workshop," uploaded May 8, 2018, by Samford Traditions and Oral History Recording Initiative, YouTube video, 24:34, https://www.youtube.com/watch?v=NBfxkGI0SGI.

2. This discussion is summed up, in the main, from Elizabeth S. Howard (no relation to Col. Howard), *The Vagabond Dreamer* (Huntsville, AL: Strode, 1976).

3. *The DeKalb Legend*, vol. 4, *1975–1976* (Fort Payne, AL: Landmarks of DeKalb County, 1976), 37.

4. This quotation and much of the material on Blanche Dean are from Alice S. Christenson and L. J. Davenport, "Blanche Dean: Naturalist," *Alabama Heritage*, no. 45 (Summer 1977): 16–25.

5. Most of the material in the three paragraphs above I got in conversations with Elberta Reid in May and June 2018. The Nature Conservancy's story can be read in John N. Randolph, *The Battle for Alabama's Wilderness: Saving the Great Gymnasiums of Nature* (Tuscaloosa: University of Alabama Press, 2005).

6. Dan C. Holliman, "Alabama's Mountain Ecology Workshop: A Model for Conservation Education," *Journal of the Alabama Academy of Science* 55, no. 2 (April 1984): 47–51.

7. Henry Glassie, *Pattern in the Material Folk Culture of the Eastern United States* (Philadelphia: University of Pennsylvania Press, 1968).

8. As this memoir goes to press, most of these stories and reflections seem to be standing the test of time. But this chapter—written when the Audubon Mountain Workshop was still a going concern every May at Camp Alpine—now seems critically dated. The cancellation of the workshop in 2020 and 2021 owing to COVID-19 broke an annual tradition, but it seems to me that changing priorities in the Alabama Audubon Society itself are the ultimate reason. I'm guessing that if the workshop continues at all, it will be on a roving basis, site to site. In a word, then, a chapter written largely as introduction and invitation to join may now be more of a memorial!

Chapter 12

1. An earlier version of this chapter was published as Jim Brown, "For the Amusement of the Boys: John Mealing, Railroad Caller," *Tributaries*, no. 11 (2009): 33–55; the nucleus of the article was first presented as a paper at the American Society of Ethnohistory conference, Charleston, SC, 1986.

2. See for an overview of Birmingfind and a list of publications, see "Birmingfind," Bhamwiki, edited November 28, 2009, https://www.bhamwiki.com.

3. You too can hear her voice! See "Oral History Interview with Eula McGill, December 12, 1974," interview G-0039, Documenting the American South (website), accessed April 2, 2021, https://docsouth.unc.edu/sohp/G-0039/menu.html.

4. See Jim Brown, "Gandy Dancer Work Song Tradition," *Encyclopedia of Alabama*, last updated February 10, 2021, http://www.encyclopediaofalabama.org.

5. In those first interviews Mr. Mealing told me he was fifteen years old when he began work on the Western in 1926, which would have had him born in or around 1911. The official documents apparently say he was born in 1908. Usually written documents are more accurate than memory, especially decades after the events. It's suspicious to me, however, that this officially recorded 1908 birth year would have made him just the legal age for railroad employment in 1926, so I'd wager a considerable amount that the foreman moved his birthday three years back from the actual 1911.

6. This direct quotation and all subsequent ones, unless specifically noted, come from two oral histories the author did with Mr. Mealing on June 17 and June 30, 1982, at his home in Pratt City. Transcripts in possession of the author.

7. "Durant Bend" refers to a bend in the Alabama River near Mealing's hometown of White Hall.

8. Steve Grauberger, folklife specialist with the Alabama Arts Council, was kind enough to upload the interview from June 17, 1982, to YouTube. For visuals, he added historical photos, primarily from a reenactment day at the Heart of Dixie Railroad Park in Calera. Mr. Mealing is the one in the white hat. See "John Henry Mealing Interview by Dr. Jim Brown 19820617," uploaded January 17, 2021, by Steve Grauberger, YouTube video, 31:22, https://www.youtube.com/watch?v=HyFwzam1trg.

9. See Albert B. Lord, *The Singer of Tales* (1960; New York: Atheneum, 1974), especially chapter 2, "Singers: Performance and Training."

10. *Seaboard System Railroad: Safety Rules for Engineering and Maintenance of Way*

Department (n.p.: n.p., 1984), 32. For a great article on Mr. Mealing that is extremely knowl-edgeable about labor organizations and railroad companies, see Edwin L. Brown, "'To Make a Man Feel Good': John Henry Mealing, Railroad Caller," *Labor History* 27, no. 2 (Spring 1986): 257–64. I got to know Ed doing the Birmingfind grant work, and in the article he makes use of my interviews with Mr. Mealing.

11. Alan Lomax, ed., *Folk Music of the United States: Afro-American Spirituals, Work Songs, and Ballads, from the Archive of American Folk Song* (Washington, DC: Library of Congress, Division of Music, 1960), LP, with text in accompanying loose sheets.

12. Alan Lomax, *The Folk Songs of North America in the English Language* (New York: Dou-bleday, 1960), 545.

13. William Ferris, "Railroad Chants: Form and Function," *Mississippi Folklore Register* 4 (1970): 1–14.

14. In my files is a copy of a *Birmingham News* article by Don Driver, "Line Crew Callers Kept Tracks Moving," March 9, 1983, describing a demonstration John Mealing gave the day be-fore—which, if I remember correctly, was the one at the Harbert Center where I introduced him.

15. Barry Dornfeld and Maggie Holtzberg, producers, *Gandy Dancers*, 1994 film, 30 min., Folkstreams (website), accessed April 2, 2021, http://www.folkstreams.net/film-detail.php?id=101.

16. The 1999 CD *Blues Routes: Heroes & Tricksters, Blues & Jazz, Worksongs & Street Music* from Smithsonian Folkways Recordings features Mr. Mealing's performance at Wolf Trap on track 1, "Rooster Call." Mr. Mealing performs to an obviously appreciative crowd, and a photo of him is on the back of the liner notes booklet that comes with the CD. For track listing and liner notes, see *Blues Routes*, SFW40118, Smithsonian Folkways Recordings (website), accessed April 2, 2021, https://folkways.si.edu. One double couplet of a lining chant I never heard him do is here:

> Down behind the henhouse, on my knees
> Thought I heard a chicken sneeze
> It only was a rooster, saying his prayers
> Giving out thanks for the hens upstairs . . .

17. See Kathy Kemp, "Farewell," *Birmingham News*, March 11, 2007, for a memorial article on the occasion of John Mealing's death. Ten years earlier, Kathy had written a very nice article on Mr. Mealing in what was then the *Post-Herald*, anchored by color photographs, including one of Mr. Mealing singing his railroad chants to his grandsons; see Kemp, "Rail Rhymes as an Art," *Birmingham Post-Herald*, June 9, 1997. She, too, got one lining verse from him that I never heard him do:

> Preacher in the pulpit preachin' mighty well,
> Then he come to find out he was on the way to hell . . .

Epilogue

1. Carl Ortwin Sauer, *The Early Spanish Main* (Berkeley: University of California Press, 1966), vi.

Selected Bibliography

INTRODUCTION

Pinson, Patricia, ed. *The Art of Walter Inglis Anderson*. Ocean Springs, MS: Walter Inglis Anderson Museum of Art, 2003.

CHAPTER 1. IMMERSED IN THE CAHABA RIVER

Keith, Todd. *Cahaba: A Gift for Generations; A Series of Historical Essays Revealing the Cahaba River Past, Present and Future*. Designed and illustrated by Guy Arello, with photography by Beth Maynor Young. Birmingham AL: Birmingham Printing, 1997.

CHAPTER 2. HOMEWOOD'S SALAMANDER MIGRATION AND FESTIVAL

Mitchell, Joe, and Whit Gibbons. *Salamanders of the Southeast*. Athens: University of Georgia Press, 2010.

CHAPTER 3. THE ARCHY CULVERT, A.K.A. ROSS BRIDGE

Birmingham Historical Society. "'Ross Bridge' Goes On the Record." *Newsletter*, June 2017. https://birminghamhistoricalsociety.com/news-and-newsletters/.

White, Marjorie L. *Shades Creek: Flowing through Time*. Birmingham, AL: Birmingham Historical Society, 2019.

CHAPTER 4. *FOXFIRE*, FOLK CRAFTS, AND FOLKCENTER SOUTH

Blount County Historical Society. *Heritage of Blount County*. Blountsville, AL: Blount County Historical Society, 1972.

Wigginton, Eliot, and His Students, eds. *The Foxfire Book: Hog Dressing, Log Cabin Building, Mountain Crafts and Foods, Planting by the Signs, Snake Lore, Hunting Tales, Faith Healing, Moonshining, and Other Affairs of Plain Living*. Garden City, NY: Doubleday, 1972.

CHAPTER 5. WHAT WONDROUS LOVE IS THIS: SACRED HARP SINGING

Carmer, Carl. *Stars Fell on Alabama*. New York: Literary Guild, 1934. Reprint, Tuscaloosa: University of Alabama Press, 1985.

Cobb, Buell E. *Like Cords around My Heart: A Sacred Harp Memoir*. Denver, CO: Outskirts Press, 2014.

———. *The Sacred Harp: A Tradition and Its Music*. Athens: University of Georgia Press, 1978.

Jackson, George Pullen. *White Spirituals from the Southern Uplands: The Story of the Fasola Folk, Their Songs, Singings, and "Buckwheat Notes."* Chapel Hill: University of North Carolina Press, 1933. Reprint, New York: Dover, 1965.

CHAPTER 6. TELESCOPING TIME: LANDSCAPE ARCHITECTURE, HISTORICAL GEOGRAPHY, AND GREENWAYS

McHarg, Ian. *Design with Nature*. Garden City, NY: Natural History Press, 1969. Reprinted with expanded illustrations, New York: John Wiley, 1992.

Montell, William Lynwood. *The Saga of Coe Ridge: A Study in Oral History*. Knoxville: University of Tennessee Press, 1970.

Sauer, Carl O. *The Early Spanish Main*. Berkeley: University of California Press, 1966.

CHAPTER 7. HERB DOCTOR TOMMIE BASS AND THE SCHOLARS

Crellin, John, and Jane Philpott. *Herbal Medicine Past and Present*. Vol. 1, *Trying to Give Ease*, and vol. 2, *A Reference Guide to Medicinal Plants*. Durham, NC: Duke University Press, 1990.

Duke, James A. *The Green Pharmacy: New Discoveries in Herbal Remedies for Common Diseases and Conditions from the World's Foremost Authority on Healing Herbs*. Illustrated by Peggy Kessler Duke. Emmaus, PA: Rodale Press, 1997.

Foster, Steven, and James A. Duke. *A Field Guide to Medicinal Plants and Herbs of Eastern and Central North America*. New York: Houghton Mifflin, 1990.

Patton, Darryl. *Mountain Medicine: The Herbal Remedies of Tommie Bass*. Birmingham, AL: Natural Reader Press, 2004.

CHAPTER 8. EXPERIMENTING WITH EXPERIENTIAL EDUCATION

Dewey, John. *Experience and Education*. New York: Macmillan, 1938.

Wells, Evelyn Kendrick. *The Ballad Tree: A Study of British and American Ballads, Their Folklore, Verse and Music, Together with Sixty Traditional Ballads and Their Tunes*. New York: Ronald Press, 1950.

Wigginton, Eliot, and His Students, eds. *Foxfire: 25 Years; A Celebration of Our First Quarter Century*. New York: Anchor Books, 1991.

CHAPTER 9. SURVIVAL OF THE GREAT SHOAL FISHTRAP AND OTHER OLD PRACTICES

Adair, James. *History of the American Indians*. London: Edward and Charles Dilly, 1775. Reprint, New York: Promontory Press, 1973.

Bartram, William. *The Travels of William Bartram*. Philadelphia: James and Johnson, 1791. Reprint, New York: Dover, 1955.

Fundaburk, Emma Lila, and Mary Douglass Fundaburk Foreman. *Sun Circles and Human Hands: The Southeastern Indians—Art and Industry*. Luverne, AL: Emma Lila Funderburk, 1957. Reprint, Tuscaloosa: University of Alabama Press, 2001.

McPhee, John. *The Founding Fish*. New York: Farrar, Straus and Giroux, 2002.

Chapter 10. River Redhorse and the Seasonal Snaring Thereof

Boschung, Herbert T., Jr., and Richard L. Mayden. *Fishes of Alabama*. Illustrated by Joseph R. Tomelleri, with foreword by Edward O. Wilson. Washington, DC: Smithsonian Books, 2004.

Mettee, Maurice F., Patrick E. O'Neil, and J. Malcolm Pierson. *Fishes of Alabama and the Mobile Basin*. Illustrated by Karl J. Scheidegger. Birmingham, AL: Oxmoor House, 1996.

Chapter 11. The Mountain Workshop of the Alabama Audubon Society

Glassie, Henry. *Pattern in the Material Folk Culture of the Eastern United States*. Philadelphia: University of Pennsylvania Press, 1968.

Howard, Elizabeth S. *The Vagabond Dreamer*. Huntsville, AL: Strode, 1976.

Randolph, John N. *The Battle for Alabama's Wilderness: Saving the Great Gymnasiums of Nature*. Tuscaloosa: University of Alabama Press, 2005.

Chapter 12. For the Amusement of the Boys: John Mealing, Railroad Caller

Lomax, Alan. *The Folk Songs of North America in the English Language*. New York: Doubleday, 1960.

Lord, Albert B. *The Singer of Tales*. New York: Atheneum, 1974.

Index

Page numbers in italics refer to figures.

Brooks, Otis, pastor, Vestavia Hills Baptist Church, 23

Brown, Andrea, and Audubon Mountain Workshop, 246

Brown, Helen and Ted, Sacred Harp singers from Derby, England, 118

Brozen, Reed, and Audubon Mountain Workshop, 246

Buck Creek, 13, 22; redhorse snaring on, 212

buckeye. *See* plants

Burlington Northern. *See* BNSF

Burlington Northern Santa Fe. *See* BNSF

Cabeza de Vaca, Álvar Núñez, on Gulf Coast fish weirs ca. 1527, 186

Cades Cove, Great Smoky Mountains National Park, 74

Cahaba lily. *See* plants

Cahaba River, 5–25; redhorse snaring on, 207–24

Cahaba Riverkeepers, 23

Cahaba River National Wildlife Refuge, 23

Cahaba River Society, 13–14, 17; at Homewood Salamander Festival, 47; and Ross Bridge development discussions, 53

Cahaba River Wildlife Management Area, 23

Cahaba Trunk Sewer, 19–20

Campbell, Olive Dame, 166

Campbell, Tommy, redhorse snaring expert, 221: detailed crafting of wire snare, 222–23; recommended by Morgan Lovejoy, 208; redhorse snaring, 216, 222–23, *224*

Camp DeSoto, former girl's camp, now Alpine Camp for Boys, 230

Camp Fasola, 118

Canticle of Moses, source of "honey in the rock" metaphor, 273

Canyon Mouth Park, 241

Carmer, Carl, description of a Sacred Harp singing in *Stars Fell on Alabama*, 98

Carnegie Hall, as venue for railroad caller John Mealing, 270, 272

Cates, Albert, Mulberry Fork shoal fishtrap owner/operator, 200–203; on the illegality of fishtraps, 285n25

catfish. *See* fishes

Cauthen, Jim and Joyce: and railroad caller John Mealing, 270; and Audubon Mountain Workshop, 239

Cheaha State Park, 36

Child, Francis James. *See* ballads

Child ballads. *See* ballads

Children's Harbor Family Center, Children's Hospital, Birmingham, 131

Childress, Rector (Rec), wagon basket peddler, Mammoth Cave area, KY, 138–39

Christian Harmony. See Walker, William

Civilian Conservation Corps (CCC), and creation of DeSoto State Park, 227

Clear Creek Falls, 232

Cobb, Buell: early interest in Sacred Harp, 115; *Like Cords around My Heart*, 116; on Hugh McGraw, 116–17; *Sacred Harp*, 116

Cold Mountain, Sacred Harp soundtrack, 116

colectivo, standard riverboat transportation on the Amazon River system, 147

Congestion Mitigation and Air Quality Improvement Program (CMAQ), 132

Conroy, Pat, influence of *The Water Is Wide* on Bob England, 170

Cookeville, TN, 135

Cooper, Elizabeth, Audubon Mountain Workshop librarian, 239

cooperage, 86

Coosa River, shoal fishtraps on, 183

Cope, Edward Drinker, 205

Cornerstone, 181

Country Boy Eddie, Birmingham early morning TV show, 91

Coushatta, and folktale analysis, 136

Coxe, Walter, Birmingham advertising executive and environmentalist: as Audubon Society field trips sponsor, 248; "Walter Coxe Blessing," 249

Crellin, John K., medical research, on Tommie

Philpott, Jane, coauthor of *Wintertime for a Backwoodsman* pamphlet, 154

plants: anemone (rue-anemone, *Anemonella thalictroides*), 49; buckeye (*Aesculus* sp.), 187; Cahaba lily (*Hymenocallis coronaria*), 15; dogtooth violet/trout lily (*Erythroniaum americanum*), 49, 143, 159; liverleaf (*Hepatica* sp.), 49; manioc/cassava/yuca (*Manihot esculenta*), 147; mountain laurel (*Kalmia latifolia*), 207; mullein (*Verbascum thapsus*), 187; red buckeye (*Aesculus pavia*), 49; rivercane (*Arundinaria gigantea*), 276; St. John Conqueror root/Solomon's seal (*Polygonatum* sp.), 158; yellowroot (*Xanthorhiza simplicissima*), 150, 156

plebeian sphinx moth. *See* insects

Porterham, Mary, Audubon Mountain Workshop administrator, 245

Powell, Polly, Samford University English professor, 163

Pratt City, Birmingham, and railroad caller John Mealing, 258

Preston, William, on Shannon's relationship to the archy culvert, 60. *See also* Ross Creek culvert

Prints and Photographs Division, Library of Congress, holder of official HAER photographs, 64

Propp, Vladimir, analyst of folktale structure, 136

Public Affairs Research Council of Alabama (PARCA), and Ross Creek culvert, 65

pump drill, as pioneer toy and Native American tool, 192–94

Rabun Gap-Nacoochee School, and the *Foxfire* project, 74

Railroad Park, Birmingham, 131, 134

railroad tools: jack, 255; lining bars, 252, *253*; rail dogs, 264; 16" spike mauls, *253*; tie tongs, 255

Rankin, Tom, co-creator of film on Tommie Bass, 144

Read, John, as writer of shape note hymns, 109

redhorse, river. *See* fishes

redhorse snare, *216*, 217

Red Mountain Coal and Iron Company, 69, 70

Red Rock Trail System, 130, 133–34

Regional Planning Commission of Greater Birmingham (formerly Birmingham Regional Planning Commission), 126–28, 132

Reid, Elberta, work with Alabama Audubon Society and Audubon Mountain Workshop, 233, 235, 236, 248, 249

Reid, Robert Raymond, Jr. (Bob), environmental lawyer in Birmingham: activities in Alabama Audubon Society, 233; connections with Camp Alpine, 234

Rhea, Claude, dean of Samford University School of Music, 112

Rigsby, Homer, basketmaker, 90, 93

Rikard, Marlene, historian from Samford University, 53

river redhorse. *See* fishes

Roden, Mary Jimm, and *Sparrow Hawk* project, 171

Rosengarten, Theodore (Ted), *All God's Dangers*, 151

Ross, James Taylor, and Ross Creek culvert, 68

Ross, Jane Reed, 129–31, 132–33, 282n21

Ross Bridge, 55, 57, 58, 65, 66, 72, 278n1 (chap. 8). *See also* Ross Creek culvert

Ross Creek, tributary of Shades Creek, 51

Ross Creek culvert (a.k.a. Ross Bridge, Ross Creek viaduct, the arched culvert, or archy culvert), *54*, 58–59, 60, 61, 64, 65, 66–67, 69, 70, 71, 73. *See also* Preston, William; Ross Bridge; White, Marjorie

Ross Creek viaduct, *52. See also* Ross Creek culvert

sucker, blue. *See* fishes

Susina, Betty, Audubon Mountain Workshop librarian, 245

Swanton, John: on Native American fisheries, 185; on Native American snaring of sturgeon, 217

tag alder (*Alnus serrulata*), *25*; Tommie Bass on, 155

tamping calls, for section gangs, 267–68

Tannehill State Park: site of the 1976 Folkcenter South folkcrafts festival, 88; site of the 1977 experiential education seminar, 127, 174, 177–79

Tate, Robert (Bob), 18

Tennessee Coal and Iron Company (TCI), 63

Terrell, Clyde, and railroad caller John Mealing, 261, 263

Thomas, Joab, coauthor of guide to Alabama wildflowers, 232

Thomas, Ron, Attic and Cellar Studios, and the 1977 Tannehill-based experiential education seminar, 180

Thompson, Mary, Folkcenter South student researcher, 91

Thompson, Stith, Proppian analyst of Native American folktales, 136

Thoreau, Henry David, 226; *Walden*, 31; on wilderness, 121, 280n2

Tipton, Katherine (Katie), and Ross Creek culvert, 60, 65, 66

trammel net, *189*, 190–91

Transportation Investment Generating Economic Recovery (TIGER), 133

tulip poplar (*Liriodendron tulipfera*), 207, 220

Tullos, Allen: coauthor of *Wintertime for a Backwoodsman* pamphlet, 154–55; co-creator of film on herbalist Tommie Bass, 151–53; work with Tommie Bass, 141, 143

Turkey Creek, 42

Turkey Creek Preserve, 64, 73

Tutwiler Coal, Coke and Iron Company, 198–99

University of Alabama at Birmingham (UAB), 14, 33, 42; medical school's research on herbal medicine, 158

University of California at Los Angeles (UCLA), 147

University of Mississippi, and Sacred Harp singing calendar, 114

University of North Carolina at Chapel Hill, 141, 149

University of Pennsylvania, 127, 205

Upchurch, Henry, white oak basketmaker from White Plains, AL, 77, 93, 108, 137

US Fish and Wildlife survey for goldline darter and Cahaba shiner, 9–12

US Steel Real Estate, development of Ross Bridge, 53

Vanderbilt University, 32, 129

Van Zandt, Pete, Birmingham-Southern biology professor, and Audubon Mountain Workshop, 247

vernacular architecture: cabins, dogtrot and saddlebag, 240; Chisholm Daniels house, 242; examples of, along Shinbone Valley, 241–44; I-house, 240–41; Len Daniels house, 242–43

Vess, David, Samford University history department chair, 57

Vestavia Hills Baptist Church, 4

Veteran's Memorial Park, Birmingham, 131

Vice, Jack, blacksmith, 93

Village Creek, 17; coal washers on, 198

Villarejo, Avencio, use of telescoping time model in *Así es la Selva*, 139

Völkeanderung, 124

Vulcan Park, 63, 64, 73